AUTO

AUTOBIOGRAPHY

by Bugs2writes

Published by www.lulu.com
in association with JM Editions

© Copyright David G Hulson, Julie Hatton (MA) Editor, Mary N Hatton, Joan Bell, Bernice Caddick, Margaret Booth, Jenny Pace, Jan Judge and Rosemary Baxter each hold the copyright to their individual stories. 2017

AUTOBIOGRAPHY

All rights reserved.

The right of David G Hulson, Julie Hatton (MA) Editor, Mary N Hatton, Joan Bell, Bernice Caddick, Margaret Booth, Jenny Pace, Jan Judge and Rosemary Baxter to be identified as the authors of this work has been asserted in accordance with the Copyright, Designs and Patents Act 1988.

No part of this publication may be reproduced, stored in a retrieval system, or transmitted, in any form or by any means, electronic, mechanical, photocopying, recording or otherwise, nor translated into a machine language, without the written permission of the publisher.

Condition of sale

This book is sold subject to the condition that it shall not, by way of trade or otherwise, be lent, re-sold, hired out or otherwise circulated in any form of binding or cover other than that in which it is published and without a similar condition including this condition being imposed on the subsequent purchaser.

ISBN 978-0-244-02207-5

Book formatted by www.bookformatting.co.uk.

Contents

SHADOWS OF YOUTH 1
David G Hulson

A MINGLED YARN 26
Julie Hatton

LEWIS'S DEPT STORE, BIRMINGHAM 72
Written by: Julie Hatton

ACCIDENT PRONE, JOAN 97
Joan Bell

DANCING TO HAPPINESS 107
Bernice Caddick

MADNESS AND MAYHEM 140
Margaret Booth

FOSTERING 159
Jenny Pace

BABY BOOMER 166
Jan Judge

AFRICAN ADVENTURES – Non-Safari 177
Rosemary Baxter

THE MAGIC RAFT SERIES: 1 The Case of the Manic Monkey 221
Julie Hatton

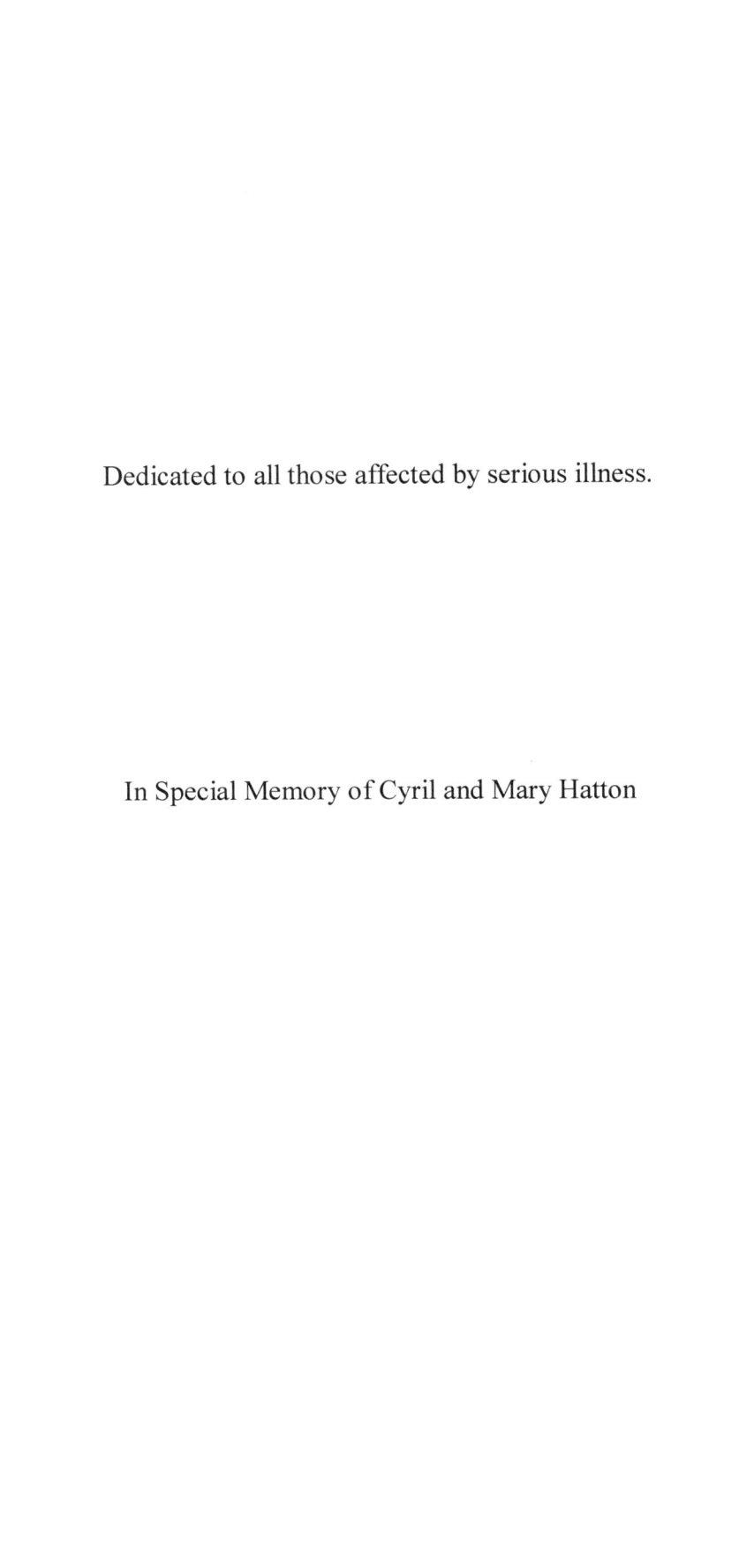

Dedicated to all those affected by serious illness.

In Special Memory of Cyril and Mary Hatton

Acknowledgements

Much appreciation goes to our *families and friends* whose unending support and encouragement help to make our work possible.

Huge gratitude goes to Tony Smith for his patience, support and participation behind the scenes.

With special thanks to Frank at www.bookformatting.co.uk who so freely and generously contributes his expertise and time to format our books in aid of Action Medical Research for Children.

Please visit our website at www.bugs2writes.co.uk where you can find information about us, our charity, other books in our collection and short extracts from the stories.

Please remember, all profits from the sale of our books go directly to the charity.

Foreword

Members of *BUGS2WRITES*: Elizabeth Allen BA, Rosemary Baxter, Joan Bell, Margaret Booth, Bernice Caddick, Julie Hatton MA (Editor), David G Hulson, Jan Judge, Sandra Knowles, Graham Mcglone, Jenny Pace, Sally Saunders and Suzanne Stack.

BUGS2WRITES was formed to write and publish books of short stories to help raise money for charity. All profits from the sale of these books will go directly to the charity. By buying this book you will be benefitting *Action Medical Research for Children*. Thank you.

This book is collection of autobiographical narratives written by 9 enthusiastic and dedicated writers. Our aim is to entertain our readers with 18 complete stories which relate the highs and lows of our lives. The tales cover the period from the 1930's through to present day.

It is the policy of *BUGS2WRITES* to publish 'clean' stories regarding language usage and sexual content. You can be confident, therefore, that the tales within our books are within stringent parameters across all age groups.

In this book, you will find an eclectic mix of personal tales from motorbike gangs, through to line-dancing troupes, to a non-safari African adventure. Some stories relate incidents from childhood through to teenage years. Others narrate experiences of early adulthood through to marriage and children. One tale explores the supernatural. A huge department store along with some of the characters who walked the floors is another. An alternative account describes the many joys and heartaches involved with fostering children. A stint in the army along with school days and childhood holidays all add to the combination of stories within. Whatever your mood, there is sure to be something to entertain, amuse and charm you.

All profits from the sale of the books go to
Action Medical Research for Children.
Thank you.

SHADOWS OF YOUTH
David G Hulson

PART 1 SAUSAGE OR BACON?

1960's: When you've been raised around motorbikes like I had and you finally reach the age where it's legal to ride one, you get one. Mine was a BSA 250cc C15 bike.

For some time, I'd been using my bike to get to and from work, but on my days off, I rode purely for pleasure.

I had been round a mate's house in Chorlton for a chat with Jed. He said, 'All the lads are going for a bike ride tomorrow. Do you want to come with us?'

'Sure,' I replied.

'Okay,' said Jed, 'we'll see you at the roundabout 4 o'clock tomorrow.'

Now with these bike trips, you could end up anywhere. It was like going on a mystery tour.

I arrived home later that evening and told Mum I'd be going for a bike ride the next day.

'Fine, son. Will you be needing sandwiches?'

'Nah, I'll be all right,' I said.

'What time are you going?' Mum asked.

'Late afternoon,' I said, 'so I'll be having dinner first.'

I slept like a log that night, well, till about 3:50 am, that is. I woke to my find the whole bedroom vibrating.

'Flipping heck!' shouted Roger, who shared my room. 'Is it an earthquake?'

AUTOBIOGRAPHY

The bedroom light suddenly switched on. 'David!' Mum shouted. 'Get out here. Now! All your friends are outside.'

'They're here now? What friends?' I asked.

'Your motorbike friends!' she shouted.

'But it's only . . .' Slowly my eyes grew accustomed to the 60-watt bulb hanging from the ceiling. I picked up the Big Ben alarm clock and focused on the hands. 'It's only 3:55 am,' I said, 'and they aren't not due until four this afternoon.'

'Well, it's now four in the morning, so someone made a muck up of their times, didn't they, David?' she said, annoyed. 'Now get downstairs and tell them to turn off their flipping engines! They're waking the entire neighbourhood!'

I ran downstairs in my pyjamas. The noise from the bike engines was deafening and getting louder and louder as I reached the front door.

Now, when you live in a little cul-de-sac that only contains twelve terraced houses the sound of a motorbike engine throbbing at four in the morning is magnified as it bounces off the walls of the small avenue.

As I opened the door, the noise was horrendous. There were about twenty motorbikes, mostly British, ticking over, and there I was in my jimjams waving like an idiot and shouting, 'Turn off your engines!' Anyone who knows British bikes from the 50's will know they have a very distinctive tone.

As I looked around the avenue, I noticed all the bedroom lights of our neighbours were being turned on and it was starting to look like the Blackpool illuminations. Finally, the last engine was turned off. The night became quiet again. I breathed a sigh of relief.

Mum's bedroom window opened and Mum and Dad were looking down at me and the bikers. 'You noisy lot,' smiled Mum, looking a little more relaxed. 'David, you best bring them into the house while you go and get dressed.'

'Come on, lads, in the house and keep the noise down because of the neighbours.' Then I realised it was a bit too late for that. 'In the kitchen,' I said. When I turned round, Mum was standing in the doorway in her dressing gown. 'I'm for it now,' I thought.

'Have you boys had breakfast yet?' she asked.

'No, Mrs,' came the mumbling replies of twenty hungry bikers.

'Arthur, light the grill will you and get out the bacon and sausages. Find a seat boys,' she said, as she slipped slices of bread under the grill.

I came back downstairs dressed for the bike ride. Mum looked at me and said, 'You can't go just yet. They haven't even started their sausages on toast and tea.'

Obviously, we didn't have enough chairs for everyone. It seemed there were bodies everywhere. I stepped over the boys to reach Mum who was now cooking bacon because all the sausages had all gone. 'What are you doing, Mum?' I asked.

'These boys haven't had breakfast yet and they need a good breakfast to start the day.'

'Mum,' I repeated.

'David,' said my mother, 'you're getting in my way. Now find somewhere to park your bum.'

'Dad,' said Roger, coming into the kitchen, 'what the heck is going on? It looks like a cafe in here.'

'Don't look at me,' he said. 'I've been put on buttering the toast. You'd best ask Mum.'

'Sausages have all gone, Roger. There's only the bacon left.'

'Not for me, Mum,' answered Roger. 'Not at four-thirty in the morning. I'm off back to bed.'

'Well, I'll have one,' I said, 'with some brown sauce, please.'

'The whole house now stinks of frying fat' was Roger's last remark as he left the room, trying not to stand on anyone's legs on the floor.

By 5am, every one of the bikers had been fed and watered.

'Thanks, Mrs H,' said Jimbo, getting up from the floor. 'We'd best be going now.'

'Yeah. Thanks for the food,' was the mumbled reply from all the lads.

'I'll see you out,' said Mum, and then the worst thing ever happened. My mother leaned over and kissed me on the cheek. 'Aww, leave it out, Mum,' I said, acutely embarrassed, but it was too late. The lads had seen the peck.

'Don't you worry, Mrs H. We will take good care of your boy,' replied Jimbo, sniggering at my discomfort.

'You all take it easy today and keep an eye on each other. You hear?' demanded my mother.

'Mum,' I said . . .

'See you tonight, son,' said Dad, patting me on the back.

The bikers piled out of the front door, pulling on their helmets and nodding their gratitude to my parents. Mum stood in the avenue to give them a goodbye wave, then asked, 'Can you start your bikes up at the end of the road, boys? It's the neighbours, you know.'

Like little children they walked their silent bikes to the top of the avenue, then the silence of the early dawn was terminated by about twenty motorbikes including BSA's, AJ's, Triumphs, Matchless and even a James and a Dot, roaring off towards Chorlton.

As the roar of all those bikes faded into the distance, my mother commented, 'What a nice bunch of lads and so polite.'

'I Just hope they don't do this again next Saturday,' said my father, dryly, 'because we're completely out of the basics now.' He breathed a sigh of relief as he closed the front door.

'Flipping Hells Angels!' said Roger, as Mum and Dad went past his room into their own and closed the door.

PART 2 DRAGON'S FIRE

1960's: When I went for a motorbike ride with my mates, the first place I'd go to was the Cafe 1010, Dickenson Road. That's where all the bikers would hangout, some lads in ordinary leathers, others wore their colours.

Jimbo and the lads were getting ready for a late evening ride up into the hills, but on this occasion, we would be joined by quite a few other bikers.

Not long afterwards, the cafe was bursting at the seams with bikers and the road outside was packed with motorbikes of various makes and cc's. Looking around the dark room and the bikes outside, I thought there must have been at least sixty plus riders gathered there if not more and all going on this late evening jaunt.

Before we left, Jimbo stood up like a general about to address his troops. 'Right boys and girls,' he said, 'we're going up on the hills tonight, but just in case we get a police escort again I'll give this signal. Jimbo raised his right arm high into the air, then clenched his fist. That's the signal for splitting up, lads, and re-joining again later on the ring-way next to the airport. Now, Jake will be Tail-End, Charley,' he added. 'If he spots anything he will come up the pack and let me know. Okay, get to your bikes!'

'My God,' I thought, 'It's like military manoeuvres!'

All the traffic on Dickenson Road came to a standstill as sixty plus motor bikes moved off from the cafe, cutting down side roads, and going through traffic lights on green, but there were that many bikes on the move, they were still going through the lights on red.

Soon we were onto Princess Road and that's where we first noticed we had company. Police motor-cyclists on their white Nortons had apparently received a tip off about our little jaunt and they had closed Princess Road to traffic so we could flow onto it without interruption.

Now it was like a game was being played by the police and the bikers for now there were three police Nortons. One stayed at the rear, and two of them moved up on the outside trying to pen us in.

Jake, Tail-End Charlie, had seen the police and pushed his way through the bikes to be at Jimbo's side. As we came up to the Southern Cemetery roundabout, there was another police officer on his motorbike who was going to try and redirect us onto their chosen route. But we had been given our instructions by Jimbo and as we reached the roundabout, he gave the signal to split.

It was like watching an explosion happen. Sixty-plus bike were splitting up and heading off in every direction possible. As we looked back over our shoulders at the roundabout, all that was left were four white Nortons with four stunned police officers on them not knowing who to follow.

Half-an-hour later it was like someone had held a massive

magnet and dangled it over Ringway Road as all the motorbikes converged as though drawn there by the force of that magnet.

Jimbo did a rough head count and said it looked like we had lost a couple of riders back at the roundabout and luckily the police as well. We waited a few more minutes for the stragglers to turn up. 'That's about it. Let's go, lads!' said Jimbo, and once again we set off without a police escort this time and headed for the hills.

As it started to get dark, we began turning on our lights and all too soon we left the city and the wide, well-lit roads behind us, and started to climb the hills on the winding, narrow roads devoid of lighting.

Thank you, Mr Percy Shaw, for your marvellous invention of 'cats' eyes.' They have saved many a life.

The clobber we wore for a bike ride included helmet, white scarf, leather jacket, jeans, boots with white Sea Boot socks folded over the top of the boots, and on the soles of our boots were steel studs.

Jimbo signalled to pull over. We stopped on the top of the hill and looked back down into the valley. We could see the long winding trail of motorbikes still coming up to meet us in single file.

It was now well past eight in the evening and the night was as black as pitch when Jimbo had his brain fart. 'I want one long line of bikes with no lights on.'

'What? You want us to go down these roads with no lights? You must be bonkers.'

'No, well, yes, sort of,' replied Jimbo. 'I'll go down first with my lights on. You can all follow my tail-light. You lot follow on behind with lights off. Put your boots on the road. That should give a shower of sparks nearly half a mile long coming down the mountain.' Well, it sounded really stupid and dangerous, but it also sounded like a lot of fun, so we all agreed.

It was spectacular. In the darkness, it looked like a long sheet of flame winding its way down from the top of the hill. It was like a Dragon had woken from a long sleep and was breathing fire as it left its lair in search of a young maiden.

The effect was so good, we did it twice more.

PART 3 THE DEVIL RIDES OUT

You just can't beat a late-night Halloween ride with all your mates. I know this may seem daft to a lot of folk, but we did it quite a few times and it was just a bit of fun, sort of.

I had joined up with the lads and some of their girlfriends for a ride from the Motorbike Club at the 1010, the cafe on the 'curry mile' in Manchester.

There were only a few of us that evening for the ride, if you can count twenty to thirty bikes as just a few. We had ridden out to Cheshire for a game of follow the leader. This is where you creep up on a car and follow it wherever it goes and whatever speed it travels. If it turns off the road you're still with it.

One car we followed ended when the driver drove up his own drive, jumped out of his vehicle and ran into his house. Jake saw another vehicle pass and when the driver gave us a dirty look, we followed him home.

The hours passed and we found ourselves going past Ringway Airport on our magical mystery tour of the north west of England.

By now the night had really drawn in and we pulled into a pub at the far side of the airport for a pint of Watney's Red Barrel. I must admit I liked Red Barrel if it came with a splash of lemonade. All the girls had Babycham, a popular drink of the day.

After refreshments, we carried on down the back lanes and found ourselves heading up towards Alderley Edge, a place of myths and legends. We've heard tales that said King Arthur's knights slept here awaiting the call from England to wake them in case the country is ever in distress. It is said, Druids also performed weird magical acts up here, and the Romans dug for tin in the area.

It must have been near enough midnight, 'the witching hour.' We all parked up near the top and strolled over towards the edge and looked down into the valley below towards Manchester. The town sparkled in the darkness. When you see a scene like this on a dark, but warm night, you sit down and enjoy the view, then you look up and see near enough every star in the heavens. It is at times like this you realise all is right with the world and think it good to be alive. You have a smoke, a cough and a quick piddle in the bushes. Life couldn't get any better.

When we got up to return to our bikes someone whispered, 'Shut up and listen.' We stopped dead and listened. We could hear talking and chanting on the breeze.

'It's coming from over there,' said Pete, pointing towards the woods. It was lucky about the chanting because thirty bikers scrambling through the bushes and falling over tree roots in the darkness was bloody noisy. Whoever was singing and chanting in the woods was so engrossed they didn't even hear us approaching.

'Get down,' Vinny whispered.

'There be rum doings going on down there,' said, Jimbo, in his best west country accent.

Well, thirty people dropping onto their bellies in the darkness was so funny. You could hear sounds like 'Ouch,' or 'Bloody twigs!' or 'Watch out!' Also heard was, 'Yuck, smell this, Terry. Is this crap from a fox or a dog?'

'How the hell should I know? Just use the grass to wipe the stuff off your hand.'

We all lay there in the deep grass, our eyes getting used to the fading light.

'So, what are they doing?' Janice asked.

'I reckon it's some sort of fertility dance,' replied her boyfriend. 'Shall we join them?' he asked, adding a wink. 'Ouch!' A punch on his arm from Janice was his reply.

'Shut the hell up, all of you,' said Vinny.

As we watched from our hiding place, we saw a roaring fire and dark shadows that were clearly human going round and round the fire doing some form of dance.

'They all be naked!' whispered Jimbo, with a snigger.

We really paid attention now, but the bright light of the fire and the dark shapes of the folk dancing and long shadows made it nigh impossible to see anything in detail.

'Told yer! They be witches and they is as naked as the day they were spawned by the devil,' added Jimbo.

'Shut up!' said Vinny, as he started to back away from the glow in the woods. We all followed suit.

At the edge of the woods Vinny held an impromptu meeting. 'Now we can have a bit of fun here,' he said. 'We can push our bikes as far as we can into the woods then when I give the signal we start our bikes with full headlights and full revs and we head for the witches. What is it? asked Vinny, in response to Bob's raised hand.

'I've got a combo.' (a motorbike and side-car).

'Well, leave your bike here and cadge a ride.'

'Okay!' was the curt reply from Bob, who felt he was being punished for having a combo.

By now it was generally accepted we were dealing with a bunch of witches. We started pushing our motorbikes through the woods. It was hard going and quite noisy, but the chanting of the witches was getting louder as we got closer to them. We pushed onwards. At the edge of the clearing we stopped and mounted our bikes.

'Now!' shouted Vinny. The woods lit up with all the bright headlights and the sound of the motorbikes roaring into life. Horns started tooting along with the loud cheering of the riders as we came through the undergrowth at speed.

The witches below in the clearing must have thought, 'Hell, Beelzebub himself must be coming after us!' and they ran. All those naked people running in and out of the trees, screaming and shouting, along with the lights and sounds of the bikes must have really put the wind up them.

They didn't stop running until they reached their vehicles on the far side of the woods.

As we reached the fire we stopped the bikes, turned off the headlights and looked into the darkness as their cars pulled away at speed, headlights sending shards of light through the gaps in the trees.

We fell about laughing as we sat on the grass around the fire. It was then we noticed the bundles of clothes under the bushes. 'Bloody hell! They were in the nuddie,' said Mike picking up a pair of knickers, 'Yuk! he said, throwing them on the fire.

'Hell, they must all be driving home in the nude,' observed Janice.

They won't be needing these clothes, then,' added Vinny, picking up a bundle of clothes and chucking them on to the fire. Everyone started picking up clothes and throwing them on the fire.

'They deserved that,' said Jimbo, removing a belt from a pair of jeans before throwing them on the fire.

It's disgusting leaving a forest in this state,' added Janice.

We stayed there for an hour or so laughing and talking and wondering what these modern-day witches would say to their friends and family when they crept into their homes in the early hours of the morning in the nude. Better still, what if they were stopped by the police?

A special note to the witches. Boo! You know who you are and what you got up to in the early 60's

PART 4 NOT JUST ANY FLAG

For my first job in 1966, I worked at the iconic Daily Express building in Manchester as a messenger boy. Sometimes you got lucky and had a relative who was well-thought of or was one of the top dogs in the union. My uncle Roy was one such person, He was the FOC (Father of the Chapel) and he worked in what was called the Wire Room. It was a room full of the latest tele-communications equipment and press agencies from around the world would send in their latest photographs.

Uncle Roy got me the job there. A messenger boy is just a name for a general dog's body. My first job was in the Art Department looking after ten artists who would touch up photographs to be reproduced for inclusion in the newspaper. I made the tea and gave them fresh jars of water so they could mix their water-based paints. My shift was 3 until 11 pm.

I was running backwards and forwards for the whole of my shift, going to the library and getting stock pictures from the files, or going to the darkroom waiting for photos that had been processed by our own cameramen. I was the guy who sent all the photographs upstairs to be turned into metal photographic images. They were then returned to me with two ink copies of the photo. I wrote on the metal plate ink images all the details of that photo and sent one ink copy and the metal image to the stone where it was inserted into a metal frame that would make up part of the page that would run in the paper.

In the press for weeks, all of Manchester, if not the whole of the country, had been force-fed information about the forthcoming World Cup. TV, Radio and even the Royal Mail were getting in on the act by producing special postage stamps.

One fine afternoon before the artists came in for their shift, I went down the stairs to the foyer with my bottle of Coke, through the front doors and sat on the doorstep for my break. As I supped my Coke and watched the trolley buses go up and down the road, I noticed a man admiring the window display at the side of the Express building.

Being a bit of a nosey sod, I got up and had a gander. I was wondering what the theme for the window would be this month. Talk about being gob-smacked. It was all about the World Cup and Umbro products dominated. There were football shirts of most of the major teams who wore Umbro kit and photographs of the England team, plus a big cut out of the English Lion World Cup Willie. Right there in the middle of this window display was a flag, but not an ordinary run of the mill flag. It was an England corner flag.

These little flags would flutter in all the grounds where the matches were to be played. It was a Union flag, with a gold Jules Rimet Cup in the centre of it and the words, 'World Championship England 1966' around the outside. It was stunning. This had to be the best-dressed window in Manchester and Umbro did it proud. I badly wanted that flag, but as luck would have it, I saw the door at the back of the display open, and a man's head poked through the opening. I ran back into the building just in time to see the window-dresser close and lock the sliding door.

'Hi!' I said. 'I just wanted to compliment you and Umbro on your window display.'

'Well, thank you, son,' he said. 'I'm glad you like it.'

'Like it? I replied. 'It's fantastic and the corner flag sets the whole window off.' You know that moment when you're pretty certain that someone is buttering you up, well this chap had that look on his face and he knew I was going to ask for something. And here it came. 'I hope you don't mind me asking, but I just have ask. What happens to the window display when the event it's promoting is over?'

The chap looked at me and smiled. 'What part of the display do you want, son?' he asked.

'That corner flag. It's absolutely brilliant,' I said.

'Look,' he replied. 'Write your name and address down on a piece of paper and I'll see what I can do.' I thanked him, as I handed over my details. For weeks after I looked at that window display and nearly drooled as I looked at the flag.

On the day of the 'England V Germany' final, I was on the front door step of the Daily Express listening to the match with about twenty others. The whistle blew. There were massive cheers and near hysteria when England won the World Cup beating Germany 4-2.

Once again, the Royal Mail over-printed their Special Souvenir England stamps with England Winners. Well, that was the first and the only time in English history that we won the World Cup. It must have been weeks later when most of the fuss over the World Cup had died down when my mum shouted, 'David are you getting up? There's some post for you down here.' You know what it's like when you are half asleep and your brain is not working yet. Who the hell could be sending me a letter?

Then it hit me. I ran downstairs and there on the kitchen table was a small brown paper parcel. I ripped it open and there inside was my 'WORLD CUP CORNER FLAG' with a covering letter from Umbro, saying best wishes. Within half-an-hour a thank you letter was written and posted.

I was sixteen at the time, but now I'm going sixty-six and still waiting for another World Cup win for England.

The flag still has pride of place on my wall.

PART 5 FORGOTTEN HERO

I was young and I worked with many men who were a lot older than me and who were in the war. Towards the end of the 60's after leaving the Daily Express, I started work for a large Security Company. After a period of training, one of my jobs was to guard factories. One I had to patrol was a large liquid natural gas storage company on the outskirts of Manchester.

Now I was working with another security officer. I'll call him Charlie. (Sometimes I wondered how they got past their initial interview). The basic job was to control who came on the site, and to patrol it. Around the clock, to assist in the patrols, we had a German Shepherd dog called Jet and he was one big dog.

On this particular night, I had just returned to the security lodge after securing Jet in his pen. As I opened the lodge door, I found the interior in total darkness which, in itself, is not unusual, as most security officers prefer to sit in the dark so their eyes are attuned to the darkness of the night. But on this occasion, there was nobody about. It looked like the lodge had been abandoned.

'Charlie! Charlie!' I shouted, just in case he was in the loo or even the back room.

'I'm here,' said a whispered voice.

'Where?' I asked.

'Down here,' replied the voice from below the table.

I turned on the lodge's lights and, as they flickered into life, I looked down at the table. I saw a hand poke out from beneath it. 'Is that you, Charlie?' I asked.

'Yeah. Keep quiet or they'll hear you.'

I quickly looked around the lodge, but there was nobody else present. 'Charlie,' I said, 'there's nobody here.'

'That's what they want you to think,' he whispered back.

'Who does?' I asked. Now this is getting weird, I thought.

'The Jap' guards. They're looking for me,' was the whispered response.

I stood up and turned on the transistor radio. Luckily Radio Piccadilly was broadcasting and the sounds of pop music flooded the security lodge. I thought perhaps the sounds of the present would snap him back to the present day.

'Ssshhhh! They'll come!' he hissed.

'It's okay, Charlie,' I replied. 'They've all gone.'

Slowly, he stuck his head out from under the table. 'Is it safe now?' he asked.

'Yes,' I said, as I helped him up from his hiding place.

'Come on, sit down, Charlie, and I'll make us a brew.' He sat down and listened to the radio.

I think it was the light being turned on, as well as the modern music, that brought him back to the present day.

About an hour later I sent him home and continued the shift by myself and, as was the practice, when I made my next contact call at 2:30 with the security company's base, I told them he had gone home sick. I never told them the real reason, but I was never to see him again.

Quite a few weeks later I was talking to another security officer who knew of him and he told me that Charlie was a Japanese prisoner of war for many years. Then it hit me: that poor man must have gone through hell and back and his brain would not let him forget the horrors he had endured.

PART 6 SHADOW MAN

'I'm one of those guys who believes there is or should be a scientific reason for everything, but –

Back in '73, I started working for a large company in Trafford Park in Manchester as a Security Officer. I was proficient in my trade as I had previously worked for one of the world's largest security companies 'Group 4' and normally nothing fazed me and, as they say - I'd seen it all before.

It was late in August and the factory across the road was as usual working flat out, but the office block had shut down in preparation for the long August bank holiday weekend. The site I worked on was extremely large and split into three sections due to its location at a crossroads. We always had at least eight officers working on a shift, all of us connected to each other via our radio system. One officer was a lodge man, the other a patrolling officer.

I was lucky, or so I thought. I was the patrolling officer of the offices. I had said goodnight to the last of the office staff as they left the building for their long weekend off. 'Right, it's nine o' clock, Jim. I'm off to do a shut down,' I said to the lodge man.

'Okay,' replied Jim, as I picked up my radio, torch and the patrol keys. As I left the security lodge, I crossed the short path and entered the offices. As I turned to lock the doors I had entered the building by, I saw the security barriers at the gate coming down and the outer gates sliding across the entrance to secure the site for the night.

It would normally take a good two and half hours to secure this three-storey glass and concrete building built in the early sixties. I secured doors and offices and started turning off lights as I went along. Even the lifts were immobilised with my master key, in fact, every single door and light was locked or turned off, I was confident it was a good lock down and everything was tightly secured for the long weekend.

As I left the building, I turned round to give the building a quick once over. 'Yup, job's a good un,' I thought, as I walked away to check the car park.

'Kilo Hotel to Base. Over,' I said into my radio.

'Base standing by. Over,' responded the main control room.

'Kilo Hotel, main office block secured. Now doing my patrol of the car park. Out,' I replied.

'Base received. Out.'

As I walked about I could hear my fellow officers confirming their night patrols with the control room. There was never any set time for patrolling buildings because you didn't want anybody to see you go in or out of buildings on a regular time slot since it was an open opportunity to thieves.

After a while, the radio chit chat stopped as the officers went back to their lodges for a brew.

Later that night, knowing the offices were really secured, I decided upon a car park patrol first, before I re-checked them again.

It was after I had finished my patrol of the car park that I headed for the offices, but as I crossed the car park I saw the dark outline of a figure watching me from a ground floor window. Even though the offices were in total darkness, the road lighting on the far side of the building shone through it and it made the man's dark outline visible to me.

I never took my eyes off the unknown watcher for a second. 'Hotel to Echo,' I called.

'Echo standing by,' replied my lodge man.

'Jim, has anybody gone in the admin offices since I left?'

'That's a negative, Dave,' responded Jim.

'Well, I think somebody's in there,' I replied.

'Do you require any assistance, Dave?' Jim asked.

'Negative, Jim. I'll check it out,' I said, but then I blinked and the silhouette in the window was gone from view. I ran to the locked building and checked out the area where I had seen the figure, but nothing. It was just an empty washroom. Everything was locked tighter than a drum. 'Is it my imagination?' I thought. Well, it was 3 am in the morning so I decided tiredness must creeping upon me. I relocked the building and left.

Curiosity got the better of me and I returned to my previous location on the car park. 'Bloody hell,' I thought. 'He's there.' He was three windows further down, just standing there watching me. As I took my eyes off him to use my radio, he was gone again when I looked up. This time I was 100% certain we had an intruder.

'Kilo Hotel to all patrol officers,' I called on my radio. 'Intruder in the admin block.'

'Kilo India on the way.'

'Kilo Golf on the way.'

'Kilo November on the way.'

Within three minutes, three other officers had joined me. I explained what I'd seen and that I had previously searched the building again looking for the man I saw but couldn't find. I was sure there was an intruder this time.

Four patrol officers entered the building and searched everywhere, locking and unlocking doors from basement to the top lift motor rooms. After an hour, nothing was found and as we left the building my fellow officers were laughing and calling me names like, 'You big daft idiot,' Or, 'Were you sleep-walking, Dave?'

'But I did see someone in there,' I protested.

'Yeah, yeah,' they mumbled, as we walked away, but Roy, the patrolling officer from the warehouse, looked back at the building and stopped dead in his tracks. In a loud voice, he said, 'Top floor. Second window along.'

We all saw him watching us walk away so now they believed me.

'Dave and Charlie, stay here,' Roy shouted. 'Keep an eye on him while me and George go back in.'

Still the road lights from the other side of the offices shone through the building. We watched the shadow man disappear and then reappear in the next window down.

Within moments Roy and George were in the building turning lights on as they went. At this rate, I thought, the building will be lit up like Blackpool illuminations and there was not going to be any hiding place for this intruder.

'Charlie,' I said, 'if they flush him out, you cover the front door and I'll do the back.'

'That's fine by me,' replied Charlie.

The third-floor lights went on. Over the radio, Roy was heard to say, 'First and second floors checked and secured.'

'We can still see him, Roy!' Charlie shouted, into his radio. 'He's now at the fourth window down.' From our vantage point we could see Roy and George enter the third floor and move along.

Now, here's the thing I don't get: Roy and George were clearly visible. We could see their uniforms quite clearly due to the many fluorescent light strips illuminating the whole floor. If we could see our lads that clearly, why couldn't we make out any features on that dark shadow man? He was just a dark shape with no visible features at all.

'Keep coming, Roy. He's just three windows down from you now,' Charlie shouted on his radio.

'I don't see him,' replied Roy, as he kept on walking along the window line.

Now I started doing a running commentary. 'Two window down. He's still there,' I said, 'Can't you see him?'

'No, I can't,' replied the exasperated voice, of the patrol man.

'He's next to you!' I shouted.

Roy stopped and looked down at Charlie and me on the car park and waved his hands.

'There's nowt here,' said Roy. The window framed Roy and the shadow man perfectly with the bright office lights behind them both.

My partner on the car park, Charlie, called on the radio, 'Roy,' he said, 'the shadow man is standing next to you. You are literally standing shoulder to shoulder with him.'

'Honest guys,' replied Roy. 'There's nobody here.' We watched as George appeared from the opposite end of the room and walked straight into the shadow man who dissolved into nothingness.

Why the shadow man could only be seen from a distance by us, and not by the officers standing next to him I'll never know, but on a final note, I don't know if it was the bright lights that scared the shadow man away, or maybe it was the presence of humans who only believed in scientifically proven things in this world. A shadow man didn't fit into anyone's view of things, but on that night, four professional security officers had no idea what was going on, even though they had hunted for the will 'o' the wisp.

They say seeing is believing, but is it?

PART 7 I AIN'T AFRAID OF NO GHOST

Being a young and green security officer was often a case of sink or swim. It was just a normal night, or so I thought. The security company I worked for was short staffed on this particular evening when I got a call from control.

'Dave,' said the controller, 'There's no-one to cover the site in Clayton and, as there's two on your site tonight, can you whip over there and let the lad who's on duty clear off home?'

'Okay,' I replied. 'Give me the address.' Previous experience proves there's nothing worse than waiting for a relief that's never going to come especially after a long twelve-hour shift.

It was dark when I arrived at the designated site at about 20:30 or thereabouts to be met at the gates by the off-going lad. 'Here's the keys. The dog's called MAX. He's been fed and he's in the pen around the back. He'll take you around the place and I'll be back at 7 in the morning,' he said, as he zoomed off on his moped.

'Yeah. See you at 7,' I said, as I gave him a half-hearted wave. I'm sure he didn't hear me over the putt, putt sound of his moped. I watched him as he disappeared into the distance.

As I stood there outside the gates looking up at the crumbling building I was to take charge of for the night, I thought, 'What a dump!' As I walked through the wrought iron gates, taking in my surroundings, my first impressions were correct. It was a dump. The site was a large red-brick Victorian goods' warehouse and stood several stories high. At one time, I think it must have been a goods' station. I could see there was a long platform reminiscent of an old railway system on the other side of the yard.

I locked the old and groaning gates behind me and gave a silent laugh at the thought that the padlock and chain I was securing them with were probably worth more than the gates themselves. Putting the bunch of keys in my pocket, I walked down a dark passageway into a goods' yard. There I saw three of those red and cream coloured three-wheeled British railways Scammell Scarab trucks parked up and their trailers loaded ready to make their delivers the next morning.

As I strolled across to the other side of the cobbled yard, I saw the sign saying, 'Weigh-Bridge Office: this way'. I looked at my large bunch of keys as I walked across the oily cobbles to the office and found the correct one for the old door.

Upon, entering the office, I noticed it was dirty with a large built in Avery scale, ledgers stacked everywhere, plus two old black telephones and a couple of chewed pencils sticking out of an old plastic cup. 'Dirty sods,' I said, to myself. After having a good look around the office I found the kettle, cups and a small fridge with a half full bottle of sterilised milk inside. 'I know there will be sugar and tea bags somewhere,' I thought, as I searched high and low and found them in the second drawer down in the old filing cabinet. Well, that was the basics sorted, but somewhere out there was a guard dog called Max in a pen, so I decided to go looking for him.

That's when I noticed the dog's leash was hung behind the door. Well, leash is the wrong word for it. It was actually a tow rope with a collar on the end. Just from its leash I knew it must be one monster of a dog! Next to the door I saw the torch hanging on a nail. Flicking it on I noticed the battery was low. It only had a dim yellow beam of light, but I thought this better than nothing.

I had a quick look around and shouted for Max. I heard him bark and followed the sound. I found him. God only knows what breed of dog it was. I guessed at a cross between an Alsatian and a rare four-legged Yeti that was mated with a long-haired Shetland cow! Well, that was possibly the best way to describe it.

Now, I'm under the impression that guard dogs are trained to respond to the uniform we wear. Well, Max bounded up to the fence ready for his walk and, to be honest, it would have been easier for me to put on a saddle and ride him, than use the tow-rope leash.

I finally managed to get him out of the pen and fixed his lead to his collar. I was dragged by this massive dog all around the place until he saw a cat and that's when Max ripped the tow rope from my grasp. I watched as Max vaulted over a crate on the platform and disappeared down what was once the rail tracks and into the darkness until his barking finally stopped.

Now the thing with these old types of Victorian buildings is they are a maze of dimly lit passageways and storage areas, so I started my patrol quickly. I was not worried about Max. I knew he would return to his pen at some time during the night. Anyway, it was an enclosed site to stop any thieves getting in.

Now, in most places I had to visit during my shift, there would be clocking points, but as I had no site map of their locations for this Victorian building, I thought, 'Sod it.'

I started my patrol on the ground floor. I opened the modern glass door and flicked a switch. The fluorescent light made its usual pinking noise before it lit up. 'Offices', I thought. As I surveyed the area, I noted the carpet on the floor, filing cabinets, typewriters, loos and photographs on the desks. Everything looked okay so I turned the lights off and proceeded around the corner. I pressed the switch on the wall and on came the lights.

I ascended the plush carpeted stairs. As I reached the first floor, the stair lights clicked off. Probably a timed-switch. The door was an old wooden type, but it was painted green. Now this floor only had a Lino floor covering and only one or two lights hanging from the ceiling that actually worked. This area was sparsely furnished with old chairs and desks: a junk room. Just as downstairs, I noted the rooms were large. Turning off the lights, I left this floor to go up to the third.

There was no floor covering on the stairs just bare wood. 'Cheap-skates,' I thought, and you know the old saying, 'out of sight, out of mind?' Well, these office areas were. 'Never mind,' I said to myself, continuing upwards. I pressed the timer-light switch. Nothing happened. 'Bloody hell. They haven't even bothered to put a light bulb in the socket, but that's not a problem. I've got a torch! I turned it on and it had the weakest possible light. Pointing the torch at the floor the beam from it barely illuminated my shoes and it was now very dark.

The third-floor door was ajar. Its hinges had seized up years ago. This floor was just bare planks of wood, cobwebs, dust, old newspapers and ledgers from the early 1900's, all stacked on top of each other. I'm sure I even saw some rats. As I walked along the wooden floor, every step I took produced a groan or a creaking from the boards.

The beam of my touch wouldn't even reach the floor, but there was a little bit of light trying to push through the grime on the side windows from the outside street lights. This was comforting as my torch was now flickering on and off. I repeatedly tapped the touch hoping it would stay on.

My nerves were on edge. I was dreading the fact there might be holes in the floor I couldn't even see. I'm sure I could feel the rats scurrying around my feet and now every creak in the floorboards made me spin around thinking there was somebody or something just behind me. Boy, was I pleased to leave that floor. I turned the corner to face the next flight of stairs.

In the darkness, I was fumbling for the light switch on a crumbling plaster wall and that's when I made my silent wish: 'Please work.' I found the circular light button. I couldn't resist. I pressed it, knowing in my heart of hearts it wouldn't work and I was right. It didn't!

'Torch, now you work,' I said, to myself. I flicked the switch. The dim glow from my torch just about illuminated the picture of a painted hand on the wall, pointing upwards. Underneath was the word: *Stores*. 'Oh, no, not another flight of stairs.' Once again, creaking boards and groaning wood accompanied me upwards. Now I was scared there was no light at all and my torch was all about useless: the bulb only lit now and again when I tapped the glass lens. Then it was of no use. All the time my hand was brushing the crumbling wall. The wallpaper was hanging off in dried up curls. I think it must have been white at some time in its past, but now it was black, grey and mouldy.

'Drat, drat, drat!' I'm sure something ran over my foot, but it was too fast and dark to see anything. On these narrow stairs, I've got a damp rotten wall on one side and a rickety old bannister on the other when my useless torch hit a closed door.

I don't know if you've ever experienced total blackness, but you sort of sense things like a built-in radar. You just know that something is close to you like a wall and your hand automatically goes out to meet it.

I could just about make out the door. I tapped the touch again. It flickered a little bit, but I forced the last bit of life out of it. As my hand touched the door, I could feel the wood was very old. It was cracked and the peeling paint was dry and blistered with age, but there was something else, something written on the door in chalk.

I kept hitting the torch. 'Work, work, you, dipstick, work!' I shouted. I was holding the torch lens so close to the door it was actually touching the wood. My torch sparked back into life. It was a very faint glow. I could only make out one letter at a time. The first letter was a B. I moved my touch right up close to the writing.

E. I moved my touch even closer to the letters: W. A. R. E. 'Oh! Beware,' my mind said, repeating the word in my head. The letters O and F were a bit faded, but were readable. 'Right, beware OF T. H. E. Beware of the G.H.O.S.T.' I said, aloud.

Beware of the Ghost!

I dropped the torch and ran. Well, you've never seen a young lad belt down so many stairs in the pitch darkness in all your life. Even to this day, I wonder why I wasn't killed coming down those stairs two at a time, but I must have scared every rat and mouse in that whole flipping building with the amount of noise I was making running blindly down the rickety stairs.

Finally, out of the building and into the cool of the night I ran through the site until I found the safety of the office again. Once inside, I bolted the door and turned on the lights and the radio. But I was still shaking. I slid the office window open and shouted, 'Max, come here, boy!' hoping the dog would hear me.

I heard the scratching at the door. It was the dog. 'Get in here,' I said, slamming and then bolting the door behind him. Terrified, I waited for daylight to return. Well, I *was* just a kid at the time and frightened nearly to death.

PART 8 DING-DONG, AVON CALLING

'Back in a bit,' said Mum, as she slung her black bag over her shoulder and left the house.

'So, where's Mum gone?' I said, looking at Roger.

'Ding Dong, Avon Calling,' sang Roger.

'What do you mean by that?' I asked.

'She's gone to sell that Avon stuff to the ladies in Sloane Street,' said Roger. 'Dad always says they are Mum's best customers for her make-up and according to him they are Ladies of the Night,' said Roger, with a knowing nod.

'Oh,' I said, 'and what are Ladies of the Night?'

'I don't know,' replied Roger, 'but Dad does.'

About half hour later, Mum returned. 'Sorry about that,' she said, as she placed her black shoulder bag on a chair. 'I'll start your tea in a mo. I've just got to send off an order to Avon.'

'Did you sell a lot of make-up to your Ladies of the Night?' I asked, innocently.

Mum put down her order book and gave me a look that could melt the tar on the road and with a shocked face, said, 'What?' You know may the look you get from your mum when she looks at you in that certain way the lowers her head. At the same time, she stretches her neck towards you as if she's totally confused by your comments?

'What did you say?' she repeated. 'Ladies of the Night?'

'Yes,' Roger said, with a know-it-all grin. 'They were the Ladies of the Night and Dad knows all about them.'

'And how would a twelve-year old boy know that?' she asked.

'Well,' said Roger, 'Dad told me. He knows all about them and sees them all the time.'

'Oh, does he now?' asked Mum, sarcastically. 'I'll be having a chat with him later when he comes home for his tea.'

'So, what is the favourite colour lipstick for the Ladies of the Night, Mum?' I asked, trying to look inside her case which was like a mobile make-up shop.

'Does it really matter?' asked Mum, slamming the lid of the case shut and just missing my fingers. 'Ask your dad when he gets home since he seems to know all about it!'

'I'm only asking, Mum,' said I. You know how sometimes it makes sense to move away from a subject? I got that feeling just then.

Not long afterwards, when Dad returned from work, the air in our house was distinctly chilly. As Mum started with her cryptic questions, Roger and I left the kitchen to listen outside the door.

'So, have you been busy dear or do you need to go to bed and have a rest?' asked Mum of Dad.

'I'm fine,' replied Dad.

'Are you sure?' Mum asked, again.

'What are you on about, love?' said a puzzled Dad.

'You know only too well,' said Mum, now standing with arms folded and a face like a wet weekend. 'Roger told me all about it.'

'Told you what?' asked Dad, who was totally flummoxed.

'Don't give me that,' said Mum. 'You know what I'm on about.'

'I flipping wish I did,' said Dad.

'Ladies of the Night,' said Mum, 'and you've been seeing them. Apparently, you told Roger that my best customers were Ladies of the Night.'

'No! answered Dad. 'Yesterday, when Roger asked where you were going, I said you sell make-up to the ladies on nights from the jam factory not Ladies of the Night! I see them going home in the morning when I go to work.'

There was a long silence till Mum said, 'Fine!' Mum would never admit she was wrong about anything and she still liked to make Dad feel guilty. 'Well, you should be more careful about what you say when the children are about, Arthur! Now sit down and I'll get your tea.'

'Ha ha. Dad got a telling off,' said Roger, looking at me and giggling.

'You two!' shouted Dad. 'Get in here now!'

Slowly, Roger opened the door and looked around it. 'Hi, ya, Dad,' he said.

'In here now, both of you, and say you're sorry to Mum,' said Dad, angrily.

'Sorry, Mum,' Roger and I said, in tandem.

Roger whispered, 'Dad, what have we done that we're sorry for?'

'Forget it, son, and let's just hope Mum does the same.'

A MINGLED YARN
Julie Hatton

1 THE CHIMNEY SWEEP

I was born in 1955 and the days Dad set about sweeping the chimney were always exciting. Much of this was due, not just to the actual event itself, but to Mom's ability to transform even the most mundane of things into an adventure.

The usual day for this exciting occasion was always a Sunday. If it was winter time, this meant Mom didn't have to get up quite so early to light the fire to warm us up before work and school. Instead, we dressed under the bed-clothes in our arctic rooms, even putting our socks and shoes on beneath the heavy, often damp, blankets on our beds. My sister and I would help our younger brother to dress.

With a clattering of feet on the bare-boards of the stairs we would tumble into the tiny kitchen only to be hustled out immediately by our already harassed mother. Three different cereals in cracked bowls were issued to three different children at the door of the kitchen. Hot saucepan in hand our mom would pour a mixture of hot milk diluted with water over each cereal. A light sprinkling of sugar and we would turn and walk into the small 60's living-room and perch on chairs to eat our breakfast. Soon a frazzled Mom would appear with a cracked wooden tray carrying three cups of tea. Not long afterwards our dad would appear fully dressed in his oldest clothes. After eating, he would sit reading the paper.

The three of us kids would slouch in a line on the settee reading our comics and occasionally pushing and shoving each other. The only tool Dad needed in his armoury to discipline us kids was something no money could buy. It was called, *The Look*. We would be squabbling or arguing and suddenly one of us would be startled by the invisible beam radiating from *The Look*. That child would stop misbehaving immediately, but the others not caught in the headlights would continue. It was the first child's job to warn the siblings of danger. Into our playmates' ears we would fiercely whisper, 'The Look! The Look!' As though shot through with a thunderbolt, we kids would become rigid and endeavour to remain calm and quiet for a few minutes before the ritual began again.

Sunday in our house was a special day anyway. Dad worked late during the week and we kidswere in bed by the time he got home and he often worked all day Saturday, too. Sunday was usually the only chance we had to see and be with him. Our Sunday dinner was special because Mom usually made a huge toad-in-the-hole in her extra-large rusty roasting tin. There was always lots of thick onion gravy to pour over it. To have sausages was a real treat for our family and we all relished the thought of them. Sunday was already a special day, but when Dad was going to sweep the chimney it was extra special.

This being the case, Mom would bake her special chocolate cake made with our drinking chocolate powder. The recipe was taken from a food-smeared, tall and slim, Be-Ro booklet, naturally sepia in colour. It had been her mother's. It's now mine. These cakes were generally reserved for birthdays, but Mom wanted to make the day special. Dad would sweep the chimney and she would make a feast.

Sometimes, Mom allowed me to stand watching her in the tiny kitchen when she cooked, but it made things awkward: there was barely enough room for one let alone two! On this special day, she would also make a few very tiny toffee apples and, to this day, I still hear her telling me repeatedly to stay away from the pan because the sugar was now terrifyingly and dangerously hot! The cake was for tea so Mom would make bread and margarine pudding with a few sultanas, a bit of sugar, warm milk and a sprinkling of nutmeg. In those early years, no egg was ever put in when I was a kid, but we loved it. Sometimes, for an extra special treat, Mom would sprinkle it with crunchy brown demerara sugar!

Dad would then enlist our help to clear the clutter from the sitting-room into the narrow entry. Next, out would come the old brown and orange curtains to cover the furniture. The best bit used to be watching him unroll the huge, dirty cream dust-sheet. In the centre were four slashes radiating from one centre point.

The three of us would be sent to the top of the garden to fetch several bricks from the neat stack by the garage. We would place them in a pile on the floor and from the door watch as dad began hanging the dust-sheet from the shelf above the fireplace putting it so the slashes hung just in front of the open grate. He kept the sheet in place with a line of bricks along the mantle.

It was about this time that Mom would pass us our toffee apples. We would squeeze in the doorway watching Dad setting about his business in his usual slow and methodical manner. As we bit into and crunched on the burnt, bitter toffee covering the small tart apples we could not have been happier!

Dad would then pop out with a 'look' and a loud staccato, 'Do *not* touch!' and trail up the long garden to the garage at the back which bordered the gully. We would watch as he came back with an enormous flat, round brush of rigid steel-spikes and a set of poles. At the back door, we would lick, crunch and watch as he deftly screwed the thin pliable bamboo poles together to make one extremely long one. We would move out of the way to let him through to the sitting-room, the pole trailing behind him. This was all utterly fascinating to us kids. No matter how many times we watched this scenario, it always remained intensely exciting.

On his knees, Dad would lift up the bottom of the dust-sheet and put the large spiky brush-head into the grate. The sheet was then weighted down all along the bottom with more bricks. His arm would go through the slashes to grab the pole. With his other hand, he would slowly pull on the pole and attach it to the head without disturbing the sheet. We would watch as he pushed on the pole. Slowly and gradually the pole would be eaten up by the chimney.

As it went on its journey, Dad would give sharp jerks to dislodge the soot-lining. Suddenly, he would shout, 'Now! Go Now!' and at his command we, along with Mom, would run through the kitchen, down the entry, and into the back garden. Pushing and shoving with the excitement of the morning, we kids raced to the bottom of the garden and looked up.

'Ready!' Mom would shout to Dad in the house and, suddenly, out of the top of the chimney, would pop the spiky brush. At this we would cheer hard, long and loud. It was like a magician pulling a rabbit out of a hat. Dad would then join us and begin munching on his toffee-apple as he stood behind us, satisfied face to the sky, his long arms encircling the three of us in front of him. As we stood there as a family with Mom and Dad it was certainly a glorious moment of togetherness to remember and to treasure.

2 DAD AND THE GLIDER

My brother had a few Airfix models occasionally for birthdays or Christmas, but wasn't allowed to hang them from the ceiling. Thinking back at the image of Dad and my brother hunched over the table, I suspect Dad was doing most of it whilst my very able brother tried to take it back. It was his plane after all!

Once, Dad made a huge glider out of balsa wood with super fine paper placed over the double wings. We were not allowed anywhere near it. It took him months of messing about and fine tuning this or that. It actually had a little motor on it. Finally, after months of waiting, on a glorious summer's day, we all went to Sutton Park to fly the monster, a monster so dangerous we avoided knocking it at all costs. I can't remember how he worked the motor, but he pointed it into the blue sky and with a gentle throw it glided into the air for a few seconds before crashing into the top of a very tall tree.

With baited breath, we watched that plane as it teetered back and forth on the branch before crashing to earth and breaking into a myriad of fragments.

None of us dared look at Dad. No-one said anything. Mom busily turned her back and arranged our picnic on the rug. We all sat down and in the uncomfortable silence we slowly ate our meal.

Mom packed away and we all walked towards the car. Looking back, we saw Dad go to the sad wreckage of his plane and stand over it. Slowly, he turned, his head hung low. Leaving his masterpiece to the elements, he climbed into the car and drove us away from the tragic scene.

Conversation was somewhat stilted and subdued for a couple of days afterwards. None of us ever said anything about it, nor did Dad. He never made another plane.

3 NANNIE MIN

As a child, I loved tea at Nan's because it was all beautifully laid out on the table. At home, we had meals on our laps. There was little space for a table in the living room, but we did have a front room. It was not a special room for having the vicar to tea or anything like many were. No, it served as a drying room on wet days with huge sheets spread over the backs of dining chairs, tent-fashion! Mom's large Singer treadle sewing machine was in a corner where she made dresses for my sister and myself. The drop-leaf-table served as a cutting table for the dresses bought from jumble sales or donated by neighbours to be cut and sewn to fit Mom's little girls. One of my favourite dresses belonged to an older girl who lived next door. Mom cut it down and added a wide waistband in a contrasting colour which tied in a large bow at the back. I loved that dress. It was one of the prettier ones I had. Others tended to be rather drab.

Nan was a great cook and baker. The cake she made for the tea was generally a Madeira Cake. This was something Nan made virtually every week until she died at 81. She took such pride in this particular cake that I knew and understood there was something very special about it, but even today, I don't know why that was so. I consider myself a 'good' cook and for me the benchmark of a good baker has always been the Victoria Sandwich. It is quite difficult to get it absolutely right and when I do! Perhaps that's how Nan felt about her Madeira cake because it was a real testament to her skill.

I'll always remember one of the best jokes I ever played on Nan when I was a kid. It was a joke bought from the joke shop. Nan was a clean and tidy freak, something which extended to our own bodies and not just the house! She seemed to have a damp flannel permanently attached to her hand. She would catch hold of you when you least expected it, hold your arm, and quick as a flash run the flannel over your face and hands.

On this occasion, we were at Nan's for tea following our weekly shop where I had chosen my joke. The whole family was in on it. Sitting at the well-laden table surrounded by the usual home-made cakes and sandwiches, I secretly inserted a thin glass bubble into one nostril. It looked so realistic, it was unbelievable. It was all I could do not to choke with laughter. My siblings were already smothering giggles. Mom and Dad tried to keep the conversation flowing. I was at the opposite end of the table to Nan. She soon spotted the bubble seemingly blown out of my nose and began trying to indicate to Mom next to me that it was there and needed wiping.

Mom ignored the hints and carried on chatting and eating, but never looking my way. By this time, all the family were in a state of choked guffaws and shrieks of laughter from us kids. Nan's look of stunned bemusement was wonderful to see. Shaking her head, she left the table, walked over to me and ran her damp flannel over my nose. The room erupted when Nan felt the glass bubble and stared at it for several seconds before removing her glasses and doubling up with laughter. The joke was on Nan, but Nan loved a joke, and in the end enjoyed it more than anyone. The story did the round of her friends at the Derby and Joan and became her party piece for many years!

4 THE MENACE

Part 1

My family nicknamed me, 'The Menace.' Not that I was in any way related to Dennis, but because I seemed unavoidably addicted to getting into trouble. I was not naughty, I just seemed to attract mayhem.

Walking to school one day with my elder sister when I was about six, I spotted a tiny car hub from a model car on the wall outside the headmistress's office. Like a magpie, I saw that shiny, silver hub glinting in the sunlight and popped it in my mouth. It tasted nice and metallic. I sucked on it like a sweet. I sucked and sucked almost to the school gates. It was only then I realised I couldn't spit it out. Instead, the dratted thing was firmly suctioned to the roof of my mouth.

I tried to prise it off with a finger nail to no avail. I pulled my sister back and told her it was stuck. There was the usual roll of eyes to heaven that I had come to expect. She stood me still, told me to open wide and tried herself to remove the hub. It resisted all her efforts.

By this time, the roof of my mouth was beginning to feel sore from all the prodding and prising that was going on. Jan grabbed my arm and hurled me through the school's doorway and told me to wait and not move.

I waited for what seemed ages. Finally, she appeared with a teacher, Mr Jenkins. Other children were milling around as he approached me. It was now his turn to try and prise the hub out. I always remember the smell and taste of stale tobacco on his fingers. The roof of my mouth was now quite swollen and throbbing so he sent me home to get it sorted.

Mom was surprised to see me. She had a go at trying to remove the darned thing, too, but no joy. Out came the huge grey pram. Mom flung my brother in and we marched all the way up to Tower Hill. Quite a long way. There, I saw two doctors in the surgery. Once again, I had strangers' fingers in my mouth trying to dislodge the recalcitrant cap. With sad shakes of their heads they told Mom to get me to Birmingham Children's hospital quickly. The swelling had almost covered the disc entirely by now.

Poor Mom scurried home and I followed as fast as my little legs would carry me. Poor Dad was in bed with double-pneumonia and Mom made him get up and take us to the hospital in his van. By this time, the hub could be neither seen nor felt. The swelling had completely encased it.

A nurse tried to dislodge it, then a doctor. I was soon whisked into an operating room and put to sleep. The doctor sliced through and prised the hub out. I was given antibiotics and sent home to bed. It hurt like hell for days, but soon I was up and about ready to give further credence to my name, 'The Menace.'

Part II

Not long before the wheel-hub incident I had already proved my title, 'The Menace,' was highly appropriate. I was five and we lived in a very long, steep street. It seemed to meander for miles. It was a pretty straight road from the bottom to the top. It was probably about three miles long in all.

From the bottom, the road rose quite sharply to the top of the first brow. I lived about halfway up this section. It was a rather wide street with houses either side. The road was lined with large trees evenly spaced. The houses were all of the same ilk: semi-detached with small front gardens and long narrow ones at the back.

Behind the houses was our playground: a wide gully. The road at the front was also a playground. We stayed cleaner playing in the front than the back. There weren't many vehicles, at least not by today's standards. Not many folk had a car. Just as many didn't have their own telephone. We had both, courtesy of Dad's work. A few vehicles would be parked outside the houses. One or two might have been stored in the garages at the back.

It was quite normal for us kids to play out on the street and in the road. Few cars passed through this way. The street was always clean and tidy. It could look quite lovely when the trees were wearing their green summer finery.

It was a warm summer's day and I was outside. With no-one of my own age about to play with I chose to play with a little three-year-old lad. He lived with his parents and grandmother directly opposite. He had a ball. We played with that ball together for a while. I became bored and decided to tease Phillip by taking the ball to my side of the road and pretending I was going to keep it.

Naturally, he set up a-crying and a-cat-a-wauling. His gran came to the front step to see what all the fuss was about. Phillip prattled something about me keeping his ball. I was nervous. I didn't want to get into trouble. His gran shouted, 'Hey, you! Get over here and give him his ball back!' Eager to oblige I ran out into the road and

Bang!

I was hit by a lady driving a white van. My body flew six feet in the air and about twelve feet forwards. I landed with my forehead hitting the pavement. I was out for the count. Unconscious. All hell broke loose. Witnesses say there was much running about and shouting.

Mom and Dad ran out of the house to see what the commotion was about. They found me lying as one dead in the road. Carefully, Dad picked me and lay me still unconscious on the couch. The white-van lady was on the floor by my side crying uncontrollably. An ambulance was called. It soon arrived and I was rushed to hospital, all sirens blaring.

I was unconscious for several hours, but finally came round in a quiet hospital ward that smelled of disinfectant. I was sick on and off for a few hours. I remained in the hospital for three days before being allowed home. It wasn't long before I was up and about again. The moral of the story? Don't play with silly little boys who cry when you steal their balls!

Part III

Occasionally, I was a naughty child and not unintentionally either. Despite the unfortunate incident when I was walloped by a white van, I was still allowed to play in the street.

When not at school, eating or sleeping I was in that darned street. It made for a marvellous playground. Most of the kids played out. The more studious ones stayed inside to read. I, too, loved reading, but not during the fun hours of daylight. Like most kids, I climbed trees and swung from lamp-posts. I particularly enjoyed skipping. Dad had a very long rope often borrowed for this purpose.

The road was very wide. The rope stretched from side to side. It was easy for five of us to skip together at the same time. We played all the skipping games and had great fun.

Something else I dearly loved was roller skating. Living on quite a steep hill made it doubly exciting. My older sister, though not such an obsessive skater, was far more elegant than I. She would zoom down the hill and stop at the bottom by way of a strategically placed lamp-post. As she approached, she would put out her right hand, take hold of the pole and swing around it as gracefully as a swan in flight. The lamp-post was the only means of stopping when you were careering down the road as though on a race-track.

I would set out slowly, my skates gathering speed and momentum until I was in full flight. I would hurtle down that hill as though chased by a rabid dog. How I loved the wind flapping my plaits as I flew along. My balance was excellent. As the houses flashed by in a blur I stayed straight and upright.

The lamp-post was looming all too fast. It ran out to meet me halfway and smacked me in the face! It hurt. An eye-brow was torn, a cheek ripped. I felt dizzy, but I began the long climb back to the house. Once there, I turned, steadied myself, and rocketed down the hill again. Once more the lamp-post hurried to meet me. Again, I tried to emulate my sister. Instead, I attacked the post like a manic bear and sprained a wrist. Over and over and over again I would practise this. A masochist? Maybe. Tenacious? Definitely. I loved the challenge. It was me or the lamp-post. The post always won.

Dad made my sister a wonderful pair of stilts and she would walk up and down the road with great panache. I wasn't very good on them so rarely had a go. No, what a dearly loved was my big scooter. It was fantastic. As with the skates, I tore down that hill as though chased by a demented lunatic. The lamp-post was not a problem. Instead I could whizz around the corner and continue on the flat. I scootered here, I scootered there, I scootered nearly everywhere. I loved the speed generated by the skates and the scooter. I was never fast on foot.

One day, aged 9, my brother's little red tin scooter was lying on the footpath. I was warned by Mom never to use it because I was too big. The devil was in me that day. I had a quick shifty around, picked it up and set off down the hill. I had to bend almost double because it was so small. Suddenly, I wobbled, fell off and broke my arm on the curb.

'The menace' was in no end of trouble again. Mom didn't quite know what to do. She was angry because I disobeyed her, she was upset because I was in pain, and she was annoyed because once again a trip to the hospital loomed. Alternately, Mom shouted at me, hugged me, then shouted again.

We had to wait for Dad to get home from work. Again, there was a lot of eye-rolling between them. My brother and sister were sent to neighbours whilst we went to the hospital. My arm was put in a temporary cast. The next day I was put to sleep, the arm was set and I was taken home to bed. As Mom was always fond of saying, 'If you did as you were told you wouldn't get into trouble now, would you?'

5 GRAN'S BY THE SEA

Part 1

In the 50's, Gran, Mom's mother, moved to Aberarth, Aberaeron, for the sea air recommended by her doctor. This meant she left her family behind in Birmingham. At the time, Mom, her only child, had just the one baby, my sister. My brother and I were but proverbial twinkles.

The little cottage, nestled amidst a small village, backed onto a rocky, stony beach. A tiny toilet with flush was reached at the bottom of a garden path. It was always filled with a huge quantity of spiders, slugs and snails.

Gran had an indoor bath and basin installed when I was about 8. It was sectioned off in the kitchen. It was on here, when we stayed, that my younger brother slept. Dad had fashioned a thick board to fit over the top. The mattress comprised a few blankets. Jan and I had a tiny bedroom upstairs. Either side of the room had a narrow cot-bed under one of which was a porcelain potty. Also under the beds were many large plastic boxes containing rice, both long and short grain, in case of future shortages to ward off starvation. Gran had lived through the shortages of two world wars. On the window-ledge were two stone hot water-bottles. On one wall hung a huge painting of Jesus amongst some fluffy white clouds. I was fascinated by this and would look at it for hours. Mom and Dad had a small bedroom next door. Gran slept on the couch.

Although Gran did eventually have a modern cooker in the kitchen, she had a fire and grate for cooking in the sitting room. Right up until she died at 79, she still used it to boil kettles and cook soups, stews and casseroles.

No matter the season, the cottage remained cold and damp throughout the year. She lit a fire every day from the early fifties until she died in the mid 70's. Gran's fire had a swing-out-stand both sides of the grate, not just one, and the kettle was always boiling away. When it had come to the boil, she would swing it away from the high heat of the fire to the front where it kept warm. This way it didn't take long to re-boil the kettle when required.

She would also use the fire to heat up soup and beans and other things like that. Since there was always going to be a fire it was a very economical way of cooking. It must have reduced her electric bills enormously. There was no bathroom in the house when she bought it. Until she died in the 70's the toilet was still always up the top of her long flat garden. It was continually full of sea snails, slugs and a mass of creeping spiders of all shapes and sizes.

There was no bolt on the rickety wooden door, just a latch, so you had to peer through the large keyless keyhole to check no-one was going to disturb you. I would watch in terror as people ambled up the narrow path towards the tiny shed. I was a very inhibited child and desperately lived in fear of someone opening the door when I was on the toilet, knickers around my ankles!

As youngsters, we spent most of the daylight hours on the beach. It was usually deserted. We loved having it all to ourselves. At the front of the house flowed the River Arth down to the nearby sea. In the narrow part of the river, we built elaborate dams like human otters. We spent the days soaking wet from the river and the sea so it never mattered it always seemed to rain in Wales.

The beach was our hide-away. No house our side of the village over-looked the beach itself. We were literally alone out there. To the right was a huge ancient fish-trap near the shore that stretched out in a wide arc into the sea and back.

One day, we three kids decided to walk the entire trap. My sister was about twelve, me ten and our brother seven. We had great fun carefully picking our way over the rocks and stones. We were tired by the time we reached about mid-way and it was quite some distance back to the shore. The wind was blowing and the waves were getting higher all the time. The tide was also coming in and coming in fast.

It was really scary out there in that huge expanse of sea and beach all alone without adult sight and supervision. The wind began to howl and get stronger, the waves higher, the air colder. The semi-circular fish-trap was getting deeper and deeper in the middle. Even I, a little dare-devil, was becoming terrified. Suddenly, there was a loud splash. My brother had vanished. He was nowhere to be seen.

Slowly, a hand rose from the water and grasped a rock. Our brother's head and shoulders appeared. He was on tip-toe. As my sister reached for his hand he said urgently, 'Leave me. Let me drown.' My sister and I leaned down and hauled him to safety. My brother was actually terrified of the water and couldn't swim like we could.

Somehow, the three of us managed to continue round the trap to the safety of the shore. Altogether it must have taken us about an hour. It was the most frightening thing ever to happen to us.

Part II

We went to stay at 'Gran's by the Sea' maybe twice a year for holidays. She came to us for Christmas. My sister was Gran's favourite and she made it blindingly obvious. I was our Nan's favourite so that evened things out a little.

To be frank, Gran didn't really like me. She preferred my sister because she was quiet and could just sit reading a book. She was no trouble to Gran. I was considered a problem because I couldn't sit still during daylight hours. I always had to be up and doing something even if it was only helping around the house and in the kitchen. At Gran's I was warned, on pain of death, never to help in the house. She just didn't trust me yet I was never clumsy or uncareful. Sadly, I loved my gran just as fiercely as I loved my nan.

Gran always intrigued us as children. She had many secrets. Many cats, both tame and wild. Mom grew up rarely hearing stories about Gran's life for she considered none of it had anything to do with her daughter even when she was a grown woman.

To me, she was terribly mysterious. I imagined her a witch with cats who brewed potions by candle-light during the witching hour. My sister didn't help. She was overly fond, in the dark hours, of telling me terrifying stories with our Gran as the principle antagonist! Her little old-fashioned cottage by the sea with its steep cliffs and haunting wind-swept beach was the stuff of many of my childish imaginings.

One day, my parents, brother and Gran were out and for once my sister and I had been left alone in the house. Swiftly and eagerly we went on a rummage to find more about out this old lady who was also Gran. Gran seemed old and she was in a way. She was unable to have a child until she was 32 in spite of being married since nineteen.

In the upstairs bedroom, we broke into a wardrobe with a key not well-hidden. On the top shelf were literally hundreds of greetings cards shoved in loosely and not in boxes. There were birthday cards, Christmas cards and Valentine's cards. Each one was addressed to 'My Dearest Darling Sweet Angel Child.'

My sister and I, eleven and nine, sat cross-legged on the floor rifling through them all. We didn't say much, but just kept looking quizzically at each other. All these cards were from one man, a man not her husband, but who according to Mom, was a life-long friend. Gran was at his bedside when he died decades later.

Gran's cats always seemed to be dying and, during many a dark night, we often wondered if she was killing them. Mom had told us the story how, when she was a little child, her mom used to drown her cat's kittens using a sack and warm water. This used to horrify Mom. It terrified us.

We put all the beautiful cards back into the wardrobe and began to look through her very old-fashioned clothes that reeked of mothballs. There was a multi-coloured brown full-length fur coat. My sister told me it was made from Gran's dead cats. Fur was expensive and since Gran was a seamstress she had, to us, clearly made her own fur coat inexpensively. I shook with horror and recoiled from the coat as my sister held it up. I was upset for the poor dead cats and hated my beloved gran for killing them just for a coat!

I stood well back as my sister continued to slide the clothes along the rail. Near the end, she picked out a long black dress. As I looked closely, I saw the collar was made out of a white dead cat! I ran as fast as I could down the stairs and into the lounge and cried uncontrollably. My sister came and put her arms around me. She left me to sob for an inordinate amount of time before explaining the brown coat was made out of mink and not dead cats. Since I had no idea what mink was it didn't bother me. She went on to say the collar on the dress was probably another type of animal altogether, but she wasn't sure what, possibly a fox. Yes, my sister always did have a cruel streak when it came to frightening her overly imaginative and naïve younger sister!

Gran, a widow, married again before I was born. She and her husband had only been married for seven months when she returned from shopping to find him dead with his head in the gas oven. No one had any inkling this might happen. It was very traumatic time for Gran

Part III

I was fourteen when Gran bought a two-berth caravan for the back garden for me and my sister to use and sleep in. I clearly remember her sitting at home with us one Christmas regaling the tale of the caravan's arrival. There was no access to the back garden so a huge crane was brought to the front of the cottage. This was perilous. The distance between the house and the river bank was barely wide enough for such huge machinery. Nevertheless, the men persevered and the caravan was swung on wires right over the top of the cottage to find refuge in the garden.

I couldn't wait for our next holiday to live in it for the usual ten-day stay. It was a very long wait until Easter. Finally, the year having dragged its feet with endless school days, suddenly quickened and we were on the long four-hour journey at last. Normally, I simply couldn't wait to get to Gran and the sea-side, but now it was those *and* a new little home in Gran's back-garden that had me overwhelmed with so much excitement it nearly made me sick.

What an adventure: our own secret and private little holiday home by the sea. The caravan was simply wonderful, so comfortable and cosy. Gran had filled a bowl with fruit and another with sweets and chocolates. Bottles of pop were by the sink. A small vase of fresh flowers welcomed us home. The beds were made up ready for sleep. I was in heaven. A great lover of Enid Blyton, I imagined myself as Anne in the Famous Five, the child who was the little mommy who looked after the others when it came to home comforts and food. Like Anne, I spent much of the holiday cleaning and sweeping our little home and keeping the vase filled with fresh flowers from the garden. My sister read a lot and enjoyed all the fuss.

Our brother could now sleep in the tiny bedroom we had slept in. By now he was very tall, though still young, and he had to sleep with his feet on the window-ledge! He didn't mind, though. The bed proved more comfortable than on top of the bath.

This holiday was the first time my sister and I had a séance. It was late evening and, by the light of two candles, (there was no electric in the caravan) we methodically wrote out the alphabet on tiny squares of paper and added one saying *Yes* and another *No*. We had learned about this game from school friends.

Now for a few months I had been madly in love with a lad called Tom. He was 6' 4", had longish curly hair and huge brown eyes He was my sister's age. Two years my senior. I fancied him to bits. My heart swooned whenever I saw him.

With this in mind, I asked our make-shift ouija board if I would ever go out with him. Slowly, the glass moved to: *Yes*.

I asked, *When*?

The glass spelled out, *Soon*.

I asked again, *When*?

After G D.

Deep down, I knew my sister was pushing the glass because it certainly wasn't me. She denied it, of course. I decided to believe her and was over the moon with happiness. I still doubted, but wanted desperately to believe.

A couple of months after returning home, Tom did indeed go out with G D for a few weeks. Then, one evening, Tom and I met in town. I was wearing a green flowing maxi dress and a green fringed poncho. He and I larked about a bit down the river. He even put my poncho on and strutted about to make me laugh. That night he asked me out. I nearly fainted from pure happiness. I had won my man, but just how had my sister or the ouija board known this would all happen as it did?

Part IV

How I loved those holidays at 'Gran's by the Sea'. Gran, the cottage, the village and Wales was an active child's every wish come true. I loved the water and swimming. I was literally obsessed. There really is no other word for it. To immerse my body in cool silky water was all I ever wanted. For this reason, I also loved rain, Sunday baths, puddles, ponds, rivers, and, best of all, the sea.

Though the seaside was right on Gran's doorstep, we couldn't swim very easily with all the rocks and stones so my holidays with Gran were filled with an uncontrollable yearning to get in seas where I could swim. Unfortunately, these occasions were dictated entirely by the weather. The adults needed dry days to sit on the sands while we children went in the water.

I'd wake early each morning and the first thing I did was to look out the window to assess the weather. The rhymes: 'Red sky in the morning, shepherd's warning' and 'Red sky at night, shepherd's delight' were indelibly printed on my brain because they gave some indication of what the weather might be like.

I loved Newquay in Wales. It was a small cove where the sea was always virtually flat and made swimming easy. Games used to be organised here for kids, too, and I loved that.

Then there was Inyslas, just beyond Borth, where it was a long trudge up and down sand-dunes to arrive at the beach. Then it was an extremely long walk again along the huge stretch of beach to the water. This sea was special because it remained shallow for a good few yards. My parents were now a mere speck in the distance, too far away to save us should we be drowning!

Another favourite was Llangranog, another small cove whose waves were always enormous on a windy day! How my sister and I loved diving into the enormous swells and swimming like dolphins. It was here we saw a large brown turd floating not far from us. We got out of the water pretty quickly that day!

Once, we went early in the year to 'Gran's by the Sea'. It was very cold. Undeterred, I still wanted my swimming fix. We had shopped in Aberystwyth. We had walked the pier. By this time, I was brimming over with annoyance. I wanted to swim. I was told it was far too cold to swim. It was snowing for goodness' sake. I insisted. I begged. I sulked. I had my costume under my clothes ready. I had my beach towel. What *was* their problem? I wasn't asking them to come in, too!

Eventually, I got my way. I struggled out of my clothes in the back seat, grabbed the towel and began my way over the shingle beach and, with a gasp, dived into the freezing sea. It was beautiful standing there looking at the grey expanse of water with huge snowflakes falling and melting on the surface. I looked back and waved happily to Mom and Gran standing on the shore wrapped snugly in their matching mink fur coats. I have a picture of this. No wonder everyone often found me so irritating and annoying!

Part V

The mink coats belonging Gran and Mom make us sound a bit rich and posh, but that was far from the case. Mom was given hers second-hand from one of Gran's many sisters who had indeed married well. I have no idea where Gran got hers from. Mom's was as good as new.

When I was 17, I didn't have a particularly warm winter coat so I would often wear Mom's mink when the weather was really icy and freezing cold. It was a couple of miles to town and it did the job of keeping me really cosy and warm. It had huge matching furry gloves. I cut a rather peculiar figure, I think, no doubt about that, especially since I also wore a thick cream woolly hat that covered my entire head and fastened with lace and pompoms!

One of our greatest pleasures when staying at 'Gran's by the Sea' were the day trips to Aberwisswiss as I called it. During the ten days, we usually stayed at Gran's, we would visit this town just the once. It was in Dorothy Perkins that Mom always bought the annual family knickers. Navy ones for us girls, white for Dad and my brother, Bridget Jones' pants for Mom herself, and knee-length nylon bloomers for Nan.

The day would be spent ambling along the crowded streets in all weathers, trudging around the many shops Mom loved, but couldn't spend in, and stopping on a bench facing the sea to have our picnic lunch. We would always take a long saunter along the prom to view the amazing perpendicular railway that climbed straight up the cliff side.

Late one afternoon, we were slowly walking back to the car. We could, by now, see the long pier that stretched out on its iron legs into the sea. The beach is a shingle one with long brown breakwaters set at even intervals down the beach and into the sea. The height of the shingles caught between the breakwaters and the promenade varied. Some came almost as far the top of stone wall whilst others were seemingly miles below. Others were at different levels between the two. When I became bored on these long ambulant walks, I would often swing and leap over the metal barriers and drop down to the shingle. I'd mess about for a while before climbing back.

I was about 11 on this particular day. My sister and I were leading the way along the prom aiming for the pier, the final pleasure of the day. As sisters do, we laughed, chatted, joked or kept silent. It was during one of these quiet moments, I became bored again, so I grasped the rail and swung myself over ready to drop down onto the shingle below.

Right at the last minute, I saw I'd made a monumental error of judgement. The phrase, ' Look before you leap' springs to mind, for below me an abyss. I had only gone and sprung over at a part where the shingle was 'miles' below me. I just hung there in terror. I called desperately to my sister as I clung onto the heartless steel rail. My body was heavy and my feet touched nothing. 'I can't get up!' My sister casually walked to me and looked over.

'Oh, my God! Quickly, swing your legs up onto the prom.' I tried as hard as I could, but I couldn't do it. 'Mom! Dad!' she called urgently, as our parents approached on the opposite side of the prom. 'She can't get up!' Mom and Dad simply rolled their eyes and carried on walking towards the pier. 'No! Mom, she really can't get up!'

Our child-weary parents continued on their way totally unconcerned as to my ultimate fate. It was a salutary lesson: parents really did not care. I was still trying desperately to swing a leg up to the top of the wall, but was failing miserably. My arms were hurting and my hands were beginning to slip. My sister knelt down to encourage me in a harsh, loud voice. 'You can do it! You can do it! You have to do it!'

Somehow, from I know not where, I finally found the strength to swing that right leg up high enough to clamber safely over the rail. I sat and shook violently. We had both been scared. She put her arms around me until I stopped crying. We stood up and made our way back towards the pier. Nothing more was said. We'd both had a major fright. I never looked at my parents in quite the same way again.

Our picnics always seemed the same: egg and salad cream

sandwiches, a slice of home-made pound cake, a huge flask of hot Heinz tomato soup and a bottle of pop. Repetitive it may have been, but to us kids, those picnics were always welcome to stifle the daily hunger pangs that constantly gnawed our stomachs.

Part VI

When we were young, breakwaters were not on Aberarth beach. They were built when I was about fifteen. We didn't like them at all. We found them both ugly and constricting. Our usual freedom to walk and run at will was heavily restricted. It meant having to clamber over the breakwaters before we could continue. Nothing ever stays the same.

Just before those monstrosities were built one thing changed for the better, though. I was fourteen at the time. As we often did, my sister and I would go for endless walks along the beach, climbing over huge slimy stones and searching rock pools for small fish and crabs.

This particular day was unusually dry and hot. We ambled, chatted and laughed for quite a distance towards Aberaeron, two miles ahead. We never actually walked all the way to this town. As we turned a corner we stopped in our tracks. We could not believe our eyes. There in front of us was an enormous patch of sand. It had appeared seemingly over-night. I call it a patch, but it was huge: about the size of a football field. It ran down from the piled-up stones by the cliff-face to the water's edge.

You may remember that prior to this, the beach that stretched from Aberarth to the next town was usually nothing but rocks and stones. Now there was this wonderful oasis. It had appeared out of nowhere. It really was quite magical to behold. No-one else was about and that was the way it had always been. It was *our* beach, our private beach and only a few villagers ever ventured forth to occasionally collect driftwood for the fires that burned summer and winter.

We were already in our bikinis, but not skimpy ones like those of today. No, these were a little more modest. Together we paddled out to see how far the sand went into the sea. Very occasionally there might be a few stones or a small rock. Otherwise the floor was clear.

Joyfully we waded out up to our shoulders and had our first proper swim on our beach. It was exhilarating. The sun beamed down and tanned our bare skin. The sky was a blue mantle high overhead with just a small fluffy white cloud or two. Seagulls screeched and fought over fish in the distance.

At this point I became very daring. Still self-conscious in front of my sister, I turned my back, ducked under the water and removed my bikini top. I watched in amazement as two huge white boobies floated to the surface as I stood up. Each time I pushed them down they just bobbed right back on up! I was entranced. There was no longer a heavy weight pulling on my neck and shoulders. It was liberating. I tied my top around my ankle and swam around thrilling in the glorious excitement of the freedom I had discovered. It remains a highlight of my life.

The next time we visited Gran's by the sea all had drastically changed, changed in so many ways it was almost too awful to comprehend. In a way, it marked the turning point in our young teenage years. Gone was our innocent freedom to roam our beach at will. Gone was the freedom to run, play and shout with outlandish glee far from prying eyes and ears of others. No. Something awful and monstrous had occurred and we were absolutely gutted, devastated.

The day after we arrived, my sister and I set off to see if the sand was still there. We felt sure it would be gone. Maybe we had dreamed it together in our minds. As we walked, we were aware of a few people here and there on our beach. This was unprecedented. From toddlers until now we were the only ones to roam that beach. How dare others dirty and sully it with their presence. As we rounded the last bend to where the sand had been we were struck dumb with horror. We stared at the sight before us.

Hoards of people with their screaming kids and yapping dogs were standing, sitting or playing games on our sand. Deckchairs were out and strangers were sunning themselves oblivious to our ownership. They were trespassing and there was not a single thing we could do about it. Those folk, those tourists from Aberaeron, had found our beach, our sand. Heartlessly, they trampled our freedom, they crushed our innocence, they smote our spirit. It was nothing short of murder, a murder most horrid. Those faceless people dared to trample on our youth, our hearts, and our minds. Oblivious like the birds, the sea and the sand, those people stole our souls.

Part VII

I have mentioned, Tom, the tall, handsome guy I dated on and off for years from fourteen until I was twenty-one, the one to whom I had been so briefly engaged to. I made a huge decision then that I would not ever date again. I assumed all men were like him. He wasn't 'bad' in anyway, just seemingly indifferent to me and there was no way I could envision myself having to live with an indifferent person. He was not without love, sympathy or anything like that, but he didn't cuddle or hug and I needed that. Holding hands and one kiss at the end of the day really wasn't my scene at all. That's why it was always so on and off with me. He didn't understand it. I never told him then. I foolishly believed all men would be the same, so from our last date together, I dated no-one for 27 years!

After a serious illness and ultimate retirement, I returned to my home town having been away for eleven years. Friends from the area were now scattered wide. I didn't work so had no way of making new friends. I was lonely and needed some companionship. I was now forty-seven.

Over the twenty-seven years I often thought about my first love and, indeed, a small part of my heart remained his. I learned he had married twice and had two children. I learned he was free. A friend from Wiltshire travelled up to help us reconnect. She made the phone call. Said I'd moved back here and was contacting old friends. He suggested we meet up. We did at his local pub with my pal in tow for confidence.

It had been twenty-seven years with no-one in between for me, but it felt I'd seen him only the previous week. I talked and talked with nerves. He listened as he had always done. I got very tipsy. I forgot about my friend. She was fine with it. She went to the loo to phone Mom to tell her just how well we were getting on!

We had been going out once a week and I had met his best friends, a lovely couple. We were in the pub. They were telling me about a caravan they stayed in for holidays belonging to an uncle and Tom often went with them. I asked where it was.

'Aberaeron,' said Tom.

Well, I nearly fell off my seat in excitement. Just two miles from 'Gran's by the Sea' and they knew Aberarth! Tom said when he was travelling down with them for the first time to somewhere he had never been before he had been overcome with an over-riding sense of deja vu. It was so strong he always remembered the feeling.

'I'm not surprised!' I interjected. 'It wasn't de ja vu, Tom. You had been there before.'

'I had not!' he exclaimed. 'I had never been that way before until then!'

'But you had. You took me to 'Gran's by the Sea' when we were going out when I was nineteen, the time we got engaged briefly!'

'No way. I would have remembered.'

'Well, clearly, you didn't!'

'We left early in the morning in your work's white transit van and we travelled all the way there without stopping.'

'No. I still don't remember it.'

I continued to try and jog his memory. 'We went cos I wanted to introduce you to Gran. I also wanted to tell her about my promotion to cook in the factory canteen where I worked as general dog's body. He remembered my excitement and pay rise at the promotion. I went on and on. 'We went into Aberaeron and bought a honey ice-cream from the shop by the corner on the harbour.'

'Love those!' exclaimed Tom. 'I have never seen honey ice-cream before Aberaeron nor since and yet when I had the first one I had de ja vu again because I would have sworn I'd had one before!'

'Well, you did and you were with me. We only went for the day and that day meant so much to me. I with the man I loved at 'Gran's by the Sea'. That's why I remember the entire day like it was yesterday.'

Gradually, during the rest of the evening, a few things started to come back to him. As a group, we were all absolutely amazed at the whole thing. I mean, my young love spending holidays so near where my gran had lived. She died when I was twenty-one so she wouldn't have been there when Tom went later with his friends.

This experience now makes me think more about deja vu. Tom was utterly convinced he had never ventured that way before, yet he did when he and I were together nearly three decades before! We had a glorious day and how I loved showing him all the things related to 'Gran's by the Sea'.

Another coincidence regarding this earlier time with Tom was when we were going to marry when I was nineteen and were looking at houses to buy. Mom and I looked at the last places we viewed before Tom and I split up. They were on a new housing estate still unfinished and with lots more to come.

When I moved back to my home town, I bought the house in which I still live. Guess where? Yes, the very same estate which had featured in this story all those years ago! And it was from here Tom and I as 'oldies' dated yet again! It makes you think! There were often weird goings on related to 'Gran's by the Sea'.

6 SCHOOL DAYS

1960's: I was 10 when I discovered my favourite teacher, Miss Doogood. The first thing she taught the class frightened me to death. The word terrified me. I had neither seen nor heard it before. On the gnarled and dusty blackboard, she wrote in large white letters: *palindrome*.

Trying to calm my nerves I wondered if it was anything like the cinema, the 'Hippodrome,' in the city centre. Mom used to tell me stories about how, as a teenager, she used to go the Hippodrome to watch big Hollywood films. This was done during her lunch breaks when working at Lewis's Department Store. Maybe this *palindrome* was the name of another cinema.

Apparently not, no. Instead, she explained the meaning of the word. It meant 'a word, phrase, or sequence that reads the same backwards as forwards.' One example is *Madam*. Another is the phrase: *Nurses Run*. This bit was easy enough to understand, but that big word itself still frightened me with its three syllables and eleven letters. It looked even bigger because it was written in capitals.

Many brighter than me, though younger, probably caught on just why the teacher had begun our first lesson with this. I was slow on the uptake. Beneath that weird word, she wrote her own name:

Doogood

Using her pointy stick, she individually stabbed out each letter forwards then backwards. Understanding finally dawned. It spelled the same forwards and backwards. How magic was that?

Before starting the class I was terrified of Miss Doogood. The joy and happiness of the summer break were tinged with a huge sense of foreboding so that by the first day back at school I was a dithering wreck.

Why? My dad and older sister had both been in her class and would constantly regale me with horror stories about what she was like. My dad couldn't stand the woman and my sister hated her. She was furious and indignant that this teacher, this gorgon, had thwacked her three times over the knuckles with a thick ruler on her birthday! Miss Doogood had been telling her over and over again to write her words closer together, but she had failed to do so. I remember when she first told me and I had unkindly thought, 'Well, put them closer together, then!' After all, I avoided trouble by doing as I was told.

Fortunately, despite my fears, I came to love Miss Doogood. She was like Marmite: you either loved her or hated her. She was about 60 years old, very prim and very strict. She took no nonsense from any of the class. Woe-betide any who dared to put a foot out of place. She could be quite nasty and sharp with some of the kids who I often thought hadn't justified it, but I was just glad it was never me on the sharp end of her tongue. On the contrary, she was awfully nice to me. One time after I had given her a chalk rabbit I had won on the shooting range at the fair she thanked me and said, 'Your wonderful eyesight helps to compensate for your deafness.' I was over the moon at her praise.

She always taught this year group to play the recorder. How I enjoyed those lessons and I excelled at them. She was the music teacher and banged away on the piano during assemblies and school concerts. At the beginning of the year, she chose the school choir. We stood in a line at the front of the class singing and she came along putting her ear to our mouths to decide who was in or out of the choir. There were to be three groups: choir, growlers and the rest. I was so envious of friends who joined the 'choir' group. The next names called out were the growlers. Jubilation: I was not one of those at least. I was a sort of non-entity. Tone-deaf. A few months later, she told me she was so pleased I was not in the choir. I looked at her astonished. 'Why?'

'Well,' she explained. 'If you were in the choir who would I have to lead the recorders?'

Just a few words, but remembered with heart-felt thanks to this day! I *was* lead recorder player. I had the confidence to swing into the music at the beginning without hesitation. She arranged with St Michael's Church in the Bullring to do a service with her choir and recorders. I had the terrifying task of doing a solo of the first verse of *Lead us, Heavenly Father, Lead us*. Loud speakers had been placed all around the Bullring so everyone could enjoy the service. In the few days leading up to it I had terrible stage-fright and I told Miss Doogood I would rather not do it. She talked quietly and calmly, talking up my marvellous, my amazing, my wonderful skill on the recorder. For her sake, not mine, I agreed to do it.

The day dawned over-cast with a slight drizzle of rain. As it came nearer and nearer the time to play my solo, my fingers trembled and shook. Then, like lightening I was off: never before in the history of human conflict has that hymn been played so fast and so furiously by so few!

It was in Miss Doogood's class that I shone at the Friday afternoon spelling tests. My general English with reading and writing was poor, but this was different. Each week she gave us ten spellings to learn. Each week I wrote them over and over and over again. I found it hard remembering. Often, I had never even heard of some words and had certainly never read them.

However, given the chance to learn them, I did. Tenacious is not my second name for nothing. Not only that, I wanted to get them right to please her, to earn a rare smile, to hear an equally rare note of praise.

I slogged at them every afternoon when I arrived home tired and exhausted from yet another school day. I badgered Mom, Dad and sister to test me on them repeatedly. I dreamed of those words. I spelled them aloud in a sing-song voice to my dolls determined to get them all correct. I wrote the words tiny. I wrote them large. I mixed up the variety of tops and tails. I lived, breathed and slept those words.

Friday would dawn and I would be ready, pencil poised. *Number One: spell scissors*. Gripping the lead tightly, I would wrack my memory and jot down the answer. *Number two: spell February. Number three: spell dolphin*, and so on to the end. I rarely got one wrong so eager was I to earn her respect.

I also had difficulty with handwriting. It was never neat enough. It was in Miss Doogood's class that we could move on from a pencil to a biro. Right from the beginning of the year other little pupils were earning the right to the much-coveted pen.

Every night I practised my handwriting over and over again. I looked at my friends' books: their writing was beautifully scripted with letters nearly all the same size and equally spaced. My pages looked like a spider had walked in some ink and scurried all over my work.

It was getting towards the end of the year and I was still using the dratted pencil. I felt so ashamed at my ineptitude. I was the last one still using the leaded stick. Two weeks before school broke up for the halcyon summer days, Miss Doogood handed me a pen with a warm smile. I was cock-a-hoop. I'd finally done it! Like Shakespeare and others before me, I took up my pen and wrote!

In a way, the following is a silly little memory, but it shows how self-consciousness can affect a full enjoyment of life. We school kids had been filled with a sort of manic excitement for days. The time for a school outing with Miss Doogood was looming on the horizon. To go with my little friends and favourite teacher on a coach, with a picnic, created an emotion barely contained. I was beside myself. It was almost as bad as waiting for Father Christmas to make his magical visit. I was the kind of child whose entire body would quiver and shake with tremendous joy and happiness. I would smile and laugh and dance just to rid myself of all that excess emotional energy.

I had been on a coach only once before. I frequently stayed with Nan in the country. She took me on a coach trip one day and I still recall it vividly. I was about eight. It was lovely riding along through the country lanes and seeing great rolling hills and fields all around us. Nan and I would chat happily, sucking on the boiled sweets she bought us for the journey. A man stood at the front expounding the virtues of the small villages and towns we frequently passed through. I couldn't hear much of what he said, but I was happy enough to just be sit there holding hands with Nan and enjoying the beautiful scenery. It was a gorgeous summer's day: the air was warm, the sky blue, nature was fecund and verdant. I was filled with great happiness and contentment.

As we continued our travels through Leicestershire, I heard one of my first horror stories and it shocked me to the core. Such was my distress I have never forgotten the occasion. As the coach frolicked along a Leicestershire country lane, Nan told me the story of Lady Jane Grey. I was horrified: that an innocent seventeen-year old girl in 1554 had been taken to the scaffold and had her head chopped off was untenable. I felt tears prickle my eyes as Nan continued the story of how she was innocent of wrong-doing, how she was charged with treason and how her nine days on the throne of England signed her death warrant. The unfairness! How strongly we feel as kids the unfairness of things! I was outraged. The comfort and security of my own comfortable world was torn asunder that day.

The school trip provided a wonderful day out for us kids. We laughed and chatted and sang as the coach gambolled along the streets and lanes to our destination. The excitement of our gang was palpable. It was alive, frenetic. The air inside the coach was electric. It felt so good to be alive! A myriad of emotions bubbled and danced as we sallied forth along the byways and highways of the journey.

Finally, we arrived. Our destination was Drayton Manor Park. It was beautiful, full of trees and green grass and an abundance of bushes and flowers. Miss Doogood settled about fifty-five of us upon the green that surrounded a huge round paddling pool. We rifled through our bags to find the sandwiches and drinks moms had packed. Some of us were lucky to find a bag of Smith's crisps containing tiny blue twists of salt. It was heavenly as we munched and drank, laughing and joking as only kids can in their undiluted, unbridled happiness.

As we gathered together our rubbish and put it in the appropriate bins provided, Miss Doogood, who had been sitting on a bench with Mrs Edwards, came over to speak. 'You may paddle if you like, children. Girls remove your skirts or tuck them into your knickers.'

Excitement like a wave rose among the group. Boys tore off their shoes and socks and raced to the pool. Girls were less hasty, more dainty. Some removed their skirts and some tucked them into their knickers depending on what they were wearing. Soon, they, too, were in the pond and having the time of their lives. I remained alone, seated. Desperation suffused me. I was desperate to join in and I was equally as desperate not to remove my skirt or tuck it in! Above all things, I *loved* water. I always had to be in it whether it was simply a puddle or the huge open sea. Miss Doogood made encouraging flaps with her hand, but I shook my head mortified. I sat watching the others for a while then decided to force myself. Nearby was a block of toilets. I went in there. I tried tucking my skirt in my pants, but it just didn't feel right, yet I was more than desperate to get into that water. I dillied and dallied. I shuffled. I procrastinated. My mind did acrobatics as it tried to persuade me to tuck up, shut up, and get in the pool!

It was not to be. Nothing could persuade me to alter my clothes in this rude way. Friends begged and cajoled, others sneered. I was hapless. Helpless. I was caught up in an emotional turmoil of complete shyness and self-consciousness. Fortunately, it was the only blip in an otherwise stupendous day, but the sadness remains.

7 SECONDARY SCHOOL

FINAL YEAR

I was in my final year of school. Fifteen years old and longing to get out of that awful place. I was not overly fond of PE. Principally because I was so very self-conscious - more than most.

It was afternoon. The sky had darkened and it was pouring down with rain, as usual. Teachers, in their infinite wisdom, decided the lesson should take place in the gym. In the changing room, we girls donned the navy PE skirts we had made in our needlework classes, some with better results than most. Mine was fine, I hasten to add, except for a slightly wonky zip and a piece of frayed lining below the hem that fluttered gaily as I walked. I was embarrassed. It needed just a simple needle and thread, but I never had time for little things like that. We laughed and joked, pushed and shoved until we were marched, crocodile style, to the huge gymnasium at the one end of the prison.

As we hurried along I prayed, as usual, that no boy would appear to spy my lily-white legs below the skirt, nor ogle my far too-generous boobs as they bounced along in front of me. Fortunately, no snotty-nosed lad loomed to gurn at me as I thankfully fled into the safety of the gym. Boys in our year were in the gym at the other end of the hell-hole. Much to my relief, rarely did the twain meet during PE.

We were forced to play a few really silly and pointless games: games so mind-numbingly boring I can't remember any of them. The second-half of the lesson was a little better. At least I could rest. I actually enjoyed netball, but only because, due to my height, I was always either goal-shooter or goal-defence. No way would I be seen running, flying and lunging to catch a ball. Instead, I would try and stand gracefully fingering my long hair or inspecting my nails whilst I waited for the ball to come near me. Depending on my position, I would shoot or save and, surprisingly, considering my boredom, I was rather good at both!

As I waited, impervious to shouts of encouragement, a friend sidled up and whispered in my ear. Being hard of hearing, she had to whisper it several times before I could hear her properly and what I heard was absolutely devastating.

I looked over to the side and saw the two PE teachers looking our way. I leapt for the ball that came thrashing through the air, and instead of shooting for goal, I hugged that ball to my chest, raced for the doors, threw it back into the room and exited in a great huff of utter devastation.

I raced to the locker room, sat on a slatted bench and cried my heart out with great heaving sobs. About ten minutes later, the rest of the girls appeared. My friend sat down beside me and asked, 'What on earth is the matter?' I dropped my head and muttered into my wet hanky. She bent down to look into my face. 'Sorry. What did you say?'

I glared at her, trembling. 'How dare Mrs W say I am like a tractor?' I hate her. I hate her. My friend threw back her head and laughed and laughed. 'It's not funny!' I said, through gritted teeth. 'I hate her! I hope a bus runs her over!'

My friend knelt down and looked me in the face. 'She didn't say you are like a tractor! She said, 'You are quite attractive!' I got her to repeat this several times, first to make sure I had heard properly this time, and second, so I could hear the heavenly words again and again! MOI? No way!

Aged 32, I found myself back in that school, not by choice, but sent there for my first taste of teaching practice. I had so hated that school I really hadn't wanted to return, but return I must. At break, I was sitting, smoking away, in the staff room with a cup of tea and slice of cake when to my utter amazement, Mrs W walked in! I learned later she was the only teacher left of those I knew.

I reintroduced myself, pleased she remembered me. We sat together and I told her this story. Next thing I knew she was standing up and regaling the staffroom with my tale of woe. She ended by telling the rest of the ghouls they should be careful what they say in the presence of pupils. Amen to that, I say.

8 INHIBITED AND SELF-CONSCIOUS

The heavy weight of inhibition and self-consciousness has crippled me all my life, but none more so than when I hit puberty. Shackled to an upper body that refused to respect nature's dictum of age-appropriate, those mill-stones just grew and grew like Topsy.

At twelve, I was the owner of two rather plump and pert appendages that stuck out like two ripe melons. They measured a 34C cup, huge for a girl still not yet a teenager, huge for a girl whose friends and elder sister were still at the fried-eggs stage. My mammary glands were of unaccountable interest to all and sundry, from the young to the old, to the girls and to the boys.

My only interest in them was a horror that grew proportionally along with their burgeoning size. Many a morning you would find me secretly tying mom's white scarf around them to bind them flatter. Now Mom was a great one for home-spun philosophy and it is to my utmost regret that she never grew out of this phase. She had the oddest of ideas rarely proven by scientific fact or even logic. When it came to my boobs she was apparently the sage of mother nature. Breasts were designed with muscles that would hold them up appropriately, apparently. Wearing a man-made bra would result in the muscles not working to yank them up. Wrong.

When I was thirteen, nearly fourteen, those mountains of embarrassment had grown even further. With the rest of my body relatively slim, I was now weighed down with 36C's and the recalcitrant boob-muscles had long packed up and run. Yet still I was not allowed a bra. Even my older sister, normally ignorant of my existence, told Mom I should have one. She was embarrassed: friends were talking, boys were sniggering, girls were flabbergasted. The once plump and pert boobs could now hold an entire pack of six pencils beneath them without one dropping out! I was mortified. I cried a lot. I thought of suicide often. I dreamed of them dropping off and being devoured by wild pigs. I walked stooped over with arms held high to disguise the great atrocities, the huge mutations of nature.

You may recall the teacher in PE whom I thought had compared me to a tractor. With her was the other PE teacher called Mrs K. Now, she and I had never seen eye to eye. She loved her sport deeply. I did not. She disliked that and showed it in every way she could fathom. This same year we had already had a right royal ding-dong, but that's another story – it had nothing to do with my now quite pendulous boobs!

This particular morning my sister had left home before me to go to college. I felt daring and mischievous. I was constantly warned to stay away from her clothes. Normally, she needn't have worried since she was a slim size 12 and I a 14. This was entirely due to the enormous growths on my chest. The rest of me was normal. She had recently bought a cream, baggy, voluminous shirt made of calico that she wore tied at the waist with a belt. Now I badly coveted this shirt. We didn't have many clothes since money was short, but I desperately wanted a shirt like this. I decided to take the risk and try it on. Brilliant. It fit like a glove: baggy on her fried eggs, but fitted to my dangles. I gleefully put it on, my navy skirt falling beneath the knee. I dragged on my gabardine and pulled it tight so Mom would not see the shirt as I left the house. I couldn't wait to show it off to the girls.

Like most schools, our gym boasted showers, showers wall-lined with white cracked tiles held together by green mould in each groove. The tiles on the floor, too, were cracked, slippery and slimy. We changed into our PE stuff and sidled along the hallway to the gym. Mrs K seemed in a bad mood. She didn't smile. She didn't laugh. All she did was frown and grimace and yell out instructions. She asked for a volunteer and, army-fashion, grabbed me by the arm: a forced volunteer, no less. I was never a happy bunny in PE and I was an even less happy one that day. Now she had me try and demonstrate how to do various acrobatics and high jinks. I did my best, but even best was not good enough that fatal day. She had us adolescent girls running around that blessed gym, and up and down the walls and ropes like demented monkeys. We yelled, screamed, cried and sweated. Finally, it was time for the locker room.

    I sauntered in and did the trick I had honed over the past years to avoid the showers. I took my clothes and slipped into one of the toilet cubicles. No, I didn't have a water phobia, but I did have a naked one. With my big boobies, there was no way I was going to let all and sundry gawp at them in the shower. They gawped as it was when I was clothed and a boy once even reached up to squeeze one and asked if the great orb was real or stuffed! The previous three years I had gotten away with my trick. I guess the teachers couldn't be arsed whether we showered or not really, but Mrs K was different. Not much older than us she betrayed a steely determination to do everything by the darned book!

    The showers did have two separate cubicles, but they lacked curtains. There really was no place to hide away from curious eyes in there. Everyone was nearly dressed when I emerged from my hiding place. Like lightening, the witch lunged forward and streaked across the room. She spun me round and asked if I had showered. I replied in the negative. Oh, my God, but that human mutation went utterly berserk. She ranted and raved, throwing her arms around as she did so. Did I, she asked, know what water was for? I nodded. The girls were now all gathered round. Then why hadn't I showered? Did I really want to pong out the classroom in the next lesson? Did someone who sat next to me really have to suffer the stink of my sweaty body odour? I just stood there. I mutely agreed with every syllable she uttered, but no power on this earth was going to part me from my clothes. Glowering, she said, 'And you can take that insolent look off your face. You are going to have a shower!' With that she took hold of the front of my sister's shirt and yanked it hard. Buttons flew across the room to the awful sound of ripping calico! Stunned silence, but for the steady tick tock of a clock on the wall. Suddenly, she spun on her heel and left the room.

    We soon began giggling, whispering and chewing the event over as we made our way out with me clutching closed the gaping shirt. I was in dire trouble now. Oh, I didn't give a jot about the school or the teachers, but I did worry about what my sister would think when I told her the story of her now-dead shirt. It was weeks before she would speak to me again and rightly so.

Earlier, I alluded to a prior ding-dong I had with Mrs K before the shower incident. As usual in Britain, it was raining torrents so we were all shoved into the library for a dry PE. We arranged ourselves around the tables in the room to gently steam after being in school-lock out during lunch break. For an hour, we'd had to shelter from the wet as best we could by turning our sodden backs like sheep against the drenching rain. Finally, we settled down with paper and pens on the table in front of us. I was sitting next to my best friend, at the back of the room. Our task was to listen to the dragon drone on doing dictation whilst we wrote it down.

Now, you may recall I am very hard-of-hearing. I wore a behind-the-ear aid, hidden by my long hair as usual. Few knew I was deaf. I kept it hidden rather well. In those not so halcyon days I preferred to be thought daft rather than deaf. It was not a good time to be deaf, if any time really can be. On droned Mrs K and I strained to hear what she was saying, but I need to lip-read, too, and it's difficult if you are meant to be writing at the same time. In the end, I began copying from my mate. It was less stressful, and she was in on my secret deafness.

The rain had made most of us start coughing and sneezing. I removed my grubby hanky and began to quietly blow my nose. Suddenly, without warning, a shout arose from the front of the class. 'Just what do you think you are doing, Missssss Hatt-on?' I looked up, pushing my hanky away. All the girls spun round and were looking at me. Again, she boomed, 'I said, what are you doing?'

I looked at her in amazement and said, 'Writing, Miss.'

She began to walk towards me. 'No, you're not. Your pen is not even in your hand. You are wasting time. Now get out!' My friend looked at me with a raised quizzical eyebrow. 'Get out! Get out now! I leapt to my feet and left the room to stand outside in disgrace. Now, normally it wouldn't have bothered me, but it was during the time of the installation everywhere of North Sea Gas.

AUTOBIOGRAPHY

At the end of the corridor, not too far away, stood six rather dishy lads installing it. Now I was embarrassed and hugely self-conscious. That these gorgeous young men could see my disgrace was absolutely awful. They did keep smiling and waving at me. I was blood red in the face from blushing so badly. I need to say at this point that this was only the second time I had been expelled from a room. This was fourth year. The other was in second year and it was for talking. Fair enough!

I could see into Mrs K's lair through the glass windows. I saw her stomping up to the door. She came through and in front of those 'Chippendales' she pushed my shoulder and ranted on. I did nothing. Finally, she ordered me to wait for her outside the headmaster's office. I did. She went in to explain the situation. Meanwhile, I was trapped in a small space used as a medical room. I was there for over an hour. Next thing I know I am in the Head's office and Mom and Mrs K are there.

Mom had only recently passed her driving test so thought to collect me from school. My friend had seen her outside the gates and told her that Mrs K had hit me. According to her, Mom shot out of the car in rage to think I had been thumped by a teacher! She apparently gave the Head and Mrs K a right telling off and we left the school together! Mom, by the way, was actually a very gentle and kind lady normally. Even I had never seen her like this. I was intrigued. It was the end of that story, but more was still to come from this tale involving me and Mrs K.

Following the sometimes, violent confrontations with my PE teacher the rest of my last year at school proved fairly uneventful in that department. In reality, I am a sensitive soul and wasn't used to arousing such dislike in people. It confused me. It annihilated me. It made me lose what confidence I had. Fortunately, I was never bullied at school by other kids, though a girl did threaten once to 'beat me up'. She was the school bully, but thankfully she never did.

Life went on after school. However, I dreaded meeting my nemesis, Mrs K, in the street. I dreaded meeting her any place I worked or anywhere I travelled. When I passed my driving test, that all changed. I looked for her everywhere. I wanted her to cross the road in front of my car so I could run her down so strong was my dislike I swear I wouldn't have hesitated.

9 TEACHING PRACTICE

Having taken O and A Levels at night college over a few years, I went to university. I studied really hard. I became an English Teacher. Part of the training for this is Teaching Practice in schools. I've told you the story of the other PE teacher when I misheard a word and was frightfully upset about what wasn't said. I hadn't wanted to go back to my old school in the least, but I had no choice, no option. I dreaded that Mrs K would still be there. All my nightmares would come true if she was.

Fortunately, she wasn't and I had a good time teaching the kids my favourite subject. But, that school's curse was still a force to be reckoned with. A report of your performance is sent to the university. The department deputy did not give an entirely favourable review. When I found this out I was mortified as were my tutors. They often came to evaluate lessons. Their reports and that of the school did not match! At my second school, I had a glowing report and an offer of a job should it become vacant.

On the first day of this second school I made ready. I was smart and tidy and arrived on the spot with the expected few packets of biscuits for the English staff room. I was getting my bearings, when out of the corner of my eye I saw *her* enter the room. I shot from my chair and scooted around a corner and waited for the bell. Trembling, I crept out and did a few lessons all the while keeping a sharp look out in the corridors between classes.

This went on for a couple of days and I could no longer stand the stress. I had to deal with this somehow. So, *screwing my courage to the sticking place* I went up to her in the staffroom. She looked surprised, then smiled. I smiled back. 'Do you remember me, Mrs K?'

She nodded. The long and short of it is we spent our lunch hour chatting, talking about the incidents and learning about each other. She had been a new teacher that year determined to do the best she could. If, as the rules stated, we girls had to have showers then she would make me have a shower! Not only that she had a problematic home life.

We became friends and I took several of her classes. She was Head of Fifth and she told me she had just used our episodes at school to illustrate a point to her pupils in assembly. Her students loved her. What a change! The moral was never to let an argument be unresolved because it could create havoc with the rest of your life! When my time was up we parted company with warm hugs of affection. She was the only one out of all the teachers' classes I took who bought me a thank you card and gift.

Years later, when I was forty-seven, I told my fiance this amazing story about me and Mrs K. On my wedding day, who do I see, but my friend Mrs K! My fiancé had invited her to the wedding. It was a wonderful surprise. Our scars were finally healed.

10 QARANC

Queen Alexandra's Royal Army Nursing Corps

Two years after leaving school, I joined the QARANC. I was just seventeen and hoped to train as an SEN the following year when I was eighteen. Meanwhile I was a ward assistant.

I was stationed at Aldershot for the first six weeks for basic training. This involved a lot of marching about the square, first aid lessons and the dreaded PE again! We did an awful lot of PE. I hated it. I wasn't fit and try as they might they never got me fit!

One of our trainers was Lance Corporal Taylor – a shortish, stocky female about twenty-five. I have no idea what it is about me and PE teachers, but she took an instant dislike to me. I always tried my hardest, I promise you, but it was never enough. Whenever she wanted a volunteer she picked me. The army clearly has no idea of the true meaning of the word, volunteer.

The very first lesson she decided to use me to demonstrate the art of the wheelbarrow: I had to put my hands on the floor whilst she held my knees. She walked me forward. Okay. She walked faster. What? My arms collapsed so she just pushed me round that dratted gym twice on my forearms taking off a layer of skin. The next day, I honestly couldn't move to get out of bed. I hurt all over. A doctor came and told me to be in class for 12 pm. The pain was horrendous especially walking up and down steps.

We girls spent our evenings together whitening our pumps, ironing their laces, and spit and polishing our shoes. There was one girl, Lynn, short, with long jet-black hair. I didn't like her at all. She was already a trained nurse. She was twenty-one and had absolutely no time for a girl who cried every night because she was home-sick, or had a migraine, or terrible period pains, or excruciatingly painful feet. In her defence, she was unaware of these at the time. I hadn't wanted to appear a wimp.

Lynn used to bustle when she walked and she walked very fast. She was fond of telling me to grow a back bone and grow up because I was so homesick. Nope, didn't like the woman at all. She was the polar opposite to me. Still, we would pass a few remarks occasionally, but that was it. I had made two very good friends. Both Scottish. I heard very little of what they said because of their thick accents and my deafness, but it didn't hamper us unduly.

Each morning at 5 am we had to rise and barrack our beds. This meant making them up with hospital corners and folding blankets on the bottom of the bed. It was the job of Lance Corporal Taylor to check the beds were correct every morning. She used to do it whilst we were at early breakfast. Every morning I returned to my room and would find the dratted bed stripped.

After a while, this really began to distress me and Lynn came across me sobbing in despair. After telling me to stop sniffing and get a grip, she said she would make my bed the following morning because hers had never been stripped. I was relieved and, though I didn't like the super-confident woman at all, I thought it a nice gesture.

Next morning, we returned from breakfast and once again my bed was stripped. If you had seen Lynn's face! It was absolutely thunderous! I watched as she strutted and marched down the long corridor, her body tight and ready for battle. After about half an hour she returned to tell me my bed would not be stripped again because Major Peabody said so. I just looked at her in amazement. Wow. What a woman! No, my bed was not stripped again. Because of this, I grew to love my new friend and when we were both posted to the same military hospital in Colchester we soon became the very best of friends.

From then on, Lynn has supported and looked after me incredibly well. I was her bridesmaid when I was nineteen and we are still in touch now I am 61. Not only that, when I suffered some brain complications following an operation aged 34, it was Lynn and her two lovely girls who helped me through the very worst time of my life.

11 A TEACHER MYSELF

The profound shock and disbelief elicited by a gruelling massacre I saw remains the stuff of nightmares. It was break-time at work when I left the building only to spy the caretakers brutally and callously attacking lovely wooden, individual, lidded-school desks with a lethal weapon. Pitilessly slaughtered and butchered, the furniture was unceremoniously slung into the greedy, cavernous mouths of giant skips.

A dangerous and desperate rescue mission was obligatory. The blood bath would continue for the rest of the day and the giant skips, those yellow perils, would be collected the next morning. With no time to lose I spent all free moments rescuing two innocents at a time and taking them home in my small car. The others were not so fortunate. They, like war victims, were cruelly taken bleeding and dying to a mass grave and buried alive, useless and crippled. They were no longer of use in this harsh world.

Before I moved house, those ten survivors recuperated intact around the walls of my double garage in which I didn't keep my car. They proudly and neatly accommodated and hid garden equipment, bric-a-brac and garage essentials. They continued a positive and productive life, ending their days with pride and dignity.

12 SCAVANGERS

It was 1997. The year Princess Diana was killed and I had been teaching for a few years. At first, home was a delightful 2-bed flat situated high on a headland. It had proved a better year than normal, so I decided to take the plunge and buy a house. The flat was rented.

By far the cheapest proved to be large three-storey Victorian terraced houses. I soon found an end-of-terrace just up the road from the sea. It had five double bedrooms, the sixth of which had been turned into a huge bathroom. It had just been renovated throughout and painted magnolia. It had a large walled backyard beyond which was a double garage. My small amount of furniture from the flat was soon lost in the cavernous rooms of the house. It was thus I began to search for bargains and to scavenge.

As usual, Mom came for her monthly annual visit and was more than happy to keep her eyes peeled for anything that might suit the house. It is a truism that often when you are looking for something you can never find it. I didn't have anything particular in mind so it was a pretty general look-out.

I often babysat a little female dachshund for friends. They frequently went away for visits and holidays. I was happy to become Whitney's slave. Mom and I loved that little dog to bits even though she ruled us with a rod of iron!

Once, when Mom was walking the dog around the alleyways that separated the rows of houses, she came across a perfectly decent pine bar-stool next to a dustbin and hauled it home. We examined this contraband with great glee, wiped it down and gave it a polish.

Another day, walking the dog again, something similar happened. Mom's beady eyes spotted a television stand and again, despite its being very heavy and only having one hand free, she managed to get it home. Again, we rubbed our hands together, cleaned it up, covered it with a cloth and popped on the TV!

During another walk, Mom spied a group of children in a park playing with a large circular rug. They said they'd found it. Mom generously offered to buy it from them for the princely sum of £1.15p, the only money she had in her purse. She dragged this home and I fell on it with great delight. True it was a little tatty and a little dirty, but my rooms were all without carpets at that point. The through-lounge and dining-room were to retain their bare floorboards. I had previously stained these, though not sanded down first. The carpet made the barren room seem more cosy. After a few days, we realised we had been itching since the rug's arrival so we blamed the rug and it was taken into the yard and scrubbed to an inch of its life and sprinkled with flea powder.

Not long after I first moved in, my dustbin was full of rubbish from the move so I sneaked out one night to put some rubbish into other bins! I found one with a carpet sticking out. It was a perfect hall-runner! It brushed up nicely and looked as though it was made for the long hallway that led from the front door.

Another time, not long after Mom had decided to take Whitney out in the evening, no sooner was back again to tell me there was a huge amount of deep maroon carpet off-cuts by and in a bin. The carpet was new. It was dark out. We got in my car and drove around the corner to where the carpet was. Quietly and stealthily, I opened the boot and we crammed in all the carpet. It took three trips. We stacked it in the garage.

Much later, I methodically cut the carpet into strips and nailed these to the treads of the stairs. There were three flights of these stairs and I thought I would never finish them, but I did. The stairs looked wonderful and I no longer had to noisily clip clop up and down. Apart from the £1.15 p for the rug, the rest of these things were *free*! Everybody loves a bargain, don't they?

13 END OF SCHOOL CELEBRATION

I was fifteen and out having a meal with my best friend, Mom. It was a lovely restaurant: bright, clean, uncluttered. I loved the red-checked tablecloths and the snowy white napkins. For me this was 'posh.' Rarely had I been out for a meal during the evening and definitely not in a restaurant. We were celebrating my finishing school for good, just the two of us. It felt so very special. I had waited years to get away from that awful school. This meal was a celebration of the end of the daily grind with its unrelenting stress and boredom of pupilship. Now, stretching before me was the future: a brand-new life in the huge, interesting and exciting world beyond those grey prison walls.

I was having a lovely time. The meal, though basic, was hot and tasty. I was in clover: it was novel having my lovely Mom all to myself without having to vie for her attention amidst the rest of the demanding family.

It was near the end of the meal. A low hum in the room was comforting. Everyone was enjoying themselves. Suddenly, Mom declared in her loud voice, 'Julie, I really do wish you would masturbate your food properly.' An astonished silence fell upon the small room as the faces turned our way. I was blood-red with sheer embarrassment and amazement at Mom's words. Sweat broke out on my forehead as my heart began to thump rapidly. I bent my head and finished the meal as quickly as I could. The hum had begun again.

Once outside in the cool, fresh air, I grabbed Mom's arm and whispered fiercely, 'Why on earth did you use *that* word in there?' Mom looked astonished.

'What word?'

I hissed the word vehemently into her ear. 'Really, Mom, everyone heard and everyone was looking!' Mom shook off my grip and laughed until the tears poured down her cheeks. 'But, Julie,' she cried, 'I didn't say that. I actually said masticate.'

I looked at her long and hard before saying, 'What the heck does masticate mean, then?' Drying her eyes, she explained it simply meant 'to chew.' Doubly mortified, I walked on ahead in a huff for a while, then hung back and linked my arm in hers. Together we leaned on each other laughing all the way home. It was a very memorable day.

At the age of 57 I was with a party of nineteen celebrating a birthday. We had all been set a task: to 'Come with a funny story to tell.' Well, this was my funniest story, and yes, you've guessed it, I won first prize and thoroughly enjoyed the bottle of wine later.

15 A SIDE ORDER OF PEAS

I was about nineteen when small gang of us had been into town to attend the local flee-pit. We dressed up for the evening: hair, make-up, nails, clothes. I wore a pretty maxi-dress with daisy print. It was ever-so slightly low-cut and embarrassingly showed off my big boobies.

It was a great film and we finished the evening with a visit to an Indian restaurant. It was late. It was dark. It was very quiet in there, rather like a library. Everyone ordered authentic food except me. I ordered chicken, chips and peas. Where food's concerned, I have never been adventurous. Nearly always strapped for cash I couldn't afford to pay for something I may not like so I stuck to the tried and tested.

I hadn't really frequented restaurants much so the evening proved a novelty. The waiters were very well-pressed and crisply clean. They would lean over from the side to serve using large spoons to ladle from gleaming silver dishes. I was entranced by the whole experience.

After a long wait whilst the food was freshly cooked, our young Indian, rather handsome waiter, began serving the food from dishes on a trolley. Even to me, the food smelled delicious.

I was last to be served. The room was hushed. Conversation muted. He leaned in. First, he lifted a golden chicken quarter onto my shiny, white plate. It looked and smelled delicious. Yummy. I was starving. Friends looked on, sipping wine and nodding at the waiter with leery appreciation.

Next came the big fat chips. Delicious: fried perfectly and lightly golden. He turned to the trolley for the dark green garden peas. Again, we avidly watched his performance. It was darkly erotic and he had such a lovely shy smile.

Close at my side he leaned in. His perfumed warmth was intoxicating. He ladled a few peas on my plate. He turned regrouped and leaned in to serve a few more when his hand shook slightly.

Peas rained down me.

There was silence before laughter broke out: three little peas nestled comfortably atop my naked cleavage for all to see. All eyes were on my boobs. The waiter looked ready to cry. He began picking peas from the table. He even looked as though he might pick them from my boobs, too, but I quickly intervened. With a burning face, I picked them off one by one and set them down on the tablecloth.

I often wonder if that delightful waiter still remembers the night he didn't just serve a chicken, but also served a lady's breast with a side order of peas!

LEWIS'S DEPT STORE, BIRMINGHAM

Written by: Julie Hatton

Narrated by Mary N Hatton.

PART 1

I was born in 1929 and went to work at Lewis's as a young teenager. Working in the Ladies' Coat Department during the last war, I found the new longer length tried on by shorter customers dragged on the floor. In the workroom where coats were shortened the ladies were inundated with work and simply could not cope. The general staff was asked if we knew of a tailoress who might be willing to do some outwork.

My mother had been a tailoress and agreed to help with this important job. I used to carry coats home on the bus. Ultimately, their number became too great for my mother so I, who had no training, was roped in to help.

This went on nicely for some time and proved a good earner in days when money was short at home. Until, that is, the day I turned up a coat which was heavily gored (pleated). As each edge of the pleat stuck out, it was impossible for me to get it to lie flat as I sewed it. Naturally, the customer complained and that was the end of that little earner.

Departments within the store operated a system whereby our

basic wage was boosted by a commission on sales: 1d in every £1. Competition was rife. Assistants vied fiercely with each other. We would race as sedately as we could to reach customers first. Each week the manager of the department that made the most money also received an added bonus.

In the Blouse Department one day, a customer wanted a refund: a £4 blouse she had bought was unsuitable. Unfortunately, she seemed not to have been given a receipt with her purchase.

My manageress was particularly competitive. Any refunds would deter from the department's weekly total and subsequently her chances to win Department of the Week and her bonus. A 'return' affected our commission. No-one liked them. My manageress's tactic to reduce 'returns' was to make the experience as uncomfortable as possible for the customers: she would keep them waiting so they would think twice before returning anything again.

On this occasion, I, as a junior, was asked to go up to the account's department at the top of the building where the store kept all the carbon copies of the store's various transactions. I knew my role in this 'deterrent' was to saunter along, taking my time. I always enjoyed any opportunity to escape my own department. Meanwhile, customers would study their watches and lean on the counter, hopping on first one foot then the other.

As it happened, the Account's Department could not find any copy of the customer's receipt. As slowly as I ascended the building, I just as slowly returned to the lower floor. I explained that no copy of the receipt had been found though it was clear the blouse WAS from our store. To keep the customer waiting even longer still and to check on me, her junior, the manageress then also made her way very slowly to and from Accounts. There was still no sign of the receipt.

The customer, very weary by this time was asked for a description of the sales girl who had sold her the blouse. My manageress realised at once that the sales assistant was actually a friend of hers with whom she had spent the previous evening in the company of two American officers. There were many American soldiers in Birmingham during the war.

Despite her friendship with the girl, the manageress knew she had to fire her for she believed her friend had stolen the money and had covered the theft by not filling in a receipt. Unfortunately, this kind of stealing used to happen quite often. My manageress was furious: not only had her friend cheated the store out of money, but had cheated herself out of departmental commission and a possible bonus as the winner of the store's weekly competition. She would have to go.

I did not see the sales girl again. For a long time, I was terribly worried in case there had actually been an error over the copies. However, I learned years later that the girl had arrived for work the next morning, but was warned by a fellow assistant at the door that she was to be sacked for theft. Apparently, she turned on her heel and disappeared.

Another theft I particularly remember is that of expensive make-up. This department was on the ground floor. Originally, all items were stored and displayed within glass cabinets. The assistants brought individual pieces out one at a time to show the customers. It was my time at Lewis's when the Beauty Department began the practice of displaying its wares *on top* of the counters. I remember being horrified at what seemed such a blatant invitation to theft.

I was still working in the Blouse Department when a teenage girl stopped to talk to a colleague and myself. For some reason, she emptied all the make-up she had just stolen onto our counter. She seemed to want praise for her ingenuity and simply could not be made to see the gravity of her actions. She repacked the stolen items as we pleaded with her to take them back, but I doubt very much that she did. Though the building did have store detectives they had the entire store to cover. In those days, there was no such thing as CCTV.

To cover absences, the store relied on 'mobiles', people who came in when we were busy especially during sale times. We called these mobiles 'scratters'. Permanent staff was often peeved at the store's initiative because busy times were when we could increase our commission to improve wages.

One day, a particularly busy mobile in my department seemed to deserve something so I gave her a chewing gum. She was very pleased by my kind gesture. During the afternoon, however, she could not stop rushing to the powder room. My ruse had worked! I had managed to get her out of the department a few times so we 'permanents' could get our commission. She didn't deserve such treatment by me, nor by the chewing-gum laxative I had given her!

I carried laxatives because in those days my mother laid great emphasis on regularity of bowel movements. From childhood, she closely monitored mine as well as her own. She would encourage what she saw as sluggishness with home remedies such as Syrup-of-Figs or castor oil. Such concern over twenty-one years ensured a life-time of dependency!

Because the structure of Lewis's was so tall, there were escalators, lifts and stairs to facilitate access between floors. I remember a few tragedies that happened around these. All buildings are dangerous, but especially large buildings like Lewis's.

At the top of our very high building, in fact, on its roof, no less, there was a farm! Like Pet's Corner on a lower floor, the farm was intended to attract more customers to the store.

While I worked at Lewis's, despite there being a high railing around the edge, two people jumped off the roof on two separate occasions. I still speculate the sadness that would make these people want to end their lives. To this day, I am surprised they did not fall on and injure people in the street below.

There was another customer who also used the height of the building to commit suicide. The lady was someone who apparently should not have been left alone. On this occasion, she requested the toilet. While her mother waited outside, she took the opportunity to climb through a window and jump from the fifth floor. Her mother was extremely upset. Her daughter had been suicidal for some time and she had not let her out of her sight for weeks. Not knowing there was a large window that opened outwards and was easy to reach, she had thought her daughter safe enough in the toilet.

Naturally, suicides from the building always upset staff and customers. For weeks afterwards we would be more conscious and more aware of the store's dangers and become extra diligent for a while.

While I was working in the Service Bureau in the Complaints' Department, I once saw an extremely famous lady who had recently made a suicide bid by cutting her wrists. The wonderful lady was Judy Garland. She walked past one day and I plucked up the courage to say, 'Hello, Judy.' She turned around and gave me such a lovely smile in return. Did she have any inkling, I wonder, of how much I longed to put my arms around her and comfort her? I shall never forget the experience of meeting, however fleetingly, one of my much-adored stars of the big screen.

Like many other department stores, Lewis's had escalators. It was here I learnt just how important safety is. Customers should always make themselves aware of the existence of the emergency button that stops the escalator. In the event of an accident, it can usually be found at the bottom on the right-hand side.

Escalators contribute towards many accidents. When I worked at Lewis's it was not unknown for someone to trip at the top of the escalators and to knock down those below like dominoes. Except for guide dogs, I am glad dogs are no longer allowed in shops. The image of a dog's feet being trapped and caught in the prongs at the top of the escalator will forever remain in my memory. To this day, I also remember the little girl who was badly injured when her red wellington'd foot was trapped down the side of the steps.

In what was known as the 'old block' in Lewis's, a young boy was fatally injured by sliding down the banisters. In those days, stairwells were open-plan. On the fifth floor, the lad began his slide happily enough. Then he slipped. He fell seven floors to the sub-basement below. He had fallen through the vertical tunnel formed by the stairs that ran the height of the building. Fortunately, the staircases in the 'new block' were already displaced to prevent such awful catastrophes.

The lifts weren't entirely safe either. During the war, the sub-basement was allocated as the store's air-raid shelter. When the warning siren blew, customers and staff alike would surge towards the lifts, including myself.

I was told once about how a nearby exploding bomb could disrupt the safety mechanism of the lifts. If this happened, it would plummet to earth killing all the occupants. From then on, I always chose the stairs. Soon afterwards, it was decided to turn the lift's mechanism off during an air-raid. Then, of course, it took quite a time for people do race down the stairs, especially from the top floor. Always apprehensive about lifts anyway, I was told how, under normal circumstances, if the main mechanism failed, two giant arms would spring from the sides of the shaft to catch the lift like a babe in arms. It didn't comfort me overly much.

In the old part of the store, the iron fretwork of the lift's gates also held untold dangers. They worked like a concertina method and needed to be pulled across by a strong hand and arm. The hand would belong to a polite, smartly uniformed lift-attendant who would chauffeur the passengers between floors. All day he would be warning them to, 'Keep clear of the gates. Keep clear of the gates.'

Despite such vigilance, sometimes coats, sleeves, arms and hands would become trapped in the fretwork and hinged areas of the gates as well as been squashed painfully against the side. Children's busy little fingers were a particular cause for concern in these lifts. Though the doors were less dangerous in the new block, lift-attendants were still used as part of the store's service.

I particularly remember what our lift-attendants would say as I approached my destination for work: 'Second Floor: Coats, Gowns, Costumes, Shoes and Millinery.' Each time I heard it, or relive it now, the joy and pleasure I had at arriving on my floor and preparing for work again, was quite wonderful. I loved working at Lewis's.

Today, of course, most lifts are operated by remote control though we still need to be careful not to be bumped by the doors. Sometimes, we are confronted with a quiet, disembodied voice informing us the doors are opening or closing. If this is a safety feature it doesn't take account of the deaf amongst us. How I miss the personal touch of the lift-attendant with his smiles, his gestures and his general care. Too many things today seem cold and detached by comparison.

Part 2

A particularly favourite place of mine in the store was Pets' Corner. Devised and designed to attract customers I used to go up there whenever I had a few spare minutes during the day. It was a wonderful place to relax. I got on well with the keeper, a very friendly man, who had very long arms and beads of sweat on his forehead. He loved his animals and was always happy to pass the time of day discussing them with the staff and customers.

In the middle of Pets' Corner was a large cage containing a flying fox. I would stand and ponder this beautiful creature with its big brown eyes, furry body and wings like a bat. It seemed incongruous that this little furry creature should have bat's wings! Along with mice, hamsters, guinea pigs and rabbits, there were different exotic birds. One I was especially fond of was a large beautifully coloured parrot. He could talk and would dance for flower seeds.

I was not so fond of another parrot. One day, he was making a lot of noise, screeching and squawking. Seeing myself as something of a Dr Doolittle, I went over to investigate. As I talked soothingly to it, I leaned too close into his cage and received a nasty bite on my long nose!

After the manager caught psittacosis from one of the parrots and died, Pets' Corner was closed, never to re-open. How sad the children were who used to come to see the animals. Pets' Corner had been the highlight of the weekly shopping trips with their mothers. Similarly, due to suicides using the roof as a jumping off point, the farm on the roof was also ultimately shut down.

Whilst it lasted, the farm was a great attraction to the public. The store, like many of its customers, lived in the city centre. Even in those days, the city and its suburbs were very much concrete jungles. Most still did not have cars to access the countryside and its animals, so it was pretty much limited to bicycle, bus and train journeys during high days and holidays.

LEWIS'S DEPT STORE, BIRMINGHAM

In spring, the farm shop had to be transported in the service lift to the roof and its waste products brought down! The animals were kept in the open, fenced areas on the roof. These were kept extremely clean. A six-foot high safety- railing spanned its outer edges.

I remember ducks, geese and chickens being there. I recall the lovely pink flamingos, the goats and the sheep. I recollect little bridges that arched tiny streams, the tufts of turf scattered randomly, and the abundance of flowers and potted trees. In spring, the roof was transformed into an Easter Farm. Extra bunny rabbits were shipped in. Great pots of golden daffodils were spaced liberally over the floor. Smaller pots of pure white snowdrops and blue crocuses adorned ledges and steps. Yellow ribbons and bows decorated the budding trees.

The farm was a truly magical place! Everyone was very sad when it was closed down and removed. I have photographs of me taken on that roof and, when I gaze at them, I am transported back in time to those giddy heights and days.

The staff restaurant was situated on the sixth floor. We would have something of a 'do' here for our annual Christmas party. The 'staff' was encouraged to do a 'turn' for the entertainment. People would recite poetry, tell jokes, play an instrument, or sing and dance. One manageress had a lovely contralto voice and I vividly remember how moved we all were when she sang 'Jerusalem' so beautifully.

Because everyone has always told me my singing was 'flat,' and because I was a bit of an exhibitionist, I had cast around in my teenage years for something else I could do instead. Thus it was that I became renowned as something of an impressionist. One Christmas, I recall doing my act whereby I impersonated some of the big stars of the day. These included: Suzette Tarri, ''allo gals, 'ow are ya? All right?' Then there was Lou Costello with his, 'Mm, mm, I'm a baaaaad boy.' I always finished with Carmen Miranda's, 'I, I, I, I, I like you verrrrrrrrry much. I, I, I, I, I think you're grand.' All flat, of course. Nevertheless, I got a rousing applause for my efforts and I beamed around basking in my glory!

AUTOBIOGRAPHY

I didn't often use the staff restaurant. I used to prefer to go somewhere different for a change and to break the day's routine. Occasionally, I would wander over to the building opposite to look around. This structure was known as Grey's, a department store similar to Lewis's, though smaller. Grey's was also a little more down-market. Film stars did not often go there and there was no roof garden. Next to the store was a pub, then a self-service cafe where I would sit quietly with a coffee and bath bun.

The main road that divided the two stores was a very busy thoroughfare. A line of bus-stops fronted our rival building so the huge red double-decker buses were stopping and starting outside all day long. The buses were a major contribution to the smell of diesel and petrol fumes that hung around the streets and seeped in through the windows and doors of the shops.

When not wandering the shops, I would often escape during the lunch hour to the News Theatre. At the time, there were two in the city. The showings lasted one hour. There would be the Pathe News, followed by a film comedy or a documentary. These would run over and over again during the day. I wish these theatres still existed today. Now I am old, it would be very pleasant to have somewhere to go and rest quietly for an hour before making the long trek home carrying heavy bags.

In the cold weather, there would be tramps sleeping inside at the front of the theatre snoring their heads off! Once they'd paid to go in, they could stay there in the warm all day. Clearly, the theatre was often the only place where they could find shelter and comfort. Tramps were often seen outside begging for money to go in. Like in all cities and towns, tramps roamed the streets and slept on pavements and in doorways.

I used to love going to the pictures. I remember it cost 10d and 1/6 to get in. One cinema, The Gaumont, was just two minutes away from Lewis's. It was a very popular cinema because it had a huge concave panoramic screen. In later years, I saw three of my favourite films there: 'Zulu', 'Westside Story' and 'The Sound of Music.'

Another thing with which I occupied myself during the war

years was knitting. I loved knitting! With money and coupons in short supply I would visit jumble sales to buy knitted garments for a few pennies to unravel, wash, skein, roll and knit up. Many were the dresses, skirts, cardigans and jumpers that unravelled through my hands. I used to imagine the people who had worn them, who had knitted them, and for what occasion. I loved clothes!

Once the garments were unravelled, I would wash the skeins to clean them and remove the wrinkles. Then, as I needed balls of wool, I would get my long-suffering father to hold the skeins as I wound the tight balls. This would prove a bit tricky, though. The wool would keep catching on Daddy's permanently bent finger. It had been broken at some point. Soon, however, my fingers would be flying again and I would daydream to the sound of clicking needles. I took great pleasure in the art of 'making do.'

Besides recycling old knotted garments, I took great pride in being able to unpick second-hand dresses to make an entirely different one out of two for myself. Washed and pressed these clothes were as good as new!

I began by knitting things for myself and I remember the first garment I knitted for my mother. How proud I was when she wore that jumper regularly. My mother and I were about the same size, 'stock size,' because we had gone through the war and food had been very short.

I began to knit for everyone in those days. I would stay in at night knitting until I was forced by tiredness to go to bed. We didn't have television then. I would knit furiously as I listened to the radio or my gramophone records. There seemed to be so much more time in those days. I often wonder if I would have done so much knitting if there had been television.

To earn extra money, I would knit garments for the girls at work. They described what they wanted and provided the wool. I would then knit each item for 10/-. I vividly remember doing a jumper that was navy at the bottom with a pink yolk in moss stitch. I did so much knitting I no longer needed patterns; anyway, they were too expensive for me to buy.

For sales girls, Saturdays were always the busiest days of the week. Thus, it was always difficult for us to get a day off to get married. I remember my manageress being most annoyed I would need a Saturday off to marry the man of my dreams. Her disapproving scowl deepened further when she learned I needed two weeks off for my honeymoon in Bournemouth! My fiancé, too, found it difficult to get time off to marry me. He was working shifts and, unable to get the night off before the wedding, he had to leave his night shift and go almost directly to the church.

Though there was still some rationing when I married in 1950 I was luckier than my mother because I wasn't forced to have a cardboard wedding cake.. She had married at nineteen during the First World War in 1917 while full rationing was in full force. There was not the money, nor spare coupons for dried fruits, sugar, flour and eggs. My three-tier creation, on the other hand, was jam packed with fruit and iced like a dream. I was so fortunate.

Again, I was terribly lucky, because after years of rationing, I was able to find and buy my own beautiful wedding dress without any trouble at all. I worked in the Gown Department on the Fashion Floor at the time, and for months I saved for one of the gorgeous dresses I was so used to selling, but never owning. With my precious savings and staff discount, I was finally able to buy one of the fairytale creations coveted for so long.

It was a white chiffon georgette number, with long fitted sleeves that came to a point on the back of the hand. The shirred fitted bodice held a full-length flowing skirt. I wore a long veil with large flowers over each ear made of soft white feathers. I felt like Scarlett O'Hara in 'Gone With the Wind.'

I had one bridesmaid, my best friend Audrey. There was no money left for a bridesmaid dress so we had to borrow one from another friend. Audrey was married and therefore was really my Maid of Honour. Later, another friend, Barbara, became my first child's God-Mother and later still, my two daughters were her bridesmaids.

Having my first daughter christened was such an unhappy experience that I decided against christening my other two children. Because I didn't attend church regularly, the vicar was reluctant to do it and showed it. His attitude cast a blight over the day that we were not prepared to be so humiliated again.

The sun shone brightly on my wedding day. The service was beautiful and the reception perfect. The best man carried me to the taxi when we left. My new husband and I waved and smiled to the guests through the back window and I promptly burst into tears: I had not said goodbye to my mother!

Part 3

In those days, a problem for the fashion-conscious woman was how to smarten the look of her white legs. Woollen stockings and socks simply would not do! Many coloured their legs with gravy and coffee powder. I used black eye-liner on the back of my calves to represent the seam in stockings.

Nylon was invented in the US in 1935 but didn't reach me until a while later. 'Nylons' as we called the nylon stockings that became available were expensive and scarce when I was young. They were highly sort after items. Many girls, myself included, would go out with Yanks simply because they often gave nylons as presents! They weren't rationed in America and the soldiers would either bring them over with them or ask that they be included in their parcels from home.

The store sold nylons, but because they were scarce. They were still not easy to obtain. Lewis's operated a system known as fair-shares for staff. This meant a certain number of rationed items were put aside for us to purchase. Each department would receive one coupon and draws would be held to win the much-coveted nylons.

Because nylons were so scarce and expensive, getting a ladder was devastating. Entrepreneurs soon saw the opportunity to make money, and places were set up in the city where ladders could be invisibly repaired for 6d! One such place was in a dry-cleaning shop. If I couldn't afford their services, I would use nail polish to stop the ladder or sew it up with fawn cotton. My nylons would be washed and dried with the greatest of care. They had to last!

As a youngster during the war and the lean years that still

followed, I was always hungry. There never seemed enough to eat. I used to eat everything on my plate whether I liked it or not. Even today, I can't bear to see food wasted. Seeing people throwing away perfectly good food makes me sad. The Food Department in Lewis's was on the ground floor. Every morning when I went into work I would stare longingly at the mounds of tempting food on display. How my mouth used to water.

Because many of the ingredients of prepared food were still rationed, they were scarce and expensive to buy. I remember the time when gateau was highly popular. These luxuriant cakes attracted everybody, me in particular. But, the customers always came first. A few gateaux were, however, put aid for staffs' 'fair-shares' and occasionally I was lucky enough to receive one. I would slowly savour each morsel before swallowing and would be greatly disappointed when the cake was finished.

Something else that always made my mouth water was the huge mound of pork dripping. In the morning, it would be tipped out of its container onto the counter, its wet, glistening jelly shivering on the top. I could but it by the quarter. Wrapped in greaseproof paper, I took it home for supper. It was a real treat. Spread on thick crusty bread and sprinkled liberally with salt and pepper it proved a connoisseur's delight!

Broken biscuits were also things you could buy cheaply, and many were the times I proudly took home a bag for mother. We would open the package and gaze at them longingly, teasing ourselves by prolonging the agony. We particularly liked a bag of broken biscuits because it was a mixed selection of many different kinds sold in the store.

Travelling to and from Lewis's proved quite a journey. It was a five-mile bus ride into the city. Every day I would climb the high step of the double-decker and make my way up the narrow steps to the top. At eighteen, I began smoking Park Drive and, since no smoking was allowed downstairs, I would always go up. I am pretty sure that smoking contributed in some way to the migraine I had every day of the working week, particularly when I was manager of the Service Bureau in the Complaints Department.

Most of the week was spent dealing with frustrated and angry customers. They would thrust their heads out, shout and bang the desk. It was very difficult remaining polite and courteous. But I did it. Hence the terrible headaches! One customer especially stands out in my mind. He was extremely angry and when I tried to help him he stabbed his finger and demanded, 'I want to see the real manager, not some chit of a girl like you!'

In the mornings, I would wait at the bus stop on the Walsall Road in all weathers. The bus was always overly full and if the conductor said, 'No room at the top,' I could usually be found strap-hanging the five miles into the city centre. Fortunately, I still had the energy in those days to go on and complete a full day's work.

After the store closed in the evenings, I caught the bus from Bull Street for the five-mile journey return to the suburbs. Because my migraines were so bad, I had to focus on one place for the entire journey. This was not easy. I have always been travel-sick so the nausea with the headaches added to the misery of the journey.

Winter time was particularly difficult. Often the journey would take an hour or more. This was because of the fogs we had; pea-soupers, we called them: dense, yellowish-green fogs. This vapour caused by the fog mixed with the thick smoke from the burning of coal, factory and crematoria emissions. It caused great disruption to our lives.

There was always a traffic jam on my way home from Birmingham, but in a pea-souper it took on a nightmarish quality. Sometimes, the smog was so dense it was impossible to see a hand in front of your face.

The bus would crawl along at a snail's pace, bumper to bumper with the vehicle in front. Horns and disembodied shouting would shatter the silence. It was a dangerous journey. Drivers, tired after a long day at work, would grow impatient and do dangerous manoeuvres like trying to over-take or go too fast for such treacherous conditions.

Once, when I was on a bus in these circumstances, the conductor was walking in front of the bus holding up a white handkerchief to guide the driver. Because I felt sorry for the conductor, I offered to guide the bus for a while to allow him to rest.

From Beeches' Road, I walked along in front of the bus holding aloft my own hanky. After about ten minutes I was suddenly confronted by a dilemma. To get home, I had to turn left into Rocky Lane, but the bus had to go straight on. For me, then, there seemed no way to let the driver know this. The smog was so thick I couldn't see the driver, not it seemed could I go to the back of the bus to tell the conductor, so I did the only thing I could: I took off into the smog! I heard a screech of breaks, then nothing. To this day, I still wonder what actually happened!

Sometimes the pea-soupers would be so bad, buses were cancelled and I would have to walk the five miles home. I remember once being tired and exhausted when the faint lights of a sweet shop glowed through the fog. I went to buy some of my favourite dolly mixtures to keep me going on the tedious journey home.

I had many other misadventures with transport throughout my life. In my pre-teens mother bought me a longed-for bike. She warned me not to go on the road, but I did. I used to go to the top of our hill then get onto the road and sail down with my feet on the handlebars. Usually, this passed off without event, until one day, mother came out, and as soon as I saw her I began to wobble in terror. I came off, all bravado swept away as I prepared to face the consequences of my disobedience.

I was working at Lewis's when I raced a friend down the road. As we passed the house on the corner where my boyfriend lived I looked to see if he was about. As I sailed around the corner, Audrey shouted, 'Look out!' but it was too later. I failed to see a parked car and my bike glanced off it. The impact threw me head first into the road. Audrey, close behind me, couldn't avoid me altogether. Her peddle ripped my head open. I must have lost consciousness momentarily because the next time I saw her she was a long way down the road, her bike wobbling dangerously.

I was fortunate the accident took place outside a doctor's surgery. Audrey came back and knocked on the door. The doctor was out, but his wife came out to me. As she prised my hand off my head, blood poured out over me and the road. She took me inside and I remember being very conscious that I was dripping red blood all over her pale carpet. She gave me a towel to press to my wound while she phoned for an ambulance. By the time it came, my father had arrived. Mother was out as usual. As we settled into the ambulance all the neighbours gathered around. They did in those days. One poked her head around the door and asked what was going on. I said, 'I've ripped my head open and I am going to hospital for stitches.

I was given a local anaesthetic and my head was shaved around the long deep wound. After a while, the stitching really began to hurt and they gave me a deeper anaesthetic. Doctors laughed and joked around me as if I wasn't there talking about a dance they were going to that night. I was mortally offended and indignant: how could they do that when I was suffering so badly?

Dad and I went home in the blackout. It was as dark as the inside of a shark's stomach. Even the bus had its headlights covered to prevent too much light showing. The passengers of the bus acted as though they thought Dad had given me a beating because I was still covered in blood.

When we got home, mother was outside with our lodger, her not so secret boyfriend for many years. She took me upstairs and began berating and hitting me over the head for hurting myself and causing so much trouble. Mr Smith had to stop her, saying, 'I think the girl has suffered enough.'

The next morning I arrived at the Fashion Floor as usual. I must have looked a sight for though I combed my hair over the scar, I could do little about my two swollen black eyes. Thinking the customers would be scared off, they made me go home. I would rather have stayed than be with mother: she would simply talk at me all day.

The next day, I took off on my holidays with Audrey. We took a train to Wales to stay with her Aunt Sally. Her husband was a miner and would come home covered in black from head to foot. A tin bath was filled before the fire, and while Audrey and I waited outside, he took his bath.

That night, Audrey and I went to a local dance and picked up two of the lads. They took us for a spin on their motorbikes all around the Black Mountains. The thrill of the speed and the danger of sheer drops on either side was exhilarating.

The next day, the boys took us to some disused mines to show us around. Audrey went down but, much as I loved adventure, I couldn't do it. I've always been funny about enclosed spaces.

Despite my head injury, I thoroughly enjoyed the holiday and returned to Lewis's refreshed and rejuvenated, ready to start again.

Christmas was my favourite time of year at Lewis's, particularly after the war, because all the festive lights were at last allowed to shine outside. During the hours of darkness when the war was on, no light was allowed to show in case enemy bombers and planes found a target.

Preparations for Christmas began weeks in advance of the season. The overall planning for the giant windows and in-store stands were designed and goods ordered and stored. There was a flurry of activity as we cleaned, dusted and mended the trimmings, lights, costumes and ornaments that had been stored from the previous year.

Missing bulbs were replaced and checked, garlands were carefully patched and repaired, costumes were washed and ironed. How I loved the build-up, the growing air of excitement and, despite tiredness and frenetic activity, the lively camaraderie between departments.

As darkness fell that first Christmas after the war, the windows acted as a beacon of hope and light, encouraging shoppers to step inside and buy Christmas gifts, free from any worry of bombs. The six years' conflict was finally over!

Customers entered a tinsel wonderland to be wooed into parting with their cash. Carols like 'O Come All Ye Faithful' were piped throughout the stores loud-speakers to raise the Christmas spirit.

The store's wrapping service was popular. Any gift could be beautifully wrapped in shiny coloured paper and decorated with matching streamers and bows.

Part 4

Santa's Grotto, situated on the fifth floor, was my favourite place, both as a single girl and later as a mother. The Grotto was quite big. It had a covered walk-way of winding paths that led you round to Father Christmas. The man chosen to play him was always a big, genial gentleman with a warm, friendly smile.

Most of the children loved him. I say most, because there were some who were frightened of Santa Claus, including my middle child, Julie. We went to see him every year when the children were little, but she always refused to sit on his lap. Instead, she would hide and cling to my skirt in terror. My other two children, had no such reservations and would sit hugging Santa for as long as they were able.

At that time, it cost 2/6 to visit the Grotto. When the children were young, I used to receive £7 house-keeping money so 7/6 was quite a lot of money. Beside Santa, in two bulging sacks, were the presents: one for the girls and one for the boys. The gifts were of high quality.

There were metal toy guns for the boys and flaxen-haired dolls for the girls. General gifts included jig-saws, post-office sets, trumpets, drums, monkey-puzzles, books and printing sets. With money short the experience wasn't cheap, but it was worth it. I used to begin putting money aside in October so I could take my children to Birmingham for the day in mid-December.

We had a wonderful time in town shopping for presents. The day's treat would include a visit to the Odeon cinema for the matinee showing of a Disney film. Hot-dogs and bath buns were washed down with lemonade until it was time for the highlight of the day. All year the children and I waited for this special visit to Lewis's to see Father Christmas in the flesh. That mommy used to work there made the place more exceptional still.

The queues for the Grotto seemed endless. The nearer it came to Christmas, the longer they became. As the endless minutes of waiting went by, the atmosphere became electric. Over-excited children became tired but, on the whole, were remarkably well-behaved.

The queues of mothers and children would wind down the stairs from the fifth floor until finally, on Christmas Eve, the queue exploded beyond the doors outside. But mothers and children were still willing to wait. It seemed they could just about put up with anything to see Father Christmas at Lewis's.

There were plenty of Santa's helpers about to relieve the monotony of waiting. The little ones loved the pixies and elves. They wore little green hats with golden bells they tinkled as they moved. Their tight, green leggings cut off at the calf, along with red and yellow tops and pointy shoes all helped create a sense of fairyland. Pretty, dainty fairies danced nimbly along the rows in their white sparkling dresses, throwing glitter and waving wands.

To finally reach Santa's Grotto was the epitome of excitement. An expectant hush would descend. As we stepped through the doors quiet carols enhanced the spiritual mood. All was dark.

Along the low-ceilinged, winding passengers, behind glass screens, were Christmas tableaux, each depicting famous figures and scenes of the season. Fairy-lights twinkled overhead like stars to guide us on our way.

Best of all was discovering that the tableau moved. There was a Santa automaton actually waving to us from his sack-laden sleigh, surrounded by snow and encircled with elves and reindeer. Rudolf's red flashing nose always caused great excitement.

Next would come the Snow Queen in her icy palace. It was startling white. Everything: her hair, skin, dress, the walls, floor and doors. Icicles dripped and froze in sharply defined points from the ceiling. An invisible wind blew doors open and closed. Flurries of snow settled in drifts against glacial furniture. The Snow Queen would nod disdainfully at us. We shivered and gladly moved on to something less chilly.

This tableau was our beloved Snow White and the Seven Dwarfs. She would wave and smile while the dwarfs worked hard in the mine. There were many moving parts. A dwarf would raise his pick-axe then let it fall. Another operated the bucket that raised and lowered itself, while other workers busied themselves shovelling two and fro. And all the time their famous song would play, 'Hey ho, hey ho, it's off to work we go.'

The children loved these attractions and so, as a very special treat, we would sometimes visit another store called Henry's. Apart from Lewis's, this was my mother's favourite shop. It was smaller and cheaper than my store.

Here the children sat in a bright red train with bright chrome furniture. A sense of movement was created by a gentle rocking of the carriages. On the wall at the side of the train, painted scenery depicting a journey to Lapland would scroll slowly along to add to the impression of travelling along tracks. At the end of this imaginary, but magical journey, the children would meet Father Christmas and receive a small gift from his bulging sack.

When I worked on the sixth floor in the Service Bureau, Christmas was an especially busy and stressful time. Many customers would decide to buy large items like furniture for Christmas, but would leave it until the last minute, then complain bitterly when their orders were slow in arriving. Among other things, we dealt with orders, refunds, lost property and complaints.

All day I sat typing with the telephone squeezed between my left shoulder and ear. At the same time, I would be fending off irate customers demanding my instant attention.

Customers came to us for refunds. To deter them doing it again I would do the same as I had on Blouses: deal with it as slowly as possible.

Lost property in the store created extra paperwork for the staff. When a customer handed in a lost item, we would give a receipt with the date, the name of the department where found and a description of the item. If it was not claimed within three months, then the finder was allowed to collect it. A note would be kept in a book to record amounts of money found in purses and wallets. If this was not claimed the money would go to Accounts.

Customers who came to enquire about things they had lost would need to give a description of the item and the department where they had mislaid it.

Lost property usually comprised a lot of single gloves and I remember sorting through odd ones to make an acceptable pair. With no money for fripperies such as these, I was glad of them to warm my hands.

My pay then was £4 a week. By the time I had paid mother for my keep and forked out for bus fares, there was very little money left for clothes and entertainment. When I was promoted to manageress of the Service Bureau, I earned £5 a week.

I had a shock a couple of years later. Preparing to leave the store to have my first baby, a general manager told me there had been a mistake: other department heads were earning £20 a week. I was not offered owing back pay and I didn't like to press. In those days, we rarely questioned anything. We certainly didn't know our rights even if we had any. It didn't stop me from feeling peeved, though.

We used to have something called Goods Waiting Instructions. Customers ordered and paid for the items, but asked us to store them until they were ready to receive them.

People began ringing and ringing to ask where their things were. Some came into the office in person to shout at us and bang the table in sheer exasperation.

Lewis's storage facility and warehouse were sited five miles from the store at the Tyburn Depot. On young salesman on Furniture used to create havoc in the Service Bureau. To get his commission on sales, he would sell to customers knowing full well the items were not even in the depot. People would keep ringing and ringing to ask where things were. Some came into the office in person to shout at us and bang the table in sheer frustration. This young salesman was the bane of our lives: he kept getting his commission while we kept getting all the flack!

I would try to contact the depot. This wasn't easy. It only had five telephone lines to cope with an entire department store ringing all day. More often than not, the lines were almost continuously engaged. With the phone to one ear and angry customers shouting, 'Where's my goods?' in the other, it's no wonder my head was ringing all day. By three o'clock, I still hadn't had time to apply my make-up.

Sometimes, though, it paid customers to make a song and dance about undelivered goods, a natural occurrence at the time. I remember on in particular whom I couldn't placate nor fob off. Instead, she demanded to see an Assistant General Manager. Once he was involved, things got moving. He spoke to the depot and had them put her furniture in a taxi right that minute. The customer had to high tail it home to take delivery!

I was very fond of this Assistant General Manager and, because he was often kind to me, I had a crush on him. During my time at Lewis's I became infatuated with quite a few of the men. The manager of Lighting and Heating was especially gorgeous. Because he looked like the swash-buckling hero, Errol Flynn, whom I adored all my life, my knees would tremble.

One Christmas he came to the Service Bureau with a sprig of mistletoe. When we kissed my legs almost gave way altogether. I was on cloud nine for the rest of the week! It was no coincidence that the man whom I was to fall in love with and marry also looked like Errol Flynn! He had a similar build, face and hair, but it was his lop-sided grin that attracted me most.

Chatting with another General Manager one day, he asked how long I'd been married. When I said three years, he had the cheek to say, 'And you've not had a baby yet!' I blushed. In those days, it was still taboo for a man to talk to a woman other than his wife about sex, pregnancy and birth. Needless to say, the shock caused me to have a baby the next year!

A scandal became attached to this General Manager. He was interrupted in the stockroom one day more than just kissing a sales girl! When he was sacked for it, I thought, 'Good!'

A while later, my husband took me to Leicester on one of his jobs and I took the opportunity to visit a Lewis's in another city. As I walked the store I spotted the very man who had been dismissed for misconduct. He had not been sacked - just moved. Clearly, he was just one of the lads!

The General Manager I did like also crossed the line. I met him in the lift just before I left Lewis's for good because I was heavily pregnant. He smiled and asked, 'When is it?'

As I said, 'Next week,' his eyes grew round with surprise. Not expecting his to ask such a personal question I'd thought he meant when was I leaving the store! As I blushed, he said, 'No, I meant, when's the baby due?' I blushed again.

I remember being shocked and horrified in 1953 when a short, middle-aged woman in the next office arrived in a see-through blouse! I was disgusted. Her blouse hid nothing! I had never seen anything like it in my life.

I was in my thirties when the sixties arrived in force so much of the excesses of the revolutionary dress passed me by. With three growing children, I didn't have money to spare for myself. I did turn up the hems of skirts and dresses a little, though.

I was working in the Service Bureau when a lovely female cat wandered into the office looking for a bed. She was heavily pregnant and settled herself down comfortably in the lost-property box on top of the soft coats, scarves and gloves. Unfortunately, the other office staff said she couldn't possibly stay so I decided to take her home.

Later I learned she had taken the lift from the Food Floor where she was kept to keep down rats. I believe she decided to go elsewhere to have her kittens because the rats usually killed her litter every time she had one.

She was a lovely little thing. At the end of the day, I carried her in my arms for the twenty-minute walk to the bus-stop in Bull Street. She was so frightened being outside amidst the traffic and noise that she pooped all over me. The smell pervaded the entire bus for the half-hour ride. She pooped again as I walked home.

I spent the evening growing to love the cat as I cuddled her on my lap and listened to the radio. At bedtime, mother made her comfortable in a box on the floor of an adjacent downstairs toilet.

That night in bed, the most awful screaming and screeching from the toilet awakened us. Mother had left the window open and our old tomcat, who had been away on his travels, had returned. In the dark, he may have thought the female was an illicit intruder. The fighting, clawing cats were separated, the female soothed and the old tom sent off with a flea in his ear.

The next day, the cat had her kittens. Two were dead, the other alive. Even now I can't be sure whether the fight had caused the deaths or not. If it had, then my Samaritan act went awry because I had brought her home. I tried to do good, but it went pear-shaped.

It wouldn't be the first time or the last time that my love and kindness brought about an unintended effect on an animal. When I was younger, I had loved my precious gold fish so much I over-fed her. Finding her body floating in the bowl the next morning was at least a salutary lesson learned the hard way.

Like others, I find the suffering and deaths of animals particularly traumatic. We had many cats at home over the years and the females were always having kittens. I would bury my head in my pillow and cry all day when mother put the mewling bundles of fluff into a stocking and drowned them in water, warm water, to be kinder, she said.

When I first began on the Gown Department I was not allowed to do any of the modelling away from the store. I was especially peeved the day all the other models went to be taken to the Grand Hotel to show the Fashion Floor's latest collection. I demanded to know why I couldn't go.

'You're too young,' said the manager. 'You are not old enough to go where they sell intoxicating liquor.'

Needless to say, I sulked all day and wished I could grow up faster!

When I was old enough, I was included with the other girls and how I enjoyed the privilege with its thrills and glamour. But later, my world fell apart again when I began to work in the Service Bureau. The manager said I could not have time out of the office to attend modelling assignments any longer. 'You work in *Offices* now,' he told me. 'Not the Fashion Floor!'

I was devastated. I so loved dressing up in the gowns and walking the restaurant or catwalk. Everyone was always very friendly and it made a pleasant change in the day. It was as if a light had gone out. Not until years later when I became a lecturer at Kidderminster College did anything else quite replace that excitement, that buzz I had missed for so long.

I found working in the Service Bureau difficult because it was an office-within-an-office. It was without much natural light and fresh air. It didn't help that the men's toilets were right next door. The smell that often pervaded our space was terrible at times and we had no windows to open.

I was a child when I first fell in love with Lewis's. I used to go shopping there every week with my mother. Most of our groceries and household ware were bought in Henry's because it was cheaper. Lewis's seemed so much more stylish and refined.

Most people who shopped there had far more money than we had. The place seemed so ritzy and glamorous and I wanted to be a part of it. The staff was smart, well-spoken and well-dressed. To me the store was something out of the classy films I saw every week at the cinema.

As I got older, I used to return home and try to emulate the sales ladies. I improved my deportment with books on my head and read aloud to upgrade my voice. I spent a lot of time in front of the mirror working on different hair-styles and trying perms, though I generally curled my long hair every night with dinky curlers. When I applied to work at Lewis's I was fifteen years old and was working underground in the tunnels at the Rover Company in Kinver Edge, near Kidderminster.

Originally, I applied for a similar office job, but they didn't have one. They did, however, have a vacancy on the Fashion Floor so, loving clothes, I accepted it. Years later, when my favourite manageress left, I transferred to the Service Bureau and did office work once more. It was at the beginning of 1944 when I began my career at Lewis's. In 1953, I was twenty-one and manageress of the Service Bureau when it ended.

ACCIDENT PRONE, JOAN
Joan Bell

I'd worked at the courts about six years when I transferred from ushering to the finance office and was put into the fixed penalty office where I spent over twenty years. Although we were called lots of unpleasant names I enjoyed my job. Never boring and it was never the same each day.

I'd only worked there a few weeks when we were told the auditors would be coming the first week in December. I was told that whatever you're doing when the auditor asks for paperwork you stop what you're doing and do as asked. As I was still learning the job I was a bit wary and jokingly asked my team leader for the week off. No way!

I did already have one day booked off to go Christmas shopping with Andrea, my eldest daughter. Charlie dropped us off in Darlington. He planned to go on to the golf club to have a practice on the driving range.

Andrea and I hadn't been in the town fifteen minutes when we were walking down three stone steps which were very old and well worn. I slipped on the first step and bumped my way down the next two on my backside. I really was in shock so didn't try to get up immediately. I think poor Andrea was mortified by the look on her face! Before I could get myself up three young men rushed to my aid and helped me up. That was when I realised I was in trouble as I couldn't put my foot to the floor.

I assured the young men I was okay and thanked them. I steadied myself against the wall and as I didn't have a mobile phone

AUTOBIOGRAPHY

Andrea found a phone box and rang Charlie at the golf club. She told him we were outside House of Fraser and he came to pick us up. Would you believe it: as he pulled up a traffic warden appeared out of nowhere and said, 'You can't park there!'

Charlie said, 'My wife has fallen and I'm picking her up.'

He says, 'Yes, but you can't park there.

Charlie said, 'I know. I don't want to park. I just want to pick her up and take her to hospital.'

The warden was still threatening to issue a ticket while I was being helped into the back seat of the car so I could put my foot up. Andrea got in and so did Charlie and we drove off with the warden still muttering.

We got to hospital and the result was a broken ankle, a pot on and four weeks' sickness. Ironically, the auditors cancelled the arranged week they were to come to us and arrived just after I got back to work. Moral of the story, be careful what you wish for.

In the Fixed Penalty Office, we would receive driving licences in all sorts of states. We had a window for the customers to visit in person if they wished, but the majority of payments arrived by post. We sometimes received damaged or burnt envelopes due to fires in post boxes. These would come with a covering letter from Royal Mail. We then had to contact the person advising them of the damage.

On one occasion, we received an old-style licence in an undamaged envelope with payment and payment slip. The licence was charred all around the edge and was very brittle and parts disintegrated. I rang the number he supplied to advise of this and he supplied the answer as to why nothing else but his licence was damaged. He used to keep his licence in his slow cooker for safe keeping. He forgot and turned the cooker on one day to heat up before using it. Then he found his licence in that condition!

After more than twenty years in that office it was decided to close the window and only deal with customers by post. I didn't like it as much as I enjoyed dealing with people face to face. Then worse was to happen: the whole office would move to Leeds as a call centre.

I was moved to the Fines Office and just sat at a screen all day. It is not good. I started suffering with migraines. The doctor gave me medication and when the offer of moving to Tribunals as a clerk came up. I accepted. I don't usually like change especially as I got older and thought I would find it hard to learn new things. But this move proved to be marvellous. The migraines stopped. I never sat long at my desk because you are up and down to meet the appellants. When the tribunal is ready to hear the case, you take them in.

There was lots of admin work to do such as phone calls, phone messages and faxes to see to. I worked in a satellite office as head office was in Newcastle so there were just three clerks for three tribunal rooms which kept us very busy. I also met some wonderful people and we still keep in touch so sometimes change is good and although unhappy at the time I'm now glad it happened.

Because I had dealings with the Courts I learned a few stories and this is one of them. One chap who was a regular decided he wanted a Christmas dinner.

He was in Littlewoods when they used to sell food. He had a black plastic sack with him and grabbed about three or four chickens, dragging the sack behind him. He had no way of cooking them, but he didn't want to cook them. He just wanted to be caught so he could have Christmas dinner in prison. Running away from the store detective, he ran straight into the court's reception so he didn't really need chasing. He was giving himself up!

These types of people can't be fined because they have no money to pay so he was sent off to the cells where he would be fed. Once charged and sentenced he would spend a few more days in prison.

He was a kind man. I had seen him looking after older, frailer men trying to keep them warm. He also used to love to embarrass the staff in the court. He was from a good family and was quite well spoken.

In 1979, my sister and her husband moved to Kirkella, Humberside. We both had young children so we would travel there for the weekend to spend time together. My niece, Rachel, and our daughter, Andrea, would sleep together in a bed. Andrew, my nephew, four, and Emma, our daughter, three, shared a blow-up double-mattress together on the floor.

Once the children were in bed we adults would enjoy a glass of wine downstairs. One evening we heard a piercing scream that sounded as if Emma was being murdered. We ran upstairs to find Andrew rolling about the floor in fits of giggles and Emma lying on a flattened blow-up mattress. Andrew had pulled out the plug sealing the air and it had slowly gone down while Emma was asleep. Within in minutes she was laughing the same as Andrew Once she'd recovered from the shock she joined in the laughter with Andrew. It took quite a while to get them back to sleep!

On another visit, Rachel and Andrew had been staying at their grandparents and it was arranged we would collect them and take them back with us. It was a long drawn out journey once you got on the B-roads. We would always check with the children if they needed the toilet before we got under-way.

Needless to say, Emma was desperate once we were nowhere near a toilet. Charlie stopped the car and backed into a place near the gate of a farmer's field. I was to get her out and take her behind a bush. It was muddier than we realised and the car got stuck.

The more he tried the more mud sprayed all over. If any of you have seen 'Keeping Up Appearances' you can picture the scene. Once Emma had 'been' we got back in the car to get on our way. Charlie managed to get out of the mud, but one of the girls was promptly sick all over Andrew. Poor lad. I undressed him to his underclothes and put Emma's coat on him. A girl's coat for a boy like Andrew! He was mortified. You couldn't imagine anything else could happen. But it did!

Please remember we had no mobile phones in those days and Linda knew when we'd left her mother-in-law's house and, because we were late, she was wondering where we were. We had only travelled a mile or so once back on the road when we realised with horror that we were behind a van of hunt saboteurs spraying aniseed about. Because we were on small country roads we couldn't get past so the usual three-hour drive took six hours altogether!

ACCIDENT PRONE, JOAN

Once we pulled up at Linda's, she saw the muddy car and poor Andrew climbing out in Emma's coat, and her face was a picture! We still managed to enjoy the weekend, though. Young Andrew was always a bit of a comedian and another joke he used to play involved a rubber finger covered in a bandage and blood. He would leave it in places where he knew we would come across it and scream!

I am very accident prone especially on holiday. Mam and Dad soon realised they would have to find hospitals / doctors / chemists as soon as we arrived! The first holiday I can remember was to Crimdon Dean situated on the coast near Hartlepool. We had hired a caravan for the duration.

We travelled there in the motorbike and side-car. Once there, mam went straight to the camp shop for milk to make tea. Dad started to unpack so I went with Linda, my elder sister, to the playground. Linda sat on a swing and asked me to push her. As I was doing this the swing came back and lifted me off the floor by catching my chin and throwing me in the air. A couple of teeth were knocked out and there was blood everywhere. I ran all the way back to the caravan screaming. Dad said he knew straight-away it was me! We had only been there fifteen minutes! I think I was four.

The following year, still with the side-car, we went to a caravan in Whitby. It takes about fifty-minutes to get there now, but I assume in 1959 on a motorbike it would have taken longer. It seemed forever to Linda and I.

Dad stopped at the top of Birk Brow which is in the moorland. If you saw 'Heartbeat' on television you will be able to imagine it. There is always a van there selling teas and coffees and dad wanted a drink. I wanted to get out of the side-car so dad sat me up on the bike. I have no idea why, but silly me slid down off the seat. You can imagine what happened next, I'm sure. I burnt the full length of my leg from ankle to knee on the hot exhaust. Dad wrapped a wet hanky around my leg and we had to get to Whitby Hospital. For the full week mam had to change my dressings. What a holiday that was and we hadn't even reached Whitby!

The next accident I recall I was seven or eight and we went to

AUTOBIOGRAPHY

Felixstowe to stay in my aunt's caravan. This was planned for one week, but dad's motorbike broke down so we had two weeks there in the end. We had been there about two days. Things were looking good so far: no accidents, until I jumped over an area that was roped off. This probably means I shouldn't have done that. No-one has worked out how I managed to get so caught up in the rope that I had to untangle myself and the more I tried the tighter it got. I had rope burns around both legs which were very sore for days afterwards.

I will now go back to being six years old. This was not a holiday. It was just a plan for a day out. Dad and my uncle had both gone to get petrol and I was sitting in the yard waiting for my cousin to finish with our outside toilet. Mam was packing the food. I sat on the bin swinging my legs. The lid can't have been on right because suddenly I fell forward and hit my forehead on the rough wall. There was blood everywhere.

We had a neighbour who had a taxi and as dad wasn't back the neighbour offered to take mam and me to the hospital. I was over the moon with that. I had never been in a taxi before! It was a real treat. We still went out that day with me wearing a large white bandage around my head. My cousin, Barbara, wouldn't come anywhere near me because I frightened her. I still have the scar today.

I was nine and we were in Scarborough for a week. Within an hour of arriving and putting our things away in the flat dad had rented we were walking down to the front and saw the Glass Maze. It probably wouldn't be allowed today because of health and safety reasons. Mam and Dad paid for Linda and I to go in while they waited outside.

Linda sensibly walked around with her hands out to feel for the glass. I didn't - bull in a china shop me - I started to run in a panic and wanted to get out of it. I banged my head on most of the glass. The more I banged my head the more I wanted to get out. Ultimately, the bump on my forehead was the size of a very large egg. Iodine was the stuff Mam used for many of my injuries. I actually loved the smell and as I write this it's dawned on me maybe that was the reason I hurt myself so much! Gosh, if that's right then I am dafter than I thought!

This wasn't an accident to me, but something I hardly dared tell Mam about. I was ten and mam had knitted me a beautiful cardigan that took her quite a long while because she worked full-time. I used to stay at my grandma and granddad's cottage in Dalton near Thirsk every school holiday.

My friend, Margaret and I wanted to go on a bike ride. We packed a picnic. We also took our Tressy and Sindy dolls which went everywhere with us. If you remember Tressy she had a very long ponytail which you could wind in and out to alter her hair length. I was very naughty. One day I cut her ponytail so that was another thing I didn't dare tell Mam about! I also stuck a drawing pin in her head so she always had to wear a hat to hide the damage!

We were cycling to the River Swale. There was an area which had a sandy bank. We would sit on this to have lunch. I was hot, so took my cardigan off and tied it to a rack on the back of my bike. Thinking it was safe we cycled on. After a while it got harder to cycle, but instead of checking the bike I kept going. Margaret was in front of me and couldn't see what was happening. A sleeve had dropped down into the wheel and more and more of the cardigan got twisted into it. By the time I realised, it was well and truly ruined. I couldn't even cycle home. Instead I had to push the bike. It probably took me the whole summer holiday to pluck up the courage to tell Mam I had ruined her lovely jumper! I am just coming to realise now that I must have been a right handful for my parents!

From about eleven onwards I had accidents when on holiday and at home, but they were usually falls and trips that were usually involved just scuffed knees and nothing mam and dad needed to worry about.

When I was twenty-three we went on holiday to Butlin's Filey with Charlie's sister, Diana, and her husband, Dave. We decided to go to York Museum for the day. Emma was two and Andrea four. We had a great time and were due to leave when we noticed it was raining very heavily. Charlie said he would get the car and bring it as near as he could to the door. We had no coats or brollies with us.

It had been a beautiful day when we set out. I saw the car so picked Emma up and held Andrea's hand and ran to it. Charlie opened the door and got Andrea inside, but I suddenly slipped, yet some how I managed to get Emma onto the front seat. I still felt myself slipping and tried to stay upright. I grabbed the rim of the car roof, fell forward and hit my mouth. I knocked my tooth out which went through my bottom lip. There was lots of blood, of course, which upset the girls. Diana and Dave were in their own car so they took the girls back to Butlin's to get them some tea and put them to bed while Charlie took me to hospital.

York has a ring road and although we know it quite well we weren't sure where the hospital was. There were no Sat Navs in those days. We saw a police officer who gave Charlie directions. We set off and drove quite a way, but Charlie thinks he missed a turning he should have taken. We were driving for about half an hour when the driver of a car beeped at us. It was the police officer who was, by now, off duty and on his way home. He told us to follow him. He managed to get us to the hospital. The only treatment I could have was to have the broken tooth coated with a substance to stop too much pain. The following morning, we had to find a dentist in Filey to do a temporary repair until I got home. You couldn't make it up, could you?

My tooth was repaired with a cap which wasn't very good. It was on the National Health because we couldn't afford to spend more until a good few years later.

About nine years later we all went to Woolacombe in Devon with my sister and her family. We were having scrambled eggs for breakfast when my tooth fell out when I knocked it with my fork. Now we had to find a dentist in Devon. Once home my own dentist had to do another repair, but even eating a cracker would cause it to fall out. Happily, when Charlie worked at ICI we managed an arrangement whereby I had two front teeth crowned and the payment came out of his wages over a few months.

When I worked at the Magistrate's Court my first job was as Court Usher. One day I was usher in the Juvenile Court. This area had two courts in session with a dividing locked door to keep the little darlings away from the adult section.

Each of these courts had two doors with just a few inches between them to keep the noise from the waiting room disturbing the court. The one leading out of court was a swing-type door, the next had a door handle.

We had a waiting room full of defendants with their families. It was like a day out for the regulars. It was difficult to keep some of them under control. I came out of court to check if anyone else had attended. There was a lot of giggling going on. I opened the outer door with the handle or tried to, but some joker had unscrewed the hinges and the door, being very heavy and solid, dropped to the floor. I still had hold of the handle which I suppose must have been comical for the little darlings and their parents. We didn't have security officers at that time, but after that happened, we had to have a commissionaire standing on the juvenile court landing. Nowadays they wouldn't even get passed the 'security arch' with a screwdriver!

Another comical happening occurred one day when I was trying to get through the locked door to the adult section and some clever wag had put a load of blue tack in the keyhole. I didn't find it very funny at the time!

Charlie is a member of a golf club and has been for thirty years. About twenty years ago, a lady who had been a very popular steward was retiring and Charlie was to get her a large arrangement of flowers. He was dropping me off at work one morning and then driving on to the club to take them as a presentation to her. On the way to my work we collected the flowers and I kept them in the front of the car with me. On getting out I was so concerned at keeping them upright I didn't see a bollard on the kerb.

I don't think I need to describe what happened next. Charlie drove off. He didn't even see where I landed. I did a beautiful forward roll. I know this because a colleague from work was standing with a coffee looking through the window. She told me she very nearly spilled it. What already was in her mouth she splattered all over the window-sill. Luckily, only my pride was hurt. Audrey told me that even if I had been hurt she doubts she could have helped me for laughing. I was told the lady who retired loved her flowers which fortunately arrived intact!

I used to make Sunday lunch for mam and take it to her. One very snowy Sunday I had wellies on whilst carrying it all. The wellies had deep ridges in the soles so I was trusting them to keep me upright. The snow got impacted into them and made them super slippery. From setting out it seemed okay, but it started snowing again and although it should have been a fifteen-minute walk it took me that long to just get a few yards. I slipped and fell.

My bag with all the food in went one way and my phone fell out of my pocket and went the other way. It was difficult gathering everything together again because of the snow. I had to search for everything. Underneath the thick layer of the new snow was solid ice. If I'd realised just how bad it was I wouldn't have set out. It also took some getting up because I kept slipping down again on the snow. I ended up looking like a snow monster and poor Mum had less dinner than usual that day.

When I was a child, my mam's parents had a small holding and Granddad got lots of old railway carriages which he put all along the side of his field. He had chickens roosting in them. They were free to roam and used to come to the kitchen door if we didn't get out early enough in the morning with their feed.

When chicks were born, we would bring them in by the black range to keep them warm. I really loved them and gave them names. I shouldn't have done that because quite regularly on Sundays we had chicken!

One day, a turkey wandered onto Granddad's land. He told the police and they said if no one claims it in three weeks he could keep it. No one did so I was given the job of looking after it and I did all summer. I didn't eat Christmas dinner that year. I was heartbroken.

DANCING TO HAPPINESS
Bernice Caddick

I was born in 1938 and lived in a two-bedroomed house with Mum, Dad and younger sister, Sandra. The house had quite a big garden. The war with Germany began in 1939 and from that time on everything in the shops was on ration.

Each family was issued with ration books so when you went to the shops you had to pay for your goods and the shop-keeper would tear a coupon from your ration book. If you did not have a coupon, then you could not buy it. That way it made sure that everyone got the same amount for their families.

All the mums and dads planted their gardens with as many vegetables as they could to help with the food scarcity and most families kept chickens. We did. Dad used to swap eggs for bread, cheese and all sorts of things. We used to eat bread cut up into cubes with hot milk and sugar on the top. We thought it was lovely. It kept us from feeling hungry and it also kept us warm.

Before I go on I am going to tell you a bit about my mother's family. Her mum's name was Ada and her father's name was James. They had four daughters. The first one they called Ivy. The second one, my Mum, was called Violet. The third they called Lily and the fourth one was called Rose. My gran always said that she had a bouquet, a leaf and three flowers!

My Mum was born with a bad heart and she wasn't allowed to play in the street or skip or run around like other children. When she was young her Dad went abroad to war. He was fighting in the battle of the Somme where he was reported missing, presumed dead. My gran didn't see him again until he came walking into the house two years later. My mum started crying because to her he was a stranger. I don't know where he had been, God knows, but everyone was overjoyed to see him. That was during the First World War 1914 to 1918. I can't tell you much about my husband Colin's family because I hardly know anything.

In those days, everybody looked out for everybody else and helped as much as they could. I started school when I was just three years old. It was an all-day school and I can remember going to sleep in the afternoons in the summer in the playground. When it was cold we slept on camp beds in the school hall. We had free milk every day and school dinners. I hated these with a passion. I always had to eat my dinner in the Head's office and she would often try to force feed me, but could never prise my mouth open.

We didn't have much money. Dad was in the fire-service and he was out all hours. Mum was very clever and used to make all of our clothes. At Christmas time, we had presents that Dad had made from wood or tin or paper. The Christmas stockings were Dad's socks and in there we would find an apple, an orange, a few sweets, a wooden yo-yo, crayons and a colouring book. That was it.

The walls in our house were painted with whitewash. Wallpaper was expensive so there was no wallpaper in most of the poorer houses. Dad got some dye from somewhere and mixed up a bucket with blue and one with pink. He dipped some rags then rolled them up the walls. That is how he put a pattern on the wall.

We didn't have radios, records, television or anything electronic at all, but we were very happy. People used to get together around a piano and sing and entertain themselves. The first big doll I had was made of celluloid. Plastic hadn't been invented then nor polythene or bubble wrap. We had brown paper carriers and brown paper bags for everything that we bought from the shops. All our wrapping could be burned easily on the coal fire and was much better and much easier for the environment.

During the bombing in Bristol all the people in the neighbourhood would go into the air-raid shelters. We each had one in the garden. Some were made of galvanised tin like the Anderson

Shelters and some were constructed of bricks. When we went into the shelter we had to go down steps because the rest of the shelter was underground. We would sleep there all night during raids. Someone would start playing the mouth organ or some other musical instrument and all the mums would sing so the children were not so frightened.

My Dad was out with the fire-service most of the time helping to get people out of the burning buildings. Other dads were away fighting the enemy away from home so mostly it was women who went to the shelters along with older men and women. We lived in Southmead and it was close to Filton Airport so the Germans were trying to bomb the airfields there. Because we were young we didn't realise really what was going on. The mums didn't let us know how bad things were. Bless them.

Food was still short so we still grew veg and potatoes in the garden. We grew beans, parsnips, carrots, onions, swedes, cabbages and cauliflower as much as we could grow. We found it very good because we could swap things that we grew for all sorts of things like soap, old clothes and old knitted jumpers.

Mum would wash it all and then knit cardigans for me and my sister. The coats would be cut into strips and then made into mats and they looked great on the floor in front of the fire. There were no carpets in the shops then only linoleum or nothing.

We were told that we were being evacuated to Weston-Super-Mare about twenty miles away because we were too near the airport and it was very dangerous. Mum, my sister and I got on the train and we stayed with a family that took us in for the rest of the war. When the war was over in 1945 we went back to our home in Southmead and thankfully our house was still there.

When I was seven we had an exchange with a woman and moved to Speedwell. It was a much better house with two bedrooms and a bathroom. Wow. We had never seen a bathroom before, but the toilet was still outside in the porch at the back of the house. Dad still kept chickens and still grew veg because meat and fresh food was very hard to get and we still had ration books so we were only allowed a small amount of everything.

AUTOBIOGRAPHY

We always had fresh eggs that Dad would sell. We only ever had a chicken on Christmas Day. Dad used to feed the chickens on cooked potato peelings with meal mixed in it. I can still smell it now. I thought it was probably good enough for us.

I started school and went to Two Mile Hill School. I loved it, but I wasn't very bright. I was very good at sports, however, and played netball and rounders for the school. My sister, on the other hand, was very bright and went on to pass her 11 plus exam and went to a grammar school. She didn't like sports at all. We were as different as chalk and cheese. She was blonde with straight hair. I had dark curly hair.

Do you know when my friends bragged about their dads being away in the army, air-force or navy I felt ashamed to have to tell them my Dad was at home because he was a fireman. Years later I realised that someone had to do the job of putting out the fires the bombing caused and save a lot of people by pulling them out of the burning houses. It was then I felt really proud of my dad.

When I left the junior school, I went to Speedwell Secondary and it was great because it was just around the corner from our house so I could go home for dinner. That's one thing I was very pleased to do because it meant no more school dinners!

Mum was very good with her hands and Dad managed to get her an old Singer sewing machine so she made most of our clothes. She managed to get some parachute silk and she made us underskirts and blouses out of it and she made other blouses to sell to the other mums, too. They loved them.

One Christmas, Dad made us a work-box each. In it were cottons, pins, needles and a tape measure. We were delighted. I learned to embroider, sew and knit at school. I loved making things. I would rather work with my hands than my head! Speedwell School was all girls. We had our own playground. The girls were on the top floor of the building and the boys were on the bottom floor. They also had their own playground. We girls had all lady teachers and the boys had men. I loved that school. I enjoyed everything about it and the school teachers were lovely.

It was about this time that I began to notice the boys. We used to go about in a group of boys and girls from the school and we always gathered after school to play games of skipping, hide and seek and kiss chase. I was chosen to join the school's netball team and also the rounders' team so I was very proud of that. I was hopeless at maths and mental arithmetic.

I wasn't too bad at English and was quite good at art and loved to act in any play in front of the school. We did the play, 'Jungle Book' and had to make our costumes in our art lesson. I can remember I was a peacock and it took a few weeks to make the tail. Once I played the part of Zacharius, the father of John the Baptist. When Mum came to see it, she did not recognise me. Where my sister was very shy I was the other way and loved being in the limelight. When I was eleven I started going to tap dancing classes with my best friend, Jean. We did everything together. She was like me: very outgoing. We often did a show on the stage together for church meetings and at other times for groups of mothers' meetings etc. We loved it. Mum used to make our costumes and we really enjoyed showing off our tap-dancing talent.

It was now 1952 and we were seeing more and more different foods and soaps and different toys made out of unusual material. We now had lots of fruit and all sorts of food coming back into the shops for sale, but we still had to use our ration books. That meant that we were only allowed a certain amount per coupon like half a pound of butter per week, a small loaf of bread and a quarter pound of sweets per week.

Dad gave us sixpence a week pocket money and we had the sweet coupon from the ration book from Mum. I would get Liquorice Allsorts and Sandra my sister would buy a quarter of Marzipan Teacakes, her favourite. We only had a chicken at Christmas then and that's why it was so special. When we were given a banana to eat we did not know what to do with it. Mum showed us how to peel it and then eat it

We all played together in our street, but I always had to go home first. I had to be indoors before it was dark. As the time went on our group started to pair up and we all had a great time. My Dad was very strict. It was the way he was brought up. His step-mother never showed him love and kindness so he found it very difficult to show his own feelings. It was a terrible shame really. I can never remember Dad picking me or my sister up, or sitting on his lap.

Mum, on the other hand, was a very loving person and we are what I call a kissing family. Mum joined the Auxiliary Fire Service and used to go with a friend twice a week for practice. We asked her if we could go with our friends and learn ballroom dancing. She agreed and said yes, we could, but she would pick us up at the dance school and walk us home after her practice. It was wonderful. I loved it and we learned the quick-step, the waltz, the foxtrot and the jive. We went there every week on Thursday and they put a dance on Saturday night which was great.

It was then I began going out with my first real boyfriend. His name was Michael and we went everywhere together for about a year. Then one night he said that he would have to stop seeing me because his mother and father said that he was too young for a long courtship. It broke my heart and when he left that evening I walked the streets crying my eyes out. I thought my world had come to an end.

Some twenty years later my husband and I went on a trip to Jersey for the weekend with the local pub and Michael was there. He was married with two children, a boy and girl. We had our three girls. Michael was very handsome, but I was very satisfied with my husband. I love him dearly still and we have had a wonderful life together. In fifteen-months we will have been married sixty years!

Well, I was in my last year at school and enjoying everything that went on there. We highly respected the wonderful teachers and enjoyed most of the classes. I know that when I was in the fourth year we had to invite two teachers to dinner. We had to cook a roast dinner and make a pudding. We also needed to serve the meal and clean up afterwards. It was great. We invited out favourites and it all went off okay.

I loved cookery lessons and, in our last year, we made and iced a Christmas cake from scratch. It took a few weeks before we finished it, but we were really proud of them when we presented our cakes to the family. I was now nearly fifteen and I would be leaving school when we broke up in the July.

I wanted to start work in a factory where some of our group were already working so I wrote away for an interview. I had to go after school on a Wednesday. I had just finished playing a netball game against another school and went straight off for the interview. The Matron who talked to me was very nice and she said how pleased to see a school girl look like a school girl. Anyway, I got the job, so I was over the moon and I began working in the cardboard-box factory the week after I left school. It was a very sad day when we said goodbye to all our school friends and teachers. I had quite a few tears.

Now I had left school and started work I felt really grown up. I must admit the first day at the factory seemed such a long day and I thought the time for clocking out would never come. We started work at 7.45am and had an hour dinner break and then finished work at 5.30pm. It was the longest day of my life! By the end of the first week I was getting used to the long day and when Friday came I was looking forward to the weekend off.

We had our wages paid to us by a clerk going around the factory passing out our pay packets in little brown envelopes. On the front was printed how many hours we'd worked and how much we had earned. Out of this was taken our union money, national insurance and tax. It also told you what you had as take-home pay. My first wage for that week was £1.19s.11d. I felt rich! When I got home, I gave it to Mum who then gave me 10/- back and kept the rest to help with the running of the house. I was thrilled to bits. 10/- in old money is 5op today.

Dad said he would take me to the cycle shop to get a bicycle so I could ride to work. I was pleased because the factory where I worked was quite a long walk. We went to the shop where I chose a red Raleigh Dropped Handlebar bike. Dad paid a deposit and I was to pay the rest in instalments which I did faithfully every week. I had that bike for years and loved it! It meant I didn't have to leave so early in the mornings which was fantastic and the days did not seem so long after I got used to working long hours.

We all got on very well and I was with many friends from

school. We used to get told off a lot by the section-leader, though. Someone would start singing then someone would join in and then someone else until the whole section was singing. Down the section leader would come and tell us to stop singing, but we started up again as soon as she was gone only much quieter.

As I got older I was put on several different jobs and sections. It was very interesting work. There were a lot of boys who had done their National Service and were coming back to work so I went out dancing with a few of them. I enjoyed the company and the dancing. I was still going to the Saturday night dances at the church hall where I had learned to dance and there was a boy there I fancied like mad, but he was courting.

One Saturday, he was there at the dance alone so I asked his friend Ronnie why he was there by himself. He said he and his girl had split up. They had what was called a 'ladies' privilege quickstep' so when that came around I went over to Colin and asked him for a dance. Of course, he agreed and afterwards he asked if he could walk me home. I was overjoyed and said he could.

While he was walking me home. He was telling me how upset he was that his girlfriend had wanted to go out with someone else. I'm a good listener so I listened and felt sad for him and when he kissed me goodnight, he said, 'Can I see you tomorrow?' His friend Ronnie walked my sister home as well and had also asked if he could see her the next day so we arranged to meet them by a pub called The Beatem and Wackem in the morning at 10 o'clock.

I thought Colin was charming, but when we got up in the morning, my sister had changed her mind and she said she wasn't going. She expected me to meet them both and make her excuses so I told Mum and Mum told her, 'You have to go and make your own excuses.' I was very glad Mum made her go. She did go for a walk with him, but never saw him after that date.

On the other hand, I was seeing Colin every night so that's how I met my future husband, Colin. I was fifteen and he had just turned sixteen. We were very young, but even then, I hoped I would end up marrying him. My Mum adored him. He became the son she didn't have and he would do all the things Dad couldn't do in the house. Although I was going out with Colin I'm ashamed to say that I went out with other boys, too. I know it was naughty, but I thought to myself if I didn't go out with other boys how would I know for sure that Colin was the one to spend the rest of my life with? Anyway, I soon realised no other boy could hold a candle to my lovely Colin.

When we were seventeen we decided to get engaged. As was proper in those days, Colin had to ask my Dad if he could marry me. Dad said, 'Yes, on one condition. You take me to see the Rovers playing football every home match on you motorbike!' Colin agreed and bought me a lovely five-diamond-platinum ring. We had a lovely engagement party with family and friends.

We were engaged to be married and we had to start saving for our wedding. We were both seventeen-years old and planned to get married in two years' time. Mum was very good to us and was always buying us little things for our bottom drawer like tea towels, egg cups, tea sets and all different things you need when you set up a home.

We didn't go out much because we were saving. Colin did not earn very much because he was an apprentice electrician. I still worked in the cardboard box factory. Every year on each birthday we had a rise so that was a great help. Mum used to treat us to the pictures sometimes. She gave us 2/-. It was 9d each to go in so we had enough to buy a couple of gob-stoppers and sherbert-dips. In the old money, there were twelve pennies in every shilling, so we had three pennies each to spend on sweets.

I remember one night sitting in the back row sucking my gob-stopper. I got fed up with it, so I was naughty and put it on the floor. To my horror, it started rolling down towards the front of the cinema! As it rolled down it stopped, hitting someone in front. They moved their foot and then it started rolling again and it went on like that until it hit the bottom, banging into the wood across the stage. I was so glad the lights were out and it was dark. I was so embarrassed!

Colin's family was much better off than my parents. They'd bought their own house and it was much better than ours. They also

AUTOBIOGRAPHY

had a wind-up record player. Colin's Dad also had a car so we used to go out on picnics or to the seaside every week on Sundays. Later, Colin bought a motorbike. It was a Velocette motorbike. It had an open flywheel by your foot. He loved it. It was his pride and joy and it allowed us to go out to all sorts of places. His Mum and Dad bought me a helmet to wear on the bike. They were not compulsory, then, but I had to wear it for safety, they said. I thought it was very nice of them and appreciated it very much.

Although I was seventeen and engaged to Colin I still had to be in by 9.30pm every night and if I was a minute late, I would have to stay in for a week. Colin had a sister. She was blonde and very pretty and we used to take her out for walks with us. She was fifteen years younger than Colin. My sister was also courting so we didn't see much of her. When she left school, she started work as an apprentice hairdresser. She was and still is a good hairdresser. When she went to grammar school she had a different circle of friends, so we didn't go about together anymore. We still slept in a double-bed together though and did until I got married.

When television came into the shops, Colin's Dad was the first to buy one. We thought it was wonderful. It was a 12" square screen and of course black and white. There was no colour TV in those days.

It was now 1955 and we had quite a shock because Colin's mum said on Saturday, 'We are taking you to see Gran.' She lived not too far away. She lived in the district of Laurence Hill. We went to see her. The family that lived two doors down her street were selling their house so she wanted us to look at it. It suddenly dawned on us that perhaps she thought that it would be okay for us. We were getting married the following year in the month of March.

It was about July when we went. It was a really big house: three stories at the back and two stories at the front with the front door leading out to the pavement. There was a really large garden for growing veg and potatoes. On the ground floor, at the back, was a lovely bathroom, and a good-sized kitchen and a breakfast room. A passage lead to a flight of stairs to the next floor where there was a front room and a lounge facing the back. There was another flight of stairs leading to two good sized bedrooms. We said we thought it was lovely and Colin's gran put a deposit on it for us and said, 'Pay it back when you can.' We thanked her very much. We were over the moon at the thought of having our very own house, but there was one snag: how could we pay our Mums' housekeeping and pay for the house at the same time?

We decided we'd bring our wedding forward as we were going to have to start paying for the new house. Luckily enough, the family that was moving out, had not found their new home yet so that gave us a while to still live at home and able to give our housekeeping to our mums.

Colin was quite a shy person and didn't want all the fuss of a big wedding in a church so I agreed to get married in the registry office. Mr Goss, the name of the man selling the house, said he would let us know when the house they wanted was ready and instead of us having a mortgage we could pay him monthly. We thought that was a great idea because there were extras like interest or solicitor's bills with a mortgage.

We booked our wedding for the 27th of December, 1957. I had a blue suit made and Colin had a grey suit made. It was all very exciting. We started buying bigger things for our home, but could not afford cash. Neither of us earned very much. Instead, we decided to buy several things on HP and pay weekly for them. Mr Goss contacted Colin and said they would be moving out in the November. He had a business so the house was decorated extremely well. He left us his cooker and carpet on the stairs. He also left some of the curtains which was very nice of him.

We got the keys from Mr Goss and he gave us a rent book so he could collect the monthly payments. We went to the house every night to do little things that needed to be done. Mum and Dad bought us a dining room suite with a sideboard with a cocktail cabinet inside. Colin's parents gave us their old TV. We had a three-piece suite delivered and we bought a square of carpet for the lounge and linoleum for the rest of the floor covering. In those days, no one had fitted carpets like we have today.

We had a lovely Christmas and Colin's Mum and Dad asked if

we could babysit Julie, Colin's little sister because they had been invited to a party on Boxing Night. Of course, we said yes. I still had to be in at 9.30 every night, but I thought, 'I'm getting married and will be leaving home the next day, so Dad can't keep me in anymore.' Colin brought me home later that night. It was 12,30. My sister was going to put curlers in my hair for my wedding the next day, but because I was home late Mum sent Sandra to bed so she could not do it for me. I thought, 'Oh, well, that's my punishment then'! It wasn't like Mum, but I didn't care.

We rose early in the morning to get ready. It was very hectic with us all getting ready at once, but it was very exciting. Sandra ended up doing me a quick French pleat and it looked lovely. When we arrived at the Registry Office, Colin was there waiting for me. He looked so handsome in his suit. He told me how very lovely I looked. Bless him. It only took about twenty-five minutes at the registry office before we became husband and wife.

We all came back to our new home where an aunt and a cousin had made a ham salad with mashed potatoes. Fruit jelly and cream was our sweet and, of course, we had our wedding cake.Once the meal was over, we went to a pub called The Glass House for drinks, coming back home for a party on the night. There, Dad set up a barrel of beer. There were also spirits like gin, whiskey, rum and brandy. We had a wonderful day and evening. The last person who left the party went at about 2.30am, so it was a very strenuous day and night. We were glad to go to bed, but we had enjoyed every last bit of it.

Next morning, Colin got up and went to get a cuppa and some toast to have for breakfast in bed. He picked up the milk left outside the front door and left the door on the jar as was the custom and brought our breakfast and tea back to bed.

About ten minutes later, we heard someone call out, 'Good morning!'

We thought, 'Oh, yes. One of the family is playing a joke!' As the bedroom door opened, I hid under the bedclothes. I didn't want anyone to see my flimsy nightdress.

A man came in carrying a black bag. When he saw us, he

exclaimed, 'Oh, I'm so sorry. I have come to see Mrs Goss's mother.' Colin told him they had moved and we owned the house now. He apologised and quickly left. We laughed our heads off and when we told the rest of our family they all thought it hilarious.

I used to catch the bus for work so I had to leave early. At this time, I was earning £7 a week and Colin was earning £5 a week. Between us we had £12 to spend. On Thursdays, when we got our pay, we put it on the table and sorted out what we had to pay out and what we had left. £2.10/- was for the monthly payments to Mr Goss for our house and £2 payment for the carpet and three-piece suite, pennies for the electric and gas meters and money for my bus fares. What we had left after all this was for food and I'm ashamed to say, cigarettes. We managed very well really.

We had decided we would start a family in five years' time, but we were married for five-months when I discovered I was pregnant with our first baby! Contraceptives were not available then. There were no pills or coils or anything else. We were shocked, but pleased.

We knew we would struggle a bit if I had to finish work, but that's life. I worked at the factory until I was seven months' pregnant. They advised me to leave because the work was very heavy. I left and the matron said if I wanted to go back after I'd had the baby there would be a job there waiting for me. I didn't have enough insurance stamps, so I went to work in Colin's mum's shop for another month so that I could claim the maternity grant of £36. That's what the government allowed us back in those days.

I saw a lot of Mum. Dad was now working shifts at Robinson's Wax Paper factory so Mum used to come to visit me a couple of times a week and I would go and see her.

I started having labour pains at home one Saturday night and at 4 pm on Sunday morning Colin phoned for an ambulance. I was terrified. They took me to Mortimer House to have my baby. The hospital was a large house in Clifton, a very rich part of Bristol. My baby girl was born at 2.10 am. She was 7lbs 13ozs and was very beautiful, of course!

Mum and Dad came to see me during visiting hours in the

afternoon, but staff would not let my parents see the baby, only the father. Well, Mum being Mum she was not going to let them get away with that! She played up merry hell until they let her in to see the baby. We named her Debra Anne. I had to stay in the hospital for fourteen days which was normal then.

Meanwhile, Colin's boss got to know we'd a little girl. Colin had won the 'Apprentice of the Year Award' so the boss put his wages up and put a house-phone in our house. He also gave him a van to use for work and pleasure which was great news and a huge advantage with a baby.

Debra, our first little girl, was very demanding and she did not sleep at night for very long. She was a very bonny baby, chubby with no hair. She was very spoilt by both our families, I'm afraid.

We visited Colin's family on Saturdays and went to Mum and Dad's on Sundays. Colin had promised Dad that he would take him to the Rover's ground to watch Bristol Rovers play the home games and he did just that. They became great friends.

When Debra was five-months old, I discovered I was pregnant again! I wasn't too pleased, but thought, 'Oh, well, I've just got to get on with it,' which of course I did. I always had trouble with high blood pressure, though. I decided to have my second baby at home. I carried quite well and got Mum knitting and making things for the baby. I still had Debra's pram and carry-cot so that was good. I still had plenty of Terry nappies. The baby was due in the middle of July, so that was fine.

We had lovely summers then. One Wednesday, I had taken Debra to Mum's. I was doing a bit of ironing for her while she played and saw to Debra. Suddenly, and I had terrible backache. I told Mum and she said, 'Don't worry. You have a month and a half before you give birth.'

I thought, 'Yes. She is right, but I think I will go home. I just didn't feel right. I carried Debra on and off the bus and by the time I arrived at our house, the labour pains were coming regularly and getting stronger. I phoned Colin's office and they told me he had already left work to come home. There were no mobile phones, then. When he came in, I told him I thought I was having the baby.

He said, 'Oh, bloody hell! Does your mum know?' I told him, no, so he went straight to Mum's and brought her to ours so she could have Debra.

By the time he arrived back, I had spread the newspaper on the floor and put the plastic sheet on the bed we had brought down into the lounge. We'd put the settee upstairs to make room for our bed. When Mum came, she could see I was in pain, so she took Debra out into the garden to entertain her.

While all this was going on, Colin found the number for the midwife and told her what was happening. She said she would be there as soon as she could and to boil some water. Colin rang her at 25 minutes past 7 and our second daughter arrived at 25 minutes to 8. When the midwife came in, she didn't even have time to take her coat off and the television was still on! I did apologise, but she said, 'Don't worry. I like Rawhide!' The baby, another girl, was 7 pounds 4 ounces when she was born. She had two inches of black hair all over her head and looked totally different to Debra. We called her Tracey June because she was born on the first of June.

Mum took Debra home with her for a couple of weeks, bringing her to our house every day, so I, at least, had a good rest. The weather was so nice. Tracey was out in the garden the day after she was born. It was on a Wednesday and Dad took Debra, dressed all in white, to see the Whitsun processions while Mum stayed with me.

It is 1960 now. We had been giving Colin's gran spare money whenever we had some. Financially, we found it very hard, but did our best and Mum was always buying clothes for our girls. They were always well-dressed and we were very proud of them.

A few years passed and a *compulsory purchase* order came in the post from the council. They were pulling our houses down to build new Town Houses or 'Upside Down Houses' as I liked to call them. These houses have a garage and a kitchen on the ground floor whilst upstairs there are the lounge and the bedrooms. So, although we were happy there, we knew we would have to move. We just had to find a new house.

I think we had about four months to find a new home. We were pleased because the council offered us £600 so that meant we could pay off what we owed to Mr Goss and have enough over to use in the new house.

I was pregnant now with our third baby. Colin's Mum and Dad came to tell us there was a house for sale in the street where they lived, so Colin was very keen to view it. The house was great and we both liked it straightaway. The couple were emigrating to Australia so they wanted a quick sale. They wanted £1100 for it. We put down a £100 deposit and went to the solicitors and started the ball rolling. They said if we treated the floorboards for woodworm they would allow us the mortgage. At this time, I was seven and a half months pregnant. While Colin was at work and Mum was looking after the two girls, I was down on my knees painting creosote on the floorboards!

The house was right next to St George's Park which was wonderful. It was so convenient for walks and games with the children. The surveyor came and said we had done a good job so we could have the money to buy the house. We were thrilled to bits.

We moved with the help of our family and friends on the 5th January, 1963. That year we had a really bad winter and the snow and ice hung around for weeks. When we moved into the house, the men had to dig the snow away from the front door so we could see the three steps leading up and into the door.

In this house, we had a large front room and a smaller back room, a kitchen and an outside toilet. The upstairs consisted of three bedrooms. One was very large, another a bit smaller and then there was a tiny box room. Colin said he was going to make the latter into a bathroom when we could afford it. I was extremely lucky because Colin was very good with his hands and could do everything that needed doing in the house.

On February 9th, I gave birth to another beautiful baby girl. Her weight was 7 lbs 14ozs. I was in hospital for just two days this time. When I came home Mum was brilliant. She helped me such a lot. She was my best friend and I loved her dearly.

Colin and I were both twenty-five by then. I did not work at all while the girls were young. Most mums didn't work, then. Instead, they stayed home looking after the home and the children. Debra, our eldest daughter, was four years old on the 8th of February. Tracey, our next daughter, was two and a half years old, and then there was our baby who we called Suzanne, born on the 9th of February. We made a lot of friends in the street and all the children played together and started school together which was lovely.

At this time, Colin became very ill and had to go for a lot of tests. He was sometimes fighting for breath. Eventually, he was sent to Ham Green Hospital for treatment. Mum came to our house to look after the children while I went on the bus to visit Colin in hospital. After allergy tests they said that he had asthma. He lost loads of weight. He went down to seven stones and could not walk very far. He was put on steroids and he took one tablet a day for eighteen years and I'm glad to say he got well and strong again in no time.

We had a very happy life together. We had a house. We also had phone put in by Colin's firm because he was often called out if someone had been broken into. He fitted burglar alarms. The different jobs he did are too many to mention, but there seemed nothing he couldn't do. We loved living there. Colin knew everyone because he had lived in the area before he married me and, of course, he moved back to the same street later in our new house.

Christmas time meant parties every night from Christmas Eve until New Year's Eve. All of the parties were in our street so everyone took the children with them and when the kids were tired they were put upstairs to bed in whoever's house we were in. Everyone was so friendly and everyone got on very well.

About this time, Colin decided he could earn more money if he was working for himself, so he started an electrical business with a friend. He was right. The business was extremely successful. Dave, his partner, moved abroad with his wife later, but Colin still kept the business going and was approached by a London firm to fit electric central heating. He started doing the central heating systems and brought his brother to work with him. He was getting so much work that when another few friends asked him for work he took them on. There were about six altogether in the end.

AUTOBIOGRAPHY

On one memorable occasion, Colin was working with his dad and was doing a job in Gwent, Wales. His Dad had a migraine so, on this occasion, his brother Jim went instead. About 10.30 that morning, I had taken the children to school and Mum and I were having a cup of tea when the phone rang. I answered it. It was the Gwent police. They told me Colin and Jimmy had had an accident and could we get over to Gwent Hospital as soon as we could. I told Mum and she said, 'Don't worry about anything. I will see to the girls.'

I rang Jim's wife. She started crying on the phone and I asked if she knew anyone who could take us. She assured me she could and would pick me up in about ten minutes. I then rang Colin's mum and dad to put them in the picture. By that time, Janet was outside the house with Jack in his sport's car, so I had to sit in the back window!

When we arrived, we asked the nurse on the desk where they were and she said, 'On the next floor.' We got into the lift. There was a nurse in the lift with a man in a wheelchair. I'm saying to Janet because she was very highly strung, 'Now, whatever they look like, however bad they may look, don't show you are shocked. Okay?'

The man in the wheelchair said, 'I'm here Bernice.' I looked at him and did not recognise him. His head was huge. He looked like a giant frog! He had glass sticking out all over his face. I could have broken down and cried, but I didn't. We went into the ward. Jim was in the next bed and he had a large cut across his neck and was badly bruised, too.

They were in hospital for two weeks. The policeman asked us who was the wife of the driver. I said, 'I am.' He told me how lucky Colin was. He said, 'If he had been wearing a seat belt he would have been killed outright because the steering column had gone straight through the driver's seat. A big lorry had gone into them. I'm just glad that they were in a big Rover car.

It took Colin and Jimmy about a month before they were fit enough to go back to work and all the while the business was still being run by the rest of the workmen. At this time, Colin had a long base big van on lease and he used that for work. The girls were growing up and we went out socialising a lot. Debra, the oldest, was now wanting Oxford-bag-trousers to wear and platform shoes. She loved David Bowie and the Bay City Rollers. Tracey was very different. She was always full of fun and playing tricks on us like when we sent her to the corner shop to get goods she would put them outside the door and make out the shop didn't have the things we had sent her for! When she kissed her dad goodnight she would kiss him on his forehead, then each cheek, then his nose. Suzanne was very different, too.

We were now into 1972. I used to see Mum every day when we moved into our new house. She was pleased because we were nearer and she could walk to our house in about twenty minutes. We went everywhere together and all my friends and neighbours knew and loved her. We went on holiday every year with my parents to Weymouth or St Ives in Cornwall. We were enjoying life and Colin was a good provider.

We were invited to London by the company for whom Colin did a lot of work. Jimmy and his wife Janet, Colin and myself were to go for the weekend. One of the bosses was a widower and he asked if we could take a lady with us so he would have someone for company. We said, 'Yes, okay. We will ask Pat, a friend of ours, but there is to be no hanky-panky!' He assured us nothing like that was going to happen so we told Pat and she agreed to come with us.

Off we went on the Friday evening. We had already told Pat the man who had invited her with us for the weekend and looked very much like Alfred Hitchcock. She was aware he was an older man and a widower. Mum and Dad were staying at our house with the girls, so we didn't have to worry about them. We arrived at Bob's penthouse flat at about 8.30 pm and after a short rest and a few drinks we went to a club. We had a wonderful night. They had a floor show of girls dancing and there were a few artists singing. We hadn't seen anything like this show before. It was marvellous. The beautiful costumes and bright lights were fantastic.

We went back to Bob's penthouse and just lounged around and talked about the show we had seen. Bob said Pat could have his room and he would sleep in a spare room. We were in another room sleeping in a single bed with Jimmy and Janet in another single bed. Colin at that time had terrible stinky feet, so I poured some perfume inside the boots and put them outside the bedroom. All was well that night and we slept quite well, though very cramped. In the morning, I said, 'Your boots are outside the door, Colin.'

He said, 'No, they aren't. I put them in the bottom of the wardrobe.'

'Oh, my God! I thought I had put them outside the door!'

Jimmy started laughing and said, 'No. They were my boots that you put outside!'

We had a wonderful day on the Saturday and were planning to go to the Sportsman's Club that night. Bob cooked us a beautiful meal of T Bone steaks with chips and salad with cheesecake for dessert. About 9 pm we all changed into our glad rags and went to the club. It was a combined club and casino.

We saw rich men giving their partners or wives £1000s to put on the gaming tables. I could not get over all the money that was being lost and won on the turn of a card. We sat at a table in the front to see the floor show. Everyone knew Bob and he was very popular.

We left the club at about 4.30 am. The man at the door went to get Colin's car for us and we were given the morning papers on our way out. Oh, I forgot to say we were introduced to Rodney Marsh and Geoff Hurst when we were in the club. They kindly autographed our programmes for us.

We had a hot chocolate when we got back and then we all said goodnight and went to bed. About an hour afterwards we heard screaming and Pat came running into our room saying Bob had tried to get into bed with her! We told him off, but he was very angry. We had already told him she was not that kind of girl. We laugh about it now, but at the time I was furious.

We all went into breakfast and it was very tense. No-one spoke. It was really bad. We were going to the famous Petticoat Lane Market that morning. We did go, but Bob was not in a good mood. Everyone shouted out to him. Everyone knew him. He took us to a baker that was icing a wedding cake. He said he wanted a cake for

Janet and myself and would the baker put our names on the top. He also said to us don't give Pat any which I thought was very nasty just because he couldn't have his wicked way with her. Of course, when we got home with it we cut it in three so she shared it anyway. We couldn't apologise enough to her. It's really funny now, though, thinking about it.

We were also invited to a Christmas party that being held in Bristol. All the bosses of the firm came to Bristol. They had a Reggae band for dancing. All the people working for the London firm from Bristol, Weston-Super-Mare and the villages around came. It was a fabulous party. They gave Christmas bonuses out to every one of their contractors. One of the bosses came over for a chat and asked me if I smoked. I said, 'Yes, I do, so he offered me a puff of his cigarette. I then realised he was offering me *pot*. How innocent was I? I said, 'No, thanks.' I had thought there was a funny smell in the air.

Colin had loads of work all over England and sometimes he had to sleep out of town if it was too far away to get home. At this time in our lives, we had money in the bank and everything was fine. We took the girls to Spain for our holidays. We used to drive to Spain, going on the ferry across to Calais in France and then we would drive down through France into Spain. There were only old roads back then. We would get off the ferry at 5 am then cross the French border at 6 pm. That was great going. I remember, at one point, when Colin that was showing signs of being too tired to go on, I persuaded him to rest and sleep for a few hours. Jimmy was following us in his car so that's what we decided to do. It was now very foggy and it was difficult to see anything.

We parked by a grass verge and Colin and Jimmy got sleeping bags out and crawled up onto the bank to have a few hours' sleep. We couldn't see very far in front of us, so with the three girls in the back and me in the front of the car, we all tried to have some sleep. We were awakened by the hooting of car horns. When we looked out of the window, the fog was gone and the men were sleeping on a roundabout with their cars facing the wrong way! Talk about being shocked.

AUTOBIOGRAPHY

Debra our eldest daughter was very rebellious and did not like the house rules at all. I won't go into that because that's another story. We had been home from our holidays for a couple of months when Mum felt ill and she wasn't getting any better. She was taken into hospital. She kept being sick and they thought she had a blockage somewhere. She had an operation to clear the blockage and was fine, but her surgeon told us that he had made her as comfortable as he could, but she had bowel cancer. It was terminal and she had about six to eight weeks to live.

Well, as you can imagine my world fell apart and I thought, 'How could this be happening to such a sweet person as my mum?' Dad told the hospital that he didn't want Mum to know, so that's how it was. She came home from hospital and felt fine. I then had to do the hardest thing in my life.

I had to write to my sister who had emigrated five years before and tell her Mum was dying and didn't have long to live and that Dad didn't want Mum to know anything about it. My sister was as devastated as I was. She wrote to Mum saying Dave, her husband, would not be able to come with her, but she was coming to see us all for a two-week holiday. Of course, Mum was over the moon.

In the meanwhile, I went to her prefab every morning after the girls went to school to get her breakfast. Sometimes she managed to keep it down, but mostly she would be sick a little while afterwards. It was dreadful. Sandra, my lovely sister, came home for a holiday for two weeks at the end of November and she knew it was the last time she was going to see Mum. Mum wanted to go to Heathrow to see Sandra off, but we would not let her, telling her the journey would be too much for her. I stayed with Mum and Colin while Dad took Sandra to the airport.

From then on, Mum gradually got worse until eventually she was taken back into hospital. That was in the May, so it was six months after she'd had her operation which was far longer that they said she'd have. At this point in my life, I am ashamed to say, I wished it was Dad leaving me, not my Mum. That's a terrible thing to think, I know, but when you lose someone so precious you want to blame anyone and everyone and unfortunately, it was Dad.

I loved my Dad although he was very strict and could not show love, but I loved him. When I was looking after Mum at her home it seemed to me that Dad would go bowling with Colin a lot. So, although I was with Mum all day, I would have to go back to her home in the evenings.

It was a long time after Mum's death that I realised Dad had to get away from the misery we all were feeling. Mum died in hospital exactly a year after the day Colin had his car accident on the 22nd of May. When she passed away we were with her all night holding her hand and talking to her. She passed at 5.30am.

I was in a dream when the taxi came to pick me up from Mum's. Dad wouldn't come home with me, though I tried my hardest. He said he wanted to be on his own. I let myself in the house. Everyone of course was still in bed. I opened the fridge and found there was no milk. I went to a friend's house a few doors down because I knew her husband would be getting ready for work. He was on shift work and had to start at six in the morning. Gill answered the door and I said, 'My Mum's just died and I haven't got any milk for a cup of tea could you let me borrow a cupful till the milkman comes, please?'

She looked at me and said, 'Yes, of course.'

When I got back to our house and let myself in, Colin was up and had put the kettle on the stove to make a cup of tea. It was the saddest day of my life. Colin took over and registered the death and did the arrangements for the funeral. Dad wanted Mum to be cremated. Mum had a thing about shrouds so we took a nightdress to the undertaker's in which to dress Mum.

Dad had to go to the hospital to get Mum's things. He looked through them and asked where her wedding ring was. She had always wanted Colin to have her ring. It was two rings made into one and was 22 carat gold so it was a very big ring. The sister in the ward was very indignant about Dad asking for Mom's wedding ring, but went and got it off her finger and gave it to him. Mum was sixty-five years of age. I think if it happened now they might have been able to save her life, but it was not to be.

It is now 1973. I had lost my Mum and best friend, but I had three daughters who loved their Nan very much so I had to pull myself together for their sakes. Life goes on, but I knew nothing would be the same ever again. I tried so hard to make things normal, but of course it was not normal. I was so lonely.

As the weeks went by, I asked Colin what he thought about having another baby! He said, 'Well, we can have one if you really want another baby in the house, but we'd better have words with the girls to see how they feel about it. That evening we sat them down after our meal and asked them what their thoughts were and they all thought it would be great. I was thrilled about that. About two months afterwards, I found I was pregnant. I was a bit scared because our youngest daughter was now eleven-years old. I thought it might be like having a first baby all over again.

My pregnancy went very well and the baby was due in July. It was a very hot summer and I had gotten very big and was suffering with high blood pressure again. The girls were very good helping with the housework. I went into hospital at 1am on the Saturday night and had bouncing baby boy at 8.30 am Sunday morning.

We were both thirty-six years old and, because I was classed as an older mother, I had to stay in hospital for fourteen days. I was moved by ambulance to a nursing home for mums and babies for the rest of the time. It was brilliant because the nurses looked after the babies and only brought the babies into us when they needed to be fed so it was a complete rest.

I couldn't wait to get back home, though. I missed the girls and Colin. We called our son, Adrian Colin. He was completely spoilt by us and his three sisters. Of course, he was totally different to the girls. He used to do things the girls wouldn't dream of doing. We were very lucky. We could continue our life as before going dancing or out for a meal at any time because Tracey our middle daughter would babysit for us. She loved babies and loved taking him out to the park all the time. The only regret I have is that Mum never saw him, but that's life, isn't it?

At that time, Colin's work was slowing down when he was approached by a man he knew who was working in Scotland on an oil refinery. The company was looking for electrical engineers and he said the wages were great. He told me about it and I said to him, 'If that's what you want, then apply for the job.' He did and got the job.

He left for Flotta, an island in the Scappa Flow. He had to work for three weeks and then he would have one week at home. The wages were brilliant. He was working for an American firm. He enjoyed it. We missed each other, but it was an opportunity he couldn't miss. He worked like that for two years.

He would ring me in the mornings to get the girls up for school and he also talked to me on the phone at night, but he always sounded tiddly to me. It was all men on the island, so they used to watch a show, or go to the pictures, or eat and drink. I think he put on about three stones in weight. He phoned me one morning and said that they were flying him home because he had a kidney stone and he couldn't pass.

We expected him to go straight to the hospital, but later that da,y a taxi turned up outside the house. Colin got out and said he had passed the stone, but did not want to go back there to work anymore. He was working twelve hours a day. It was a long day for him and I was glad he was coming home for good. We had plenty of money at that time. It was the first time I ever saw a £50 note.

We went to the local pub near our house and were very friendly with the landlord and landlady. When the pub closed, she would put out a lovely meal for about eight of us and then we would cook a meal for them. We all took it in turns. It was great.

Just after that Colin was offered a job as work's manager at Consol Designs who designed electrical and electronic equipment. He was chuffed and took the job. It paid good wages. My sister and her family were home living in Bristol so that was lovely, too, but she was working in her friend's hairdressing shop and had to work on Saturday so we didn't see much of each other which was a shame.

We bought a caravan at Brean on the south coast and we used to go there every Friday night until Sunday evening. We made a lot of friends from all over England. We used to meet in a local pub called The Beachcomber where several of us would get talked into singing

AUTOBIOGRAPHY

on the mike. We looked forward to these weekends where we could let our hair down. Because we had a caravan and spent a lot of time down there, we had a golden pass for Pontin's Holiday Camp.

We are into the 1980's now and we went to Pontin's Holiday Camp at Brean with our gold card. It was a Saturday morning and when we walked in we were shocked at the scene in front of us. There were American Indians, Confederate soldiers, Yankee soldiers, saloon girls and southern ladies in crinoline dresses.

As we walked around the camp we were astounded. There were western undertakers making coffins on the green. There were flags of all the different states in the USA. It was just like walking onto a film set. We were amazed. We were told that Pontin's had the western people there for two weeks: one week was for Westerners' re-enactment and gun shooting competitions etc. The second week was for the Western dancing.

We thought it was really great and of course wanted to join in. There were several stalls there so we bought Stetsons for Adrian and Colin and the rest of our friends also bought hats to wear.

The first week was for the Westerners and we eagerly watched everything that was going on. It was really fascinating and Adrian, who was about six years old, loved every minute of being there. I was so disappointed, though, when I asked an Indian chief if I could have my picture taken with him. He smiled and said in the broadest Welsh accent, 'Yes, of course you can.' Walking around the camp they had put tepees up for the Indians and there was a log cabin for the Trading Post. There were a lot of men and you could tell who they were portraying by looking at them. There was Doc Holiday and Clint Eastwood both playing out their fantasies. All harmless fun.

The following week was for the dancers. We did not know at that time that being there that week would change our lives again and point us on a different path. The bands were wonderful, playing Western music all the nights and afternoons. We loved country music and enjoyed it tremendously. The people were still dressed in Western clothes and the women were also dressed in shirts and denim skirts or jeans. There were stalls with lovely clothes for sale.

I bought myself a gypsy blouse and a denim skirt to wear in the evening. Colin bought Adrian a bolero neck tie and a checked shirt. He was loving it and so was I.

In the evening, the dancing started and they announced that Dick and Geneva from the USA were going to teach a Western-partner dance so Colin got me up straightaway to learn it. That's when we got the bug, I'm afraid. We loved it. When we were there we asked where we could learn this sort of dancing and the nearest class to Bristol was in Weston-Super-Mare so Colin and I started going to classes every Sunday afternoon.

We made many friends there so we and about six couples from Bristol started to learn the dancing. We found a club to go to. It was brilliant. By now we had many outfits and proper Western boots in which to dance. The club was also in Weston-Super-Mare and we loved it. I had started to make my own clothes by then and trimmed things with fringing and other things. I really enjoyed doing that. The clothes were very glamorous and as I was now in my fifties I enjoyed all the glamour.

We were more or less made to go through the dances at our house after class on a Sunday so our friends could learn the dances we were taught at class. Lots of couples got to hear about revising the dances we learned and more and more people wanted to come back with us to our house.

We had a through lounge, two rooms made into one big room, but it was not big enough for loads of people so they asked us to find a church or school hall where we could practice our dancing. That's what we did and we had more and more partners coming to our practice nights. We bought a big tea urn and took it in turns to make a cuppa for everyone to have halfway through the evening.

We were asked by so many people to teach them the popular dances because no-one was teaching them in Bristol or surrounding areas. We asked our teacher how we could become dance instructors and he put us in contact with The Dick and Geneva School of Western Dancing. We went on from there and took exams in London, Scotland, and the Midlands. When we had finished our training, we were qualified dance teachers. We went to

America with other teachers on a tour of California, visiting Western dance clubs every night finishing in San Francisco. It was magical. One night we went to one club where they were having a black and white ball. It was amazing and we loved it.

In 1980, we were in the USA having a wonderful time visiting all the highlights like Marine World and Disney Land and a few other attractions like the Grand Canyon. Every night we would go to a Western dance club that had been arranged by the leader of the group. We went to Kansas City, Rawhide, Sacramento, Boot Hill, Sedona and along the way we went to enormous stores as big as our biggest supermarkets full of Western wear and boots in all different colours and styles. We bought so much: Colin had two Western suits and I had wonderful dresses and we bought boots and hats. Colin had a Charles One-Horse Stetson with a snake-skin strap around the hat and boots to match. It was the holiday of a lifetime.

Our two-week holiday was over all too quickly and soon we were home with presents for all our family, the clothes and everything were so much cheaper in the USA so we were able to bring some nice presents home. We felt now that we were qualified to teach. We could charge our classes a fee to cover the cost of the halls and anything else that came along. We had already ordered the magazines to be sent over to us from the USA so we could keep up with the current dances.

The word had gone around about our classes and we were getting more and more people wanting to learn this new dancing. We had to buy lots of records to use and a PPL licence to be able to play the music in public. We also had to buy radio head mics because a lot of the partner dances had different hand movements so it was very hard to hold a hand mic and dance at the same time. We had to buy a player and an amp and speakers. It was quite a lot to start, but within a few months we had a Monday night partner-dance class and Tuesday, Wednesday and Thursday we had line-dance classes and Friday we went to a Western club in Weston-Super-Mare for social dancing. It was great and we loved every minute of it.

It wasn't long before we were being asked if we could organise a dance weekend away in a hotel somewhere. We hadn't thought about doing one ourselves because we always went to other people's weekends, but all the others that were advertised were camping in school fields or on social club grounds. We said to the classes that we would do one if we could find a hotel we could take over and we would fill all the rooms. A couple in our partner-class said that they had a relative working in a hotel in Teignmouth, Devon. They thought it would be ideal so we went with them to see it. We thought it would be great.

Colin did all the business with the owner of the hotel and came to an agreement. We thought it would be nice to do a Valentine Weekend commencing on the Friday afternoon and having the evening meal served in the hall so everyone would have their seat for the weekend.

We would have breakfast, teaching and social dancing in the morning, a break for a couple of hours to go out and have a look around Teignmouth, social dancing in the hall for an hour and then clear the hall so the tables could be laid for dinner. We thought it would be nice if we could put a bottle of wine and a silk red rose on the pillow in every room for the ladies with the programme for the weekend.

We and six of our friends come to the hotel on the Thursday evening to help us dress the dance hall as it was Valentine weekend. We had red balloons and huge red hearts made by ourselves, edged with a frill of gold and silk hearts and a red rose on each table. It all looked very nice. Across the ceiling hung all the colourful American flags.

We are now in the year 1985. Our first Western Dance Weekend was a great success and all the couples who came re-booked for the Valentine's weekend the following year. We were really pleased that it all went off so well. We had a wonderful Western disco that played all day for social dancing as well as teaching. We employed three other couples to teach as well as ourselves. We also had a stall there selling Western gear and flags of the American states plus collar pointes for Western shirts and, of course, Western boots. Ladies wore mostly white boots. When all of our people arrived, the hall was dressed appropriately for a Valentine's dance. All the tables were set and the names were on the tables, so everyone had a seat for the weekend. Dinner was served at six o'clock and everyone changed into their Western wear ready for the evening dance.

The band arrived and did the sound check. Colin took them to the bar for a pint. He then gave me the key to our room to change and then it was time for a great night of dancing. It's funny, you know, because we realised we had to be very careful when booking in the guests. Some people turned up with the wives of others so at times it could be a bit dodgy. Colin, I remember, booked in a lady from our class who we knew was living with her boyfriend, so naturally, he booked them into a double room with a double bed. She hit the roof and told Colin they did not sleep together! See what I mean? How was Colin to know?

The weekend was such a success we decided to do more weekends after being egged on by many friends. The next one we did was Halloween. We had lots of friends helping us to make decorations. You could not buy decorations like you can now, so we made them. We bought white sheets to make ghosts coming out of walls and one of our friends managed to get a coffin. Colin put a skeleton inside and also put in some magical stuff, so as the lid rose the skeleton's head came out looking out at the audience with red lights in its eye-sockets. So, that's how our Western weekend started and we loved every minute of it. We ended up doing a Valentine spring break, Halloween and New Year. We also did a longer weekend during Millennium 2000. Four days and three nights. It was very expensive, though. The band wanted more money as did the hotel, but we managed it. All our teachers had free weekends, but that was part of their payment and after teaching a few dances they gave out the dance sheets so other teachers could teach them all over England, so it was perfect.

We thought it would be a novelty to hold a competition for the line-dancers, so we decided to hold the very first under-water line dance competition. Well, you should have seen the costumes that everyone had! I made a stipulation on the booking form that all entering had to be dressed in old fashioned swimwear. We made our costumes. Men wore leggings and vests sewn together as one garment. Ladies wore baggy pantaloons and a top with puffed sleeves and a mob-cap. Wearing these costumes, we larger ladies didn't mind dancing with everything covered up so that was fine. Some of the men turned up wearing snorkels and other funny get ups. We had a great time. The top storey of the hotel had a huge swimming pool so and you can imagine how everyone ended up in the pool at the end including the four judges!

All our classes were going great guns and we were enjoying ourselves very much and it was lovely meeting new people and making new friends. We were still going away nearly every weekend ourselves to venues. It was a very special time for us and we made lots of wonderful friends, many have now left us, but we have some marvellous memories and we have them forever.

My husband and I began a new hobby called Eggery in 1989 after I saw some of my cousin's eggs decorated beautifully. I was impressed and thought them fabulous. 'I wonder if I could do that sort of thing?' I thought. I decided to send for a book to teach me how to cut an egg and how to decorate it. Colin, had a look at the instructions and then sent for a special cutting-drill with cutting discs to cut the eggs.

We went looking for farms selling goose eggs and found one not far from where we lived. They had some for sale so we bought eight. The eggs were fresh so, when we blew the insides out, I used them for making cakes. To blow the eggs, we make a hole with the Dremel drill at the top and bottom of the egg. We then put a knitting needle in to break the yoke and stir it up so it can come out of the egg more easily. We had to blow and blow until the egg was empty. After blowing the eggs, we soak them in disinfectant to clean them. Before I started to use expensive goose eggs, I practiced on chicken eggs. They were much smaller and much more fragile.

Colin suggested I spray the eggs with car spray to make them stronger. So, that's just what I did and it worked. The eggs were much stronger. I actually surprised myself because, apparently, I was quite good at decorating the eggs, but I couldn't master the drill so Colin took over the cutting of the eggs. He is brilliant at it and works out the easiest way of doing things.

We had no Internet back then so we asked my cousin for information. She gave us the address of a craft firm where we could buy braids, stands, gem stones and everything else that you could need like tweezers and small hinges if you want to cut doors in the egg. It was very exciting and very new, but it became a lovely hobby and, with my husband, I have been doing 'Eggery' ever since. I went on, after some practice, to make all sorts of goose eggs. I did some with two doors, some with one door and some with no doors at all. Some were made with lots of cuts in the eggshell to make patterns and windows. I lined the inside of the egg with velvet or silk or satin and then decorated the edge of the cut in the egg inside and out.

After I had done quite a few goose eggs I thought I would like to try an ostrich egg. We sent for one from the craft firm to see what I could do with it. Gosh, when it arrived in the post it was huge and we were thrilled to bits. It was already blown and cleaned. Colin is an electronic engineer so I asked if he could put some lights in the egg. He could. We went looking for tiny wall lights and found them in a shop that sold lights to put into dolls' houses. We thought they would do perfectly.

I lined the inside of the ostrich egg with a doll's house wall paper. I put velvet on the floor and made a lady out of bread and PVA glue. I put her in an old-fashioned long dress and bonnet sitting on an old- fashioned settee.

I used a tooth-paste top, painted gold, for a pot and put a Christmas tree in it. Colin managed to put some lights on the tree, too, so we had wall-lights and lights on the tree. They flashed, too.

In the early 90's craft items were fairly limited so I used anything I could find to put inside the eggs. The eggs were very expensive so we could not buy them very often, but when we had any spare money we sent for an ostrich egg. The first one we finished is still in my cabinet on display. It's a Victorian-lounge decorated inside and trimmed up for Christmas. I'm still very proud of that egg because it was our first one. Our first baby.

We went on holiday to Egypt in 1990 and with the eggery in

mind we looked for Egyptian decorations we thought we could use to create an Egyptian egg. We found many tiny statues of the gods so we thought it would be good if we could do an egg with the tomb of a king inside. We found everything we needed and when we got home we couldn't wait to start the egg; however, it had to be put on hold because Colin's dad was taken ill on the plane going out and he wasn't allowed to fly home so Colin stayed with him in Egypt.

It was a few years before I started doing eggs again, but the next one was our Egyptian egg. On the plane, I was reading a magazine and saw pictures of Tutankhamun, gods and hieroglyphics so I tore the page out. I'm so glad I did because I used it for the walls of inside King Tut's tomb with some papyrus pictures we'd bought in Egypt.

We now have quite a collection of decorated eggs. We have a very large family and I have made one for each wedding. I have many in my display cabinets and I have made quite a few Disney ones for my great-grandchildren. Now we are both retired and knocking on a bit we are still doing them. It's something we can do together and it's not very strenuous. Now as technology has progressed Colin can get lovely things for our craft on the Internet from all over the world. It makes things much easier like buying LED lights. Magical.

I have other hobbies like crochet and knitting, but I love eggery best of all.

MADNESS AND MAYHEM
Margaret Booth

Let me say before I start that these memories are mine so since I have a chequered past where my memory is concerned I might get it a wee bit wrong, occasionally, but you won't know that, so no worries.

My first memory is of the first time I saw a television set, at least I think it was a television. It was in the back of a van. I had to stand on a step to see in. I remember a few kids were around and all were very excited because it was in black and white. It was a cricket match of all things. I hate cricket now, too. I wonder now if this is part of the whole picture? I was about three, so I must have decided to tell Mum.

I set off running, calling, 'Mummy! Mummy!' but the next thing I know I am flat out on the Tarmac and I start screaming again. 'Mummy! Mummy!' I was in a lot of pain, but what I forgot to mention was I was bare to the waist and bleeding. I don't remember much after that, but I do remember being bound up with a crepe bandage, but not bound up as in kidnapped, but bound round and round my tummy, or as my daughter says, 'It's stomach, mother, not tummy.'

Every time I see a crepe bandage now I remember that day when I saw a cricket match in black and white. I can't remember if it was actually in black and white, or I think it was because of the year. It was probably 1948. Yes, I am pretty sure it was that year.

When Mum had finished bandaging me, she laid me on her bed amongst pots and pans, but lying there, too, was my baby sister wrapped up so she was warm and safe. I must have cried myself to sleep because the next thing I remember is we were in a new house. Wow, don't things happen quickly in 1948? But at three, I don't suppose they thought they needed to consult me.

We had been in a two-bedroom prefab and had moved to a three-bedroom prefab because of my sister, I reckon. There were four of us kids: two boys and two girls. The perfect family. I remember far more about the second prefab, naturally, because I was older.

I went to the primary school at five. I remember my first day. Mum took me. I don't think I cried because I can still hear this boy crying. He was the same boy I went all through school with. I remember thinking what a cry-baby he was.

Miss Smith was the name of my first teacher. Even at the tender age of five I thought she looked stern and mannish. She was strict, but I can remember on our first day that she introduced us to Mac and Tosh, two Highland Terriers, one black, one white. They were toy dogs with tartan collars. I have only just remembered this, but I can see them clearly in my mind. I also remember we had coloured counters to help us add up during sums. Later, joy of joys, we learnt to take away. We were each given a small slate and a piece of chalk to write with. Talk about modern aids, but we did improve on it with paper and crayons. I can still imagine those counters: red, blue, yellow and green and, whenever I think of small sets of numbers, I still see them as counters set out like the spots on playing cards.

We now leap to the point in my when I engaged and soon to be married. Roy and I went to an MOD Christmas party. It was my first formal outing with him and that sealed us as a couple.

We joined in the silly games. The one that should have spoken volumes to me was where a lady was in the middle of two men. The one man would run over to a lady, tap her, and then they would run to the space he had left. I said it was silly!

All was going well until Roy was tapped and he set off across a really well-polished floor at a heck of a speed. I watched him with pride, eyes shining, only to see him slip and shoot under a chair. To say I was amused would be rubbish. I could not stop laughing, nor could a few more. As they helped him up I was relieved to see he was laughing, too!

We got married in July 1966. It was a lovely day. The only blip was my wonderful Dad. All through the wedding he was carrying a pair of ladies' gloves. I asked him afterwards why he had them. He said he found them on the table and thought the owner would be grateful he had looked after them. They were actually my spare pair!

We lived on a caravan site in a small van we bought from my brother. It was good because it meant we could keep the van on the site as we were family. Not long after we were married, I had the fright of my life. Now I had had prior warning that something like this could happen, but I was still startled.

Roy used to have active nightmares. One night, he suddenly leapt up in bed. He went down on his haunches and, like a runner at the start of his race, he was off. I was in shock when he did a hell of a shout as he started, then set off down the bed like a runner in Chariots of Fire! This all happened in seconds and finished even quicker. As he ran full-pelt into the side of one of our wardrobes, he automatically woke up. But neither of us could go back to sleep because we couldn't stop laughing. Fortunately, the only part hurt was his pride and his throat from laughing when I had relayed all his actions!

I want to tell you that, although Roy and I divorced many years later, I always loved him and we had many more such 'moments.' For instance, while we were newly-weds we used to love to welcome people into our home. This included my sister and her new boyfriend, Fred. This was his nickname and I really have no idea why, but Fred it was. He was really tall, really handsome and really shy. He had really big feet, too! They used to visit quite often. Fred used to sit on one of the long seats with his elbows on his knees, his chin in his hands. His hair was styled like one of his idols, Brian Jones, from the Rolling Stones. This meant we could not see his face after the initial hello. Incidentally, he had to stoop because he was so tall and our caravan was not.

I used to offer him a glass of sherry when he sat down. Why I kept sherry in the van I don't know. It is a horrible drink unless served with lemonade. Now, upon reflection, he took the sherries just to be polite. He used to walk to our van from his home about four miles away. Roy used to take them home after their visit. He dropped my sister off locally and then Fred.

One particular night, when I was pregnant with my daughter, I had an awful sense of foreboding and begged Roy not to go. I remember getting quite hysterical about it. Very melodramatic. I kept throwing my arms round him and sobbing, 'Don't go.' He tried his best to pacify me. I have wondered since if I was over dramatic for the extra attention it gave me. I kept saying, 'Don't go. I just know something is going to happen to you.'

He just kept hugging me saying, 'Don't be silly. Nothing is going to happen to me.'

I sat down. I said goodbye to my sister and watched them go through tear-stained eyes. Roy, who was ahead, walked out and flew down the metal steps we had and sprawled face down on our lawn! Well, I said something was going to happen to him, didn't I? I was still laughing when he came home. I must add that my sister is still Mrs Fred. They have three children, six grandchildren and four great-grandchildren. I reckon it was the sherry, Fred!

When I look back on my life, of course, I think of Roy. He was a quiet unassuming man. For many years, we didn't have many, if any rows, and any disagreement was soon forgotten. I won't talk of the later years now because we later found our voices, but back to this recollection.

We left the caravan and to move four and a half miles away to live with my sister and her husband, Fred. We were to discover later it was not the best of moves. It was a big farmhouse and was plenty big enough to hold two families. This farmhouse was one of two on the farm. Originally, it had been one large single farmhouse, but it had, at some point, been renovated and divided into two-separate homes. The farmer lived in one side and we in the other. We bought our eggs from the farmer's wife.

My sister had a son by then so two families in a large farmhouse may sound ideal, but not when the females are sisters. My sister is two and a half years younger than me. We can be oil and water or sugar and spice. At this time in our lives we are both senior citizens and I love her dearly. We are very close now. She helped me to get my bedsit in my home town. After a few years of letters to my Housing Association with doctors' notes, and finally, a 'begging letter' from my sister and a lady doctor's letter, I finally had a bedsit. I will not forget how pleased my sister was when it all came to fruition. It helped both of us. Me because I was back in my home town where I came as a babe in arms, went to school and grew up.

I am in heaven: it's a great bedsit in a huge house that has played a big part in locals' lives. It is an old nursing home. It is a lovely old building. I have lived here in this big house now for a year. I love it. It's very big and inhabited by twenty-five other people, a mixture of older men and ladies. I can truthfully say I get on with all of them. The reason it helps my sister is, if they go away, which they do quite often, because they have a small touring caravan and often take off for a week or a weekend down south. I stay at their lovely bungalow. It is my pleasure because I not only house-sit, but look after Coco, their beautiful one-eyed Siamese cat. He can't go into a cattery because he gets too distressed, but since I love him, it's not a problem. He can't be allowed to roam with so little sight. I live just a stone's throw from the bungalow so it works out fine. We do still have the occasional spat, but we realise life is too short for bad feelings, but I am home.

The television aerial played a big part in our lives at the farmhouse. It was brought with us from the caravan and was fully portable. Now that is a joke shared by all who lived there during that memorable time because the aerial caused us to either see a programme on the television clearly or nearly kill us!

Let me explain. Living in the farmhouse meant we lived out in the Wiltshire countryside, but it wasn't all it seemed. Fred fixed the aerial in such a way that we could watch the black and white set, but would often need one of us to go outside and try and turn the aerial to get a good picture. However, when we went outside we were usually in a hurry to get back to the programme, so we often dashed out quickly only to be caught around the forehead by the taut wire stabilising the pole with the aerial attached! That one was me. Roy had marks around his nose and Fred had marks around his throat. This has given us a lot of laughter over the years saying everyone would know where we lived because we all had the mark of 'the wire.'

The television itself is another topic of laughter, but before l tell you this, I want to state categorically that the electricity collector left the lock undone. Honestly! Times were hard and when an opportunity presents itself you grab it, don't you?

The lock was on a meter round the back. It had a slot for sixpence pieces and, as I said, times were hard. Just the men folk were in employment whilst we women stayed at home home-making and minding our babies. In later years, we did both, as they do now.

Because the meter box was unlocked, the same sixpence could go in and through the meter that many times we nearly wore the Queen off the coin! Someone dropped it one night and we were on all fours looking for it!

When Roy and I left the farm house, we omitted to give the man who collected the coins our new address. We did have a licence for the television, though, with the correct address on it. The collector apparently came to the farmhouse after my husband and I had moved back to our home turf. This set the standard by which we would live for years to come. I think the emptiness of the meter made the original collector realise we no longer wanted it. We heard no more. Fred and my sister lost a TV set, but gained an aerial!

Before I leave the peace and quiet of the farm in Wiltshire I really can't forget the event of the put-u-up and I do want to share this hilarious happening. We took very little to the farmhouse for two reasons: We lived in a caravan with fixed fittings and my sister didn't need any more stuff. However, we did take our two cats and although they had been toilet-clean in the van, they weren't in the farmhouse.

I really did try, but they were used to climbing in and out the caravan's windows when they needed the toilet, but of course the farm was different. What annoyed Fred and my sister was the smell when the cats did their business indoors. I totally agree. There is nothing worse, but it is often difficult to find where the smell is coming from.

One particular night the smell was bad and I couldn't find the source. Tempers were frayed. I suddenly realised that it was behind the put-u-up. I was getting annoyed because I was being taunted. I said, 'Okay, I will clear it up.' I had wanted Roy to do it, but no, they were my cats.

I went behind the settee still grumbling and making a fuss when suddenly my feet went from under me and I slipped on the muck! Yuck. Down I went and landed heavily on my iron. I had put it out of the way. That hurt, but what hurt me far more was that as I slipped I caught hold of the back of the settee and it folded down into a bed. All they could see was me sitting upright at the side of the bed stunned! To say they laughed themselves stupid would be a total understatement. There was only one person not laughing, me, but I did see the funny side of it when I stopped crying, more out of embarrassment than pain, but I did have a nasty bruise on my bottom! The best part is, I had to clean my slippers as well as wash the floor.

Now I have told you how hard times were for us in those days in '68. Heating in the farmhouse was very expensive. Anyway, this is a story Fred told us. One particular night, they fancied eggs for breakfast the following morning. There were dozens of chickens, but my sister and Fred had no money and the farmer's wife didn't believe in credit. So, in the dead of the night Fred crawled all around the chicken shed, found the opening and crawled through. Bear in mind he was over six feet tall.

He kept feeling chickens by mistake and making them squawk. This could easily have alerted the farmer's wife and she might come to investigate. Fred was feeling around when he saw the yard light come on. He scrabbled, found an egg and crawled out as fast as his knees would take him. He took the egg into my sister and, holding it up, says, 'One egg!'

My sister stared at it. He was covered in straw and says, 'It's a china one!' He'd only gone and picked up the china egg farmers put in the nests to help make the hens broody! They did laugh eventually. They had been thinking of the eggs they thought they would be enjoying for breakfast the next morning. There must be a moral in all this, but I do know that never again did Fred go hunting for eggs, no matter how hungry we were!

Another story from that time in our life is that my sister had a run in with the farmer's wife. I cannot remember what it was about, but I went to stick up for my sister, as you do. She was younger, so I went to go and help, but she sent me back inside. I thought I would keep quiet since she could look after herself.

I went into the bathroom which was level with where they were rowing. I stood and hid inside ready to run to my sister's aid should I be needed, but she came back in laughing. I knew the quarrel hadn't ended with a hug, so I asked why she was laughing. She said, 'You! It was your fault I had to come back in, because all the time I was out there, I could see you leaning towards the window obviously listening.' I felt a little bit silly to say the least, but it was another reason to laugh.

We did try to brighten our men's days, though. Soon after that incident, people over a certain age will remember how plastic tulips and daffodils were free with soap powder at one time. My sister and I had accumulated a couple of bunches. I don't know which one of us suggested it, but it was probably me. It was the daft sort of thing I would do. We went outside and stuck all the flowers in the narrow strip of garden under the window! The men didn't get home till it was dark so we thought they would definitely be fooled into thinking we had planted some daffodils and tulips that had shot up in a day! Anyway, we waited impatiently for them both to come home. It was such an anti-climax when they did because neither of them were fooled and there we were, giggling like schoolgirls, and our husbands were now totally convinced we had finally lost the plot!

Roy and I weren't really too happy being with my sister and her family. There were no big rows. There were no major disagreements as such, but there were niggles and a growing feeling of discontent. Roy and I were seldom on our own and I missed cooking for us. I used to confide in my mum and she understood. I didn't want to hurt my sister, but I did want to go back to the town where I grew up and, most of all, be on my own with Roy. Mum was a star. She heard of a bedsit to rent. We saw the landlady and soon found ourselves moving in. My sister was surprised, but relieved, I thought. She was definitely all for it and so began another era.

Our daughter was very mobile by then. I can't remember if I had been painting, but I have a vague memory of a loaned suitcase being splattered with white paint. I was probably in the process of removing the paint before giving it back. Saying that, it was my fault the accident almost happened. I had a small bottle of turps on the floor. My daughter was crawling around and keeping herself amused. We had all-sorts of things all over the room, mostly clothes, and I was in the process of putting them away when I noticed my daughter had a bottle top in her mouth. Straightaway, I grabbed it back. She smelled of turps, but I didn't know if she had drunk any or not.

I was beside myself with panic it was a Friday night and Roy played darts. I then remembered my brother was opposite our home in the Town Hall so picked her up and ran over. I entered a meeting, searched the room and saw him smiling at me. I called him outside. He drove me to the doctor's surgery and we were sent to Bath Hospital. We drove straight there and sat in the waiting room and although she smelled of turpentine she was really happy, calling out to other people. My brother was trying to buck me up, but I was terrified.

The nurse came and took my baby away. My brother went with her because a doctor had called me into his office, but I could hear her screaming as they pumped her stomach. I was so upset and the doctor had no sympathy for me. Instead, he said, 'Because of your stupidity your daughter nearly died and it would have been your fault!' I wasn't crying; I was so distraught I was wailing really loudly, apparently.

They kept her in hospital overnight and said, although they couldn't be sure, there seemed to be no turps in her tummy. My brother was a treasure that night and took us back to the hospital the following morning. As you will imagine, Roy and I had no sleep that night, but the minute we walked into the ward my beautiful little daughter shot up in her cot calling, 'Mummy! Mummy!' I am crying now at this memory. I was so relieved. To this day, I cannot bear the smell of turpentine.

We were worse off living in the bedsit with both money and space. We obviously had a lot more room in the farmhouse and it was cheaper pooling our money to buy groceries. The landlady of the bedsit was a pure dragon and kept knocking at my door for one thing or another. The house was rented from the Lord of the Manor. He owned a whole street and still does, at least his relatives do. I spoke to the MP of our area in my quest to get a council house. He did help me get a move and was also instrumental in getting the landlady to stop her continuous knocking on my door every time she had a problem. As the town was full of art students in need of accommodation I wondered if the landlady wanted us to leave. Initially, it had been the caretaker who'd offered us the room.

My biggest embarrassment happened one particular night. When this incident occurred, we had been out during the day. Everything was lovely until we came home. I remember we had been on a picnic and my little girl had walked for the first time and we were in good spirits.

Before leaving the bedsit, we had sprinkled a thin coating of flour on the floorboards. You may think this a strange thing to do, but we had been fairly certain that the landlady had been going into our room while we were out. Since we didn't have any proof we decided to get some. I was an avid crime book / film buff and knew a way to prove it one way or the other, hence the fine coating of flour, but when we came back from our outing we totally forgot about our 'trap.'

The landlady had followed us upstairs and was saying I had made a mess in the communal kitchen which I hadn't been in at all. Quite nicely I said I hadn't, but she was having none of it. I was getting quite fired up with indignation. By this time, I had opened the bedsit door. All of a sudden, she said, 'What is all that white stuff all over the floor?' I could have cried. I had been in and out of the room several times and the 'trap' had worked only not in the way I had anticipated! I made an excuse of tipping up the flour. We didn't worry because by that time we had been offered a two-bedroom house in a village two miles away. This turned out to be perfect because it was near Roy's place of work. It also became available just in time because I was pregnant with my son who made my pigeon pair!

Well, here we were. It was 1968. It was late autumn and we were in our new house. We were so excited. Our first real home together. I must admit it took a time to furnish it as we had started off with very little. The good thing about living there was that it was only a short walk for Roy for work. It became very handy for me, too, a couple of years later, when I re-joined the workers. But that was to come. I had seven months to go before I had my son and some how I had to get a home together. I should mean 'we,' but Roy was so laid back I thought it was cute. However, the novelty of this soon wore off. I soon realised I couldn't rely on Roy to do the garden or decorate. He was a lovely, gentle man, but really didn't have much of a clue about being a husband! I hope you will understand what I mean by that.

We gradually got things for the home with a little help from our parents, more Roy's than mine, since Roy's were still working. They had come down from Lancashire with the Military of Defence when a large number of people had migrated to Wiltshire. Houses were ready for them when their wives joined them.

Roy's Dad worked in a surface job in the Machine Shop, as did Roy. His Mum worked nearer to us on a trading estate in a white overall environment. Because this was the MOD you weren't privy to the details. It was all secrets. Roy's mum was a fiery woman who stood five feet nothing and one of those people you do not upset.

Roy's dad was a really quiet gentleman who towered over his wife at six feet tall. He was a lovely man and he did as he was told, or at least seemed to, but when push came to shove he wasn't so soft. If Roy ever needed anything he would get it, but was always lectured on the error of his ways by his wife. This made things uncomfortable so Roy was reluctant to ask for help and, in fact, he seldom did. However, they loved my daughter and she didn't want for a thing, and boy, as she grew older, she knew how to get every single thing she wanted.

As far as mother-in-law was concerned, it was very different with my son. As a mum myself, it really used to rile me, but there was no answer to it. I couldn't have discussed it with her so I just used to over-compensate my son. He still mentions things now that hurt him way back forty-odd years.

My pregnancy with my son was not an easy one. I ended up having a caesarean and he was only tiny at 3lbs. Apparently, the afterbirth was in front of him, so he could not be born naturally. He started putting on weight immediately and went from strength to strength.

That was until one July day when he was two weeks from his second birthday. He was very lethargic that day. It was so hot I bought the children an ice lolly each. He was moaning and very floppy. I walked quickly to Mum's. She said as it was too late for the doctors it would be better to call in on one of the two chemists we had, but he said go into the doctor's immediately. I did, but the doctor, a young new one, said to take him home and bathe his head in cold water.

However, that night my lovely boy had awful fits and I only knew this because he had been so sick. I pulled the cot over to my side and held his tiny hand. During the night, I felt him having a fit so Roy raced down to our vicarage because it had a phone. An ambulance took him to Bath Hospital and he was diagnosed with meningitis. We so nearly lost him, but from that day, he started getting well and he honestly never looked back. We had a very close call, but my family was still complete. Thank God.

Things in life are not always what they seem. No-one can ever know just what goes on behind closed doors. This is an absolute fact of life. My husband, as I have mentioned, was a good, quiet and unassuming man. We had settled into family life in our two-bedroom house on a very small housing estate in a Wiltshire village and life was okay, not brilliant, but okay. I had enlisted the help of my neighbour, a big and independent lady, married to a huge man who was Ukrainian. He was a lovely man who worked in a rubber factory on the nearby trading estate.

My female neighbour had agreed to help me decorate my kitchen so I needed to buy wallpaper and paint. The end result will stay in my mind forever. It was so beautiful. Most of the adults from our estate worked on the trading estate one way or another. Later, I would work in the same factory as Roy. I had actually returned several times on different occasions, one time going there daily, but in the end, I had to leave again because it was affecting my children too much. Once I had sorted out a good babysitter I went back again.

I could easily have hanged for the creature who minded them for me in the village. She was a relative of my neighbour. My daughter never wanted to go to her after a while. Because she was only three and my son a baby, I thought it was just my daughter playing up. This was confirmed by the babysitter. She said my child was always fine once I had left the house.

She was a clean woman and her house was always clean and tidy. She was enormous in build and so were her children. They all looked alike and seemed nice kids. My daughter has since told me they were, but they lived in total fear of their mother. I would leave my two with her until, one particular day, out of the blue, she told my daughter to tell me she wouldn't be minding them anymore. When I went around to query this, she simply said, 'Just because . . .

I said, 'You can't just stop. I have to give my notice at work and do it.' I also couldn't afford not to work. I had financial commitments by then. Workmates ran a couple of clubs for Christmas presents for the children and I was also buying some fashion items for myself. This was so easy to get into when you work with younger single girls. However, regardless of what I had got, I couldn't afford not have that bit of extra money. I knew I had to try and get 'her' to change her mind.

I was desperate and went running around to her house. I banged on her door and to this day I don't know why I opened her door and attempted to shout, but I was silenced as her 'ample' fist engaged with my mouth! I could have cried with the shock and pain.

'Right,' I shouted. 'That's it. I am ringing the police!' With that I took off, my lips throbbing. We still didn't have a telephone, so I had to run quite a distance to a phone box. Panting, I went inside and phoned our local police station. I managed to say what I needed, but didn't expect any support, but to my amazement I had some. The policeman asked after I explained the attack, 'Did you step over the threshold?' I could answer, no, quite honestly. 'Right. Well, she is wrong for hitting you . . . '

Right at that moment I saw 'her' at my house. I could see it well from where I was so I told the chap on the phone that she was there. He said, 'Go back and tell her to expect a visit.' This was not a message I was in any hurry to relay to the big fisted one. Nevertheless, I went home only to find a note pushed through my door.

It said in words to the effect that she was very sorry and hoped I was okay. She had changed her mind about no longer babysitting if I wanted to continue with the arrangement. If I agreed, could I please tell the police all was well. I thought about it. I asked Roy and he said, 'Well, we need the money, so it's up to you.' That saw me going down to the phone again. I rang the station and told them I had changed my mind. The policeman did try to make me stick by my complaint, but by that time I just wanted peace to reign. I went home. It was a Friday night and nothing would change now. Wrong!

Sunday afternoon there was a knock at the door. The woman had sent her husband, Mr Meek and Mild, around. With a 'don't blame' me look, he said, 'She don't want your kids no more' and just turned around and walked away. Well, you could have knocked me down with the proverbial feather. I had been so sure it was okay, but apparently not. That meant I had to search for someone else to babysit. Eventually, I did find someone else for a short time, but meanwhile I had to finish work again.

We did manage because my sister-in-law helped out. Again, I went back to work, but that was not the end of 'her.' My daughter and son told me a long time afterwards, that 'she' had burnt my daughter with a poker from the fire. At the time, she had told me my son had done it. When I had asked my daughter when it happened she had been too terrified to tell me the truth. Apparently, the woman was forever smacking them, too. Why had I been oblivious to all of this? My God. I would have laid into her for hurting my babies. When my children told me the truth she had long since died and so had three of her children. They say God works in mysterious ways and they also speak about karma.

I experienced a bad day only recently. I am staying at my brother's house dog-sitting. He is on holiday. His son is a barber in Bath and works long hours. I was asked a few weeks ago, if I could stay with my nephew while my brother was away. I had reluctantly given him my little dog a year ago when I became incapacitated. It really was the only thing I could do. I'd had an accident at home and had broken a couple of ribs. As I lay on the floor being smothered by Fearne's kisses, I realised I had a bigger problem than being licked. Thus, my brother and nephew took charge of Fearne. I still see her occasionally and I miss her very much. She is a very strong dog and has pulled me over several times and this is why my family were so relieved I had at last been sensible and allowed them to look after her.

The reason I am telling you this tale is because I want you to understand why I have put up with staying out in the country miles away from shops, my sister and friends. It is for the sake of Fearne and my family.

Tuesday 31st of January 2017 was a very traumatic day. It started like any other. I had an appointment at Bath Royal United Hospital. As the bus-stop is just down the road from my brother's house it was perfect. I mean, what could possibly go wrong? If you have read previous tales from the 'Land of Margaret' you will realise there is never a perfect day!

I caught the bus to Bath without a problem and arrived thinking I had plenty of time to have a cup of tea, but looking at the time, I had a shock. It was later than I thought, so I had a mad dash to catch the connection to the hospital and caught it just in time. I sat down thankfully, looking out on a grey, wet, miserable day, though the sun did peep out for a short while.

Still rushing, I arrived at the hospital where I checked the time of the appointment and the room number. Too late, I remembered that where I needed to be was 'miles' away: over the other side of the hospital, in fact, and no, there wasn't short cut.

As I made my way over the long distance, I avoided looking at my watch because l didn't want to arrive at the correct department panting and crying. As l neared the reception window, two ladies appeared out of nowhere and approached the window very swiftly and jumped in front of me in the queue. Being late made me extremely irritable, but they were soon seen to and sat down.

I had gone over in my mind just what excuse for my tardiness would be plausible for reception, but in the end decided truth was perhaps the best policy. Hurriedly, I began my explanation. 'Sorry to be so late,' I said, whilst shooting a knowing look at the two 'pushers in.'

The receptionist looked up confused. 'Oh, but you are an hour early, Mrs Booth.' I looked again at my watch. I had stupidly misread the time, but I knew the reason why I hadn't looked properly.

I had taken my brother's golfing umbrella. It is huge and clumsy and I had raised my arm with difficulty so my view of the watch was distorted. Hence, I had an hour to wait, but at least I wasn't late!

Soon, I was in and out of the hospital, but then, I had the march back to the bus-stop. I was soon in the bus-station waiting for the bus. I nearly died when thought I had just missed one and had an hour to wait for the next, but I hadn't missed it at all.

Before my nephew had left for work in the morning, I had called out to ask him to leave his keys because I had left mine at home. He left them saying, 'Whatever you do, don't lose them.' He even put them on a long cord to hang around my neck. Not wishing to be treated like a fool, I removed the cord, little knowing what lay ahead and how much of a fool I obviously am.

The bus journey home was soon over and we were nearing my stop. I say we were nearing my stop, but I didn't know quite where I was. It was dark now and I thought I'd better watch out or I would miss my stop altogether.

A young man who had irritated me for the whole journey by loudly talking on his phone asked a young lady opposite him for directions to a certain pub near his new home. She told him it was the next stop, so, straightaway, I realised I had missed my stop. As it turned out, I had indeed missed it by about a mile. The young man thanked her warmly as he got off the bus. She giggled flirtatiously and said, 'I know all the stops along here as I have been on this bus for four years.' They both laughed at that.

I asked the young girl if it was also the stop I needed and gave her the name of the estate. She just stared at me and she said, 'I don't know, do I? How am I supposed to know?' With a giggle, she rolled her eyes heavenwards. Fortunately, a nice young man who was sitting nearby, rushed to the front of the bus and asked the driver to stop because I had missed my stop. He asked the driver where the estate was. As I drew level with the driver he said, 'It's a long way back there.'

I nearly fell off the bus as I departed. The bus had stopped by a bank and, as it was still raining, it was very wet and muddy and I had to stretch to get off. As I was leaving, the spiteful young woman said something nasty about me being old and the she couldn't understand me asking her about my stop. 'I mean, for God's sake, how am I supposed to know every stop?'

I stepped a little way back and said, 'I thought you had been on this bus route for four years?' I didn't quite catch what she replied. but I know it wasn't nice. She laughed. I said, 'It's not funny!' I was so mad by then because I also knew I had a long walk along the road in front of me in the dark.

She'd a good laugh at my expense, yet I am nearly 72 years old. I have arthritis and hydrocephalus which both affect the speed at which I can walk. I had very sore feet before I began walking, but my word they were throbbing by the time I reached my brother's house. I have swollen feet at the best of times.

The walk was very unpleasant and very creepy. It is a lonely road with very little pavement and devoid of street lighting. When I finally got to the estate, I was crying and really cold and wet. I had narrowly been missed by a couple of cars who obviously were in a hurry. I turned into the estate and was so glad my ordeal was nearly over.

Under the lamplight, I thought to get the keys out ready, but no, my ordeal had just restarted instead. I dropped two little keys and picked them up, but didn't notice the two others I'd also dropped.

I went back the day after looking for the two keys. I won't go into the palaver I had with getting back into my brother's home, but certainly had to eat my words about not having the keys around my neck. Fortunately, they were found by my sister who had driven over to give me a hand looking for them and she found them where I had stopped to get them ready. Even in Margaret's world this had been a chaotic day. I have actually left out some other things that happened because you would just never believe a person could have so much bad luck in one day.

I have told you in previous tales about ex-husband, Roy, and how he made me laugh about the accidents he had. It makes it seem like I was forever waiting for him to fall over, but he *was* very clumsy when we first got married, though he did improve as time went on. I don't think for a minute he did these things to amuse me. The trouble is, I do have a very loud laugh!

One particular evening, my fairly new husband was taking me out, but because it was to a pub I'd never been to, he warned me of an obstacle. As we were walking in the side entrance, he said, 'Go carefully, Marg.' As we walked through the double-gates that were permanently open, he added, 'There is a stop in the middle on the ground to keep the gates from shutting, but it's very dangerous and if you aren't careful you will fall over it'. He put his arm protectively around me, kissed my cheek and, as we walked through the passageway, he promptly tripped over the stop! To say I laughed would be putting it mildly. Luckily, he was unhurt except for his pride. I'm pleased to say we laughed, but whenever I walked that passageway later, I couldn't do it without smiling and thinking about Roy and his concern for me that evening in August 1966!

As I said, Roy did improve as time went by, but he did have one last accident that I remember. Fortunately, he was never hospitalised. The last one gave me plenty to laugh about. He was playing cricket with the locals in a field very close to home. A few of the lads had suggested a game so they gathered together one Sunday afternoon on a bright, sunny day.

I am not and never have been a lover of cricket, but as we had been married a few years by then, I played the dutiful wife and stood on the side-lines clapping with an occasional wave when he was fielding. I knew when it was over he would hurry back to get changed in the Men's Institute by the field. Because it was his local he knew he would need to hurry so as not to be last at the bar.

I stood waiting for the stampede. When they all started running with Roy in the lead, he ran past me and, forgetting he was wearing regulation white leather shoes, he slipped and skidded down the path straight into a big bunch of stinging nettles! As I helped him up, I was laughing again, of course. His arms were soon covered in stinging-nettle rash!

I ran around searching for dock-leaves and finally found some. I returned to help treat his stings. By this time, he'd been served at the bar and was sitting down. Not wanting to appear a sissy in front of his mates, he brushed off the dock leaves and gave me a wink. I sat down with my half of lager and we were there for the night. Men!

FOSTERING

Jenny Pace

Over the years, we've fostered many children. During one particular period, we had a set of three siblings. There was a fourth, a baby, who eventually went to someone else. The original plan was for the four children to be adopted together. Sadly, it didn't work, so the two girls and a boy stayed with us.

The family who had hoped to adopt the four children took in the baby first. Later, all four of the siblings spent the day with the family. It soon became clear, though, that this family was not a suitable match for the children. For instance, in just one day, the family decided they didn't want the youngest girl simply because she had been upset, and quite naturally had kept asking for me the entire first day they had them all on their own. All the children stayed with this family for a while, but sadly they all came back into our care, but very quickly, the baby went out to a lovely family.

The social eventually found a family who would have my three. I had doubts then, but things seemed to be going well. We had a meeting on the Thursday morning with the family at their house. The plan was they would have the three children for the day and bring them back on the night and the next day move to their new home with a memory-box each, but again, sadly, all the siblings came back into our care.

The family was clearly not happy with the children. One gripe was the adults were irritated that the little girl, who was just three-years old, asked for me all the time and wouldn't do what they asked. The little girl kept saying to me through tears, 'I have to say sorry to new mummy and daddy all morning.' I told the couple to get in touch with their social worker and discuss things.

The next morning, I phoned our own social worker and explained that I really didn't think this match was going to work. As I thought, the arrangement failed miserably, and once again the three children were back with us. We never saw or heard from that family again.

Social services said they would have to rethink the children's situation. They came up with the idea that would, after all, spilt the children up. The older girl would be placed go on her own whilst her two siblings would stay together.

We begged them not to split them up. It may have worked for the older girl because she would get all the attention on her own and probably enjoy that, but it would be disastrous for the other two children, especially the little girl who still blamed herself that the intended new mummy and daddy had never come back.

Unfortunately, our fears had to be ignored. The social went ahead with their plans to split the children up further. They were already separated from their baby sibling. A lovely lady was teamed up with the eldest girl and it all went very smoothly, like clockwork. We keep in touch still and eight years on I am still Nanny to her.

A search then began to find a new mummy and daddy for the other two children. We asked if we could simply just keep fostering them, but were told, no. The little girl was most distressed and unhappy. She kept saying, 'I don't want a new mum and dad. I want to stay with Nanny. Mummies and daddies aren't nice. She even got us to help her write it on her review form because, by now, she was nearly five years old.

Eventually, a couple was found who might adopt them. We met with them. They seemed a nice couple, but lived miles away. The 'Introduction' process began, but still the little girl said she wanted to stay.

At my twelve-monthly review, the reviewing officer suggested we put in for 'Special Guardianship.' We did. The reply came back: 'If it doesn't work with this family, then you can take one of the children out.'

Things went well for a while. We took the children to see their new house. Luckily, my son lived only an hour away from the family so we stayed with him. We needed to stay down in the area for almost a week. This is necessary for what we call, 'The Moving On' work.

We were with the children during the Thursday when there was a meeting to ascertain everything was going ahead with the process. The night before, the little boy asked his new daddy, 'Are you going to be our forever mummy and daddy?'

'Yes,' he answered, 'we are. You are going to stay here forever.'

Over the next few weeks everything went well. They let me know they'd started school and liked it and seemed to settle. I was so relieved, but I still kept their rooms free just in case. The little girl could be very loud if she was upset. You knew it when she was mad. She'd shout if she was unhappy or she'd be swinging off lampshades in joy. The little boy was the exact opposite. He'd go quiet and you had to figure out what was up. He was the thinker. I found the little girl easier to handle, but not everyone agreed. I used to say at least you knew where you were with her.

We had two other children living with us at the time, too. They knew the siblings well and always asked after them. The plan for these other two children was that one was going back to a family very shortly with the other to follow.

One day, we had a phone call asking if we could take in a little eighteen-month old boy. Of course, we said, yes. I still didn't use the other set of siblings' rooms, though. Somehow it didn't feel right. Daft really. We'd had the little lad a few days when the siblings' social worker turned up.

She sat down and the look on her face said something was up. At that time, we had only just discovered my husband had lung cancer. The social was unaware of this because we needed time for the awful news to sink in. I asked what the problem was. She told us the little girl had come back into care. I asked when could we collect her, but she said the child was already in care and had been for a couple of days and was with other carers.

We were gob smacked. We couldn't take it in. Why wasn't she back with us? They'd said if the worst happened we could have them. We were furious! I got in touch with the manager of the foster team and asked what was going on. She said she would find out for us. Then a couple of weeks later the boy came back.

The day of the phone call came. The little girl I knew was usually very loud and bubbly when the phone rang, I picked it up and said hello like always, but nothing. I said hello again and a very quiet, sad and flat little voice spoke to me. 'Nanny, can I ask you sumfin?'

I said, 'Of course you can, darling. You know you can ask me anything and I'll do my best to answer you.'

There was silence for what seemed a life time, then she said, 'Why did you lie to me about finding the best forever mommy and daddy and why didn't you come for me like you said?'

I couldn't get my words out. I was absolutely devastated. Tears rolled down my face. She needed me to answer her, but I didn't have the words. What could I say? I'd broken my promise to this little girl who I loved so much, but I had to say something. I spoke words, but not the words I wanted to say. I wanted to say, 'I'll come and get you now. I'll be your mommy. I'll make it right, but of course I couldn't.'

All I could say was, 'I am so sorry that I have not been able to keep my promise. I really thought I had found you and your brother a really good forever mommy and daddy. They said they wanted you so much and they would keep you safe forever, but they were unable to do so in the end. No-one told me. Had I known I would have come straightaway. I'm so, so sorry, darling.' I could hear her crying, but all she said was, 'But you didn't come,' and the phone went dead.

I got straight on the phone to my social worker and asked her, 'Do you realise what you have done to this child?' I was so upset. She asked me to calm down and explain myself. After I managed to control my tears and anger I repeated the phone call I'd just had from the little girl.

'Oh, my God,' was all she could say. I wanted answers. I needed answers. She said she'd get back to me and let me know when the disruption meeting was taking place and that she'd make sure I'd get some answers. I really hoped I would. I was distraught.

After the phone call from the little girl I was told I would get regular contact as I am Nanny to them both in the children's eyes. The carers weren't that keen and asked if we could pretend to just bump into them for first time. I agreed.

By this time, my late husband was having chemo and it was making him really ill so he couldn't attend the meeting. It was nearly Christmas, so I arranged to meet them in town and get some Christmas shopping at the same time. The carer said to meet by Blackpool Tower, then go for coffee and see how it went.

We met up and I pretended to be surprised to see them. They both ran up to me and gave me a hug. We went to BHS for coffee. Both children wanted to sit on my lap. When they called me Nanny, the other carer said, 'She's not Nanny, she's Jenny and please sit on your own seat. I was totally taken back by this attitude. Needless to say, the meeting proved uncomfortable and I just hoped the children didn't pick up on it. I kissed them goodbye and said I hoped to see them again soon. It never happened. Our Xmas presents came back as not collected from the post office.

We were really upset by this. I wanted answers. The day of the disruption meeting came and I went armed with lots of questions I wanted answers to. They all introduced themselves and started the meeting.

I sat listening to each one of them. The children's social worker never once mentioned that the plan for the children was to come back to us if anything went wrong. By this time, I was getting really mad. I'm normally quite easy going, but not any more I was so angry.

I asked the chair if I could now have my say. Everyone turned to look at me like I'd got two heads and were shocked that I even wanted to speak. The chair said, 'Yes, of course, if it is relevant to the situation.

I said, 'Oh, yes. It's very relevant indeed. I addressed the chair. 'I would like to know why, when I was told that if the adoption broke down the children would come back to me and we'd be allowed to keep them under special guardianship because we worked with the children. Moving them to the adoptive parents' house and letting them know we would always be there for them and if anything happened they would come back to us. We didn't even know they had left those carers until they were with another carer. Why didn't they come back to us as promised?'

The room went quiet. The chair looked at her paperwork and spoke to the social worker then said, 'It was because we had a new placement the day before the little girl came back and you were full.'

I said, 'That's rubbish. I did have a little one come in, but he is in a cot. Also, one of the other children was going home within that week followed by the sister. The bedrooms belonging to the children we are discussing were empty and left as they were when they left. But, if it is like as you said that it's about numbers, then I have two questions to put forward. Why wasn't the new child put with someone else as he hadn't at that time settled and why was I given four more children a couple weeks later?'

The chair asked, 'How many children do you have in your household now that are fostered.'

I said, six and that's three more than when the children came back into care. How then can it be down to numbers? We are talking about children here that had lived with me for nearly four years.'

No-one could answer that. But I was told that now the children were settled in their new placement then it would not be in their best interest to move them now.

The next day I had a phone call telling me the little one who came in the day before the siblings came back into care was moving to a new placement. No reason why was given, yet he had settled with us by then. So why and what was the difference? It didn't make sense and there has been no contact since.

Some years ago, we had a little boy 18 months old to be exact. He had lots of problems when he came and his behaviour was one of them. Over the next year or so one of the main problems was that he'd throw temper tantrums for no real reason and it didn't matter what we did. It made no difference.

One day, I was out shopping with him in a supermarket when he kicked off. Customers kept looking and tutting. One lady shouted, 'Can't you control your son? If he was mine he'd have had a smacked bottom by now.'

It had been one of those days when you would like to go back to bed and start the day all over again. I'd just about had enough of the comments and the lad's tantrum. I promptly got down on the floor next to him and proceeded to copy him by kicking and hitting the ground much to the horror of the shoppers.

He stopped what he was doing, sat up, looked at me and said, 'You are stupid, you are,' and stood up quietly.

I straightened up, too, and said, 'Well, that makes both of us, love. Come on, let's finish the shopping.' He never did it again. He was three and a half years old!

BABY BOOMER
Jan Judge

I'm Jan, but my full name, Janice, was kept for Sunday best and when Mum was cross. I was born in 1958. I have one brother who is seven years older than me called Clifford (Cliff) or Fiff, as I pronounced it as a young child. I was born into a post-war family, but it wasn't until recently I realised how close to the war it still was when I entered the world.

I can't remember much of it, but we moved from our two-bed house to a big three-bedroom house in Perry Barr. This is where I grew up. The house had a lovely front garden with a wall and a big, old, iron fancy gate which, until I was old enough, was as far as I was allowed to go.

This was good fun. There were three ways to get there. The first was a sloped path. The other was along the train (as I called it in my head), a retaining wall which started off like the front end of one of those round-fronted steam-trains normally blue in colour. The wall was wide enough to walk down and you could jump down at the end, run back up the path, and do it again. The other way was across the grass and along the castle wall which stopped all the earth from escaping the raised garden.

I loved this old 1930's house with its bay windows, archway door and side-entrance. In the archway, there was an old gas meter which had a cupboard around it. It always smelled funny. In the cupboard was the biggest spider I had ever seen. The baker used to rest his basket on the meter box when he came to the door for Mum to choose her bread and the milkman used to leave the milk on it.

BABY BOOMER

The doorstep had black and white tiles and the front door was painted dark blue. The back garden seemed massive, but probably wasn't that big. There was a large coal shed at the end of the side entrance. By the back door was a meat safe with fine mesh so the air went through, but no flies got in. That went in the early 60's when we had a fridge.

You went up two steps from what we now-a-days call the patio, but then it was known as the yard to the garden proper. Then up another step to the next bit of the garden and right at the top was Dad's garage where the car lived and he spent many hours up there tinkering and repairing whatever he was running on a shoe-string at the time.

Idyllic days of small child-life went on and my days were filled with mud pies, collecting worms and Mom saying I should have been a boy. I was always playing in the dirt, not like my brother who was known as the Teflon kid because nothing ever stuck to him. Me? I was always dirty.

Halfway up the back garden was my favourite spot as there were two concrete bird-baths. If I got there before Mom it was sheer bliss to play in the water and empty the baths ready for clean water. I really enjoyed myself doing that. Days passed as they do when you're a child. Everything seemed to happen in a warm and rosy glow.

In the spring, Mom used to wash all the blankets off the beds. I would help. We would stand down the entry with the mangle and a dolly tub. Mom would lift the blanket out of the water and take it up to the mangle. Turning the handle, she fed the blankets through with me on the other side guiding the blanket into the basket. I always wondered how all the water came out of the blankets when it was simply passing through the rollers.

We used to go and see my maternal gran and grandpa. I always found that exciting as it meant a two-bus journey. One on the 51 or 52 cream Corporation bus down to Perry Barr then over the road to the number 11 on the Wellington Road. These were big blue and yellow buses with a driver and a conductor and a lovely bell. I loved buses. I loved the smell of them and the noise they made.

AUTOBIOGRAPHY

When we went on short journeys we didn't go upstairs like we did when we went to town because, as Mom used to say, no sooner had we got on to the top deck, but it was time to come down again.

Gran's house was a little two-up-2 down with a scullery, a big old iron stove in the corner and a fire place in the back room. We never went in the front room since that was for best. It was all big sofas and chairs in red leather that had a pattern on with chair-backs and hand-embroidered cushions. A few family photos were scattered about. It also contained the front door which was never used. We always came and went via the entry to the back door. This had a porch with a trellis for the roses to grow on and this was where shoes, boots and wellingtons were taken off.

Gran's backyard and garden were places of wonderment to me. They had a wash house with a copper, a couple of stone sinks, a big old fire to get the water warm, a mangle, a tin bath, a smaller tin bath, a long-handled posher and a short one and behind this was an outside loo. It was cold and spidery with a huge over-head flush. The rest of the garden was put to use for veg, chickens and some flowers. I can't remember much about Grandpa only that he was a kindly old man. He died of cancer in '64. Gran carried on living in the cottage until the early 70's when the cottages got knocked down and she moved to Tower Hill in Great Barr.

The ever-changing life of a small child carried on in blissful ignorance of what really was happening. I remember going to see my gran, but Grandpa was not there anymore. I remember wondering why everyone was so sad, but never asking why. There were no more stories from days gone by when Grandpa was a lad and how he met gran. When I look back I hadn't been to see them for ages. Mom took me next door to be looked after while she went to see them. It was only much later that I was told that he had died, whatever that meant.

Christmas that year was strange. Everyone was trying hard to be happy for my brother and I. It was the first of many Christmas's that Dad fetched Gran to come and stay for a few days. She never went to Mom's brothers. Always us.

After Christmas, it was the run up to me going to school in the

September. During this year, we went on a big family holiday to Weston-Super-Mare. We took the train. With the family came Gran, Mom, Dad, Mom's two elder brothers, their wives and children. We always had a good time with picnics on the beach, rides on the donkeys, going to the boating pool to sail our boats and, best of all, ice cream.

We stopped at a bed and breakfast place up the other end by a nursing home. This Gran told me was where she came to convalesce during the war after a major operation. The holiday all came to an end too quickly and it was heading for me to go to school.

I was looking forward to it. I didn't know what to expect, but it sounded very grown up. Mom took me to town to get a blazer in blue with the school badge. I felt very posh in it and a pleated skirt with braces and buttons and a white shirt. Mom and Gran had been busy knitting cardigans for me to wear to school.

The thing about going to school is I already knew Karen from over the road. We had played as we grew up and were the same age. I was just a few days older. The school days flew past. I was milk monitor and put the holes in the top of the milk and Karen put the straws in. There was Music and Movement and a Mrs Whitehouse, who was at least a hundred! She was a lovely lady.

Christmas was soon upon us and parts were given out for the play. I helped behind the scenes which suited me fine. That Christmas was a much brighter one than the year before. Dad had encouraged Mom to put the tree up early. It was fantastic. I would go into the front room to look at it. All the lamps, the baubles and the fairy on the top would make me sit on the floor in wonderment.

This Christmas was even better still because it snowed and it continued to snow for a while afterwards. Jack Frost drew pictures on the inside of the windows. We still had an open fire in the back room, but in the front Mom and Dad had fitted a gas fire. This came in useful because shortly after Christmas I came down with measles and Mom and I slept downstairs. Mom had rigged up a tent-like structure over me so the light couldn't get to my sore eyes. The doctor was coming in three times a day. It wasn't till much later in life Mom told me how touch and go it had been with me during the measles.

My Dad's parents lived around the corner from my gran. Nan was a sharp no nonsense kind of woman. Both Nan and Granddad were only five feet tall and they were like a double act. Their house was a lot bigger than Gran's. It had a room at the front which was full of junk and a fabulous old soapstone owl which I loved. The middle room had an upright piano in which everyone always stopped and played a few notes on the way upstairs. The house did have an indoor bathroom and these stairs led up to it from behind a door up the corner.

The back room where they lived mainly had a long box above the door. In it were six little windows and a bell. The little curtains in the box opened when the buzzer was pushed to say the person in that room needed a servant! It hadn't been used, though, since Nan and Granddad lived there with my dad, brother, two sisters and a couple of cats.

From the back room, you went down a few steps to a scullery where the was a big old green gas cooker, a Belfast sink, a boiler for the washing and a door to the outside. Here was a yard, the outside loo and the wash house.

The back garden was long and there were three sections to it. The first part was the garden with grass and plants around the edge. The second bit was a vegetable garden. The final section, as Granddad used to say, was a Nan-free place. It was his Slippery Elm! His shed was here and it is where he used to smoke his Players' cigarettes without Nan knowing. Well, that's what he thought, but Nan was an all seeing-eye, all-knowing eye! He used the shed as an escape from Nan when she got too much for him. He would vanish off down there regularly. She was a very bossy person!

The piano came into its own where Dad was concerned. He loved music and was always late picking up Mom for a date even though he only lived around the corner. The lure of playing a song or two before he left to pick her up was too much. He would often end up playing three or more songs. Nan used to come in and say, 'I thought you were taking Jean out tonight? You're late!'

Dad had a rough war and this affected him for the rest of his life. As he put it, 'I was a guest of the Jap's Emperor.' It wasn't until much later I realised what he had actually meant. Before then I had thought he had lived in a castle during the war.

During reception class I had to go to Birmingham Children's Hospital in the middle of Brum. It was a large impressive building and very old. Amazingly, it had managed to come through the blitz unscathed. I don't know if it had been hit, but the front was like an old workhouse.

Mom took me and we went down into the dungeon as I called it. It was the Orthopaedics Ward. I had a problem with the cartilage in my left leg (still have a problem now). I had to go every so often to have it checked. This ward did very strange things. Some children had large wooden crosses plastered to their feet and legs plastered as well. This was for clickity hips so the nurse said. Others had braces on their legs. I was so grateful I didn't have to have anything like this done.

We used to travel to town on the bus. I loved the bus and when I grew up I wanted to be a clippie as they had the ticket thingy and rang the bell! When getting on the bus, the step was at the back and there was a pole to help you on. Mom used to grab me and push me onto the bus as I was too short to get up myself. We then would go downstairs on the journey into town and I liked to sit on the side seats. My feet didn't touch the floor, but that was most of the fun.

I remember going past where the new underpass was being built in Perry Barr. The bus used to sway over the rickety road, past the end of Wellhead Lane - one of the roads that led to where Dad worked at ICI, Kynock Works. It became IMI. This was also the way to Gran's and Nan's, but we got off the bus by the New Crown and Cushion and crossed over to get on the number eleven outer-circle bus, but going into town we carried on up through Birchfield past the new blocks of flats and the Trinity Church on to Newtown then up into town itself, stopping outside a shop called the Beehive.

When I was about seven, we had a lovely Christmas. Dad had managed to get Mom to put the tree up early in the week before

Christmas. It was exciting because we went down to Hampstead to the village to choose and collect the tree. We went in Connie the Consul because it had plenty of room for the tree and me on the back seat.

We arrived home and the tree went into the front room in the big bay window. Dad climbed into the loft and brought the tree decorations down. I loved the pretty balls. The ones I loved most were the lovely concave ones with a star or a flower in them. The other one I liked was bright blue glass with rabbits around it. I still have some of these on my tree. Some are almost sixty-five years old because they went on my brother's first Christmas tree.

Dad and my brother, Cliff, put the tree up. After tightening each individual little bulb and testing them, the strings of lights were hung into festive shapes around the tree and the room. Mom and I checked and made sure the hanging balls had the cotton loops through them so they could be hung on the tree's green branches. We also had the job of unravelling and hanging the sparkly tinsel. We all worked until the tree was resplendent. I was utterly overcome and enchanted with the tree and the room. It was truly magical.

It was time for tea on a Saturday, the night we could sit and have our meal round the TV. Gran had prepared the tea. We had buttered crumpets, fruit and cream and cake. After eating, I went to see the tree and just sat on the floor looking at it. I was mesmerised. It was like fairyland.

It wasn't long until Christmas Eve when we put our pillowcases up. That year I had asked Father Christmas for a Sindy doll and some outfits with which to dress her. He didn't disappoint. In my sock, I had a chocolate Santa, some shiny pennies, an orange and some nuts. A number of small games added to my surprises and delight at the gifts. To make that Christmas really special, it snowed. The whole world was a true winter wonderland. I have never forgotten that particular Christmas.

Looking back my parents must have struggled in the 60's. They were buying their own house, the first of the family to do so. There was me and my ever-growing brother to buy clothes for. I wasn't so difficult because Mom used to get the old 'treadle' out and run up my dresses. Gran knitted cardigans and jumpers for me. Cliff was now in long trousers and these very often fell out with his shoes he was such a tall gangling youth.

Mom was good at making something out of nothing to eat and having lived through the war knew how to fill our tums with good nosh. She was not a fancy cook, but plain and simple with meat and veg and fish and chips on a Friday. There was often neck of lamb stew, braised skirt of beef and lamb ribs, but we always had a roast on a Sunday.

One Saturday night, Mom made a 'chicken' casserole. She put it down in front of us and we all sat at the table. Family meal times were special. Every night we always sat down together to swap news, crack jokes and as the dining table was in the front room we would take the micky out of the people walking up and down the road. There was spring-healed Jack, Jimmy Jesus, Fangio and his daughter, Pash, short for passion-killer. She looked as if she had fallen out of the ugly tree and hit every branch on the way down, but she wore the brightest red lipstick. Her Dad Fangio drove a sit-up-and-beg Ford Pop and this poor car never got out of first gear, but he used to get in with driving gloves and a flat cap. Dad said he looked like a racing driver but couldn't drive for toffee.

But I digress. Casserole is what this is about. I was a very fussy eater and was often got threatened with, 'If you don't eat it you will have it for your breakfast, though I never did! This plate of food was put in front of me and it looked like chicken casserole as usual so, being a meat-eater I dived straight into the meat.

I took a taste and said, 'Mom, this tastes funny.' Mom assured me it was fine so, with some trepidation, I had another mouthful. It was the right texture for chicken, but it had a funny fishy taste. I said, 'I don't like it and it's making me feel sick.'

Mom said, 'Don't be daft. Now eat it up.'

I looked at Dad and said, 'It's not right. Sorry.'

Dad said, 'Look, she knows it isn't what it's supposed to be so tell her. She might eat it, then.'

Mom took a deep breath and said, 'It's rabbit.'

AUTOBIOGRAPHY

The words still stick in my head. We were eating fluffy bunnies! No. This was so wrong. I ran upstairs and was sick. Mom came up to me and said, 'Don't be silly,' but I had a reaction to it and was ill for a few days afterwards so no more 'chicken' casserole for me.

My maternal Gran loved the pictures and musicals. She simply adored them and once a month or whenever a film that took her fancy came to the local flea pit, it was, 'Catins come and see -' Catins was her pet name for me. I never knew why, but it stuck and this is how she referred to me and so my love of films was born.

She moved from her cottage in Wood Lane to Tower Hill just behind the library to a modern bed-sit that had a bath, inside loo and hot and cold running water. It was, as she said, 'proper posh.' All she had been used to till then was an outside loo, cold water and a tin bath. She moved there in the late 60's and just around the corner was The Clifton Cinema. It was wonderful for Gran. She was in her oil tot.

We went to see My Fair Lady, Mary Poppins, Hello Dolly, The Jazz Singer and too many others to mention. She also she took me to see Gone with the Wind. My bum was numb when we came out after that one.

Once or twice a year we ventured into Birmingham town centre to The Gaumont Cinema. It had a huge concave screen. The most memorable film we saw there was the new release of The Sound of Music in 1965. We came home on the 51 bus, singing the songs. It was a magical time.

When Gran moved to Tower Hill I used to pop in on the way home from school to see her. Sometimes Mom was there especially if they had been shopping or Mom had done some cleaning in the places Gran couldn't reach.

Gran was born in the 1800's and had lived through some bad times, but she was a very down to earth lady with the motto: what will be will be. She died in 1973 at the age of 86. I missed really her.

A few surprises were to come about Gran. When the flat was cleared, Mom came upon a handbag in the back of her wardrobe with over £2000 inside. It was in white fivers. Also, in a tea caddy, there was about another £500. There was also the money for the funeral from the 'Pru.' Gran was clearly a money-hoarder and may not have trusted the banks too much. Mom and her brothers didn't realise she had all this money. She was a very canny lady.

This was a standing joke in our family, Nelson stood by the Bull Ring shopping centre in Birmingham in the middle of a large open island where the market traders stood. Dad had been born and brought up in Brum and had driven round Birmingham many times. In 1935 he passed his driving test, had a motorbike and worked for a garage on cars.

When we went on holidays in the car before the advent of the M5, we had to go through town on the way to the coast. We would drive past the Digbeth Bus Station and Bird's Custard Factory. Dad always gave us a bit of a history lesson about various places and shops that we passed, but looking back, this must have distracted him from where we were going.

We duly set out after the usual, 'I just need to see what that noise is in the car.' Mom would get more and more infuriated with him because he could have done that during the week beforehand. He would have mentioned it a few times, but still did nothing about it. So, it was always a last-minute thing.

Mom hated getting ready to go away on holiday. She was a proper home bird and would have preferred not to go. Dad messing around with the car didn't help and it would be after a few terse words that we would set out. In the back of the car would be me, my brother and Gran with Mom Dad and the dog in the front.

Off we would go down the Walsall Rd into Perry Barr, then down the underpass, over the fly-over and into the town.

I don't know how Dad managed it, but we always seemed to come upon the statue of Nelson from different roads. We went around the island as usual, but Dad missed his turning. This mistake was a fair one because a car cut him up on the inside.

The second time around, he got distracted and went back down the road we had just come on. Dad turned round and headed back onto the island again. Because Gran was teasing Dad so much and we were all laughing, he went and missed the turning again, but eventually he managed to get to the right exit and off we went.

Holidays were never quite the same once the M5 was built because previously when we went to Devon, it was always 'Twice around Nelson'. For us, that was the fun part of a very long journey!

Walking the Dog Today: Since the clocks have gone back taking the dog a walk is earlier before the light goes because 'living in the sticks' with the only a lamp-post outside the pub. It is the only source of light for the village.

I am walking up the lane and musing on winter coming and looking across the fields seeing the sun setting in a watery, grey-blue sky. The low mist is rolling over the fields. This is no brilliant sunset like the summer affords us, but still pretty in its own way. The muted oranges are more like peach and the reds are just insipid pink with the smudges of clouds diffusing the light even more.

In the distance, a pheasant calls. It's a strange noise. The crows cackle no more and the skylark sings no more. Owls hoot into the evening sky. The swallows have left. Yes, summer has gone and a sadness spreads over me like the rolling mist.

Looking up the hill, the trees on the top are all in varying stages of undress. One is now just plain branches. The leaves have all fallen. The next one is showing a last glow before the leaves tumble to the floor like a firework of oranges, reds and yellows. Fortunately, a couple of fir trees are still standing fully-clothed with a copper-beech standing proudly beside it.

We turn to walk back to the village. One of the houses has lit a fire. The smoke is lazily spewing out of the chimney pot with the gentle breeze taking it, curling it and sending it on its way. The jackdaws are making a noise as they fly into the tall conifers next to the church for the night. The church bell signals that it's four-thirty. The light is failing fast. Yes, winter is on its way.

AFRICAN ADVENTURES – Non-Safari
Rosemary Baxter

PART 1

'Come To Sunny Zambia!' shouted the advert in the Jobs' Section of Mum and Dad's Daily Mirror. It grabbed my attention straightaway.

It went on to say that, following its recent independence, Zambia (formerly Northern Rhodesia) was in dire need of British nurses in their hospitals and shorthand-typists in their government offices.

'I could do this job!' I said to Mum, as she fried my breakfast of bacon, eggs, mushrooms and tomatoes.

'Sounds like a dream job!' Mum replied, probably thinking in her heart that it would remain just a dream. Her shy little daughter, going across the world to darkest Africa? It would never happen in a month of Sundays!

It was true. I was very shy. I had been working for Marconi, first as a clerk-typist, then a secretary for nine years and in all that time I had never had the courage to find another, better paid, job. I felt safe there: I knew everyone and everyone knew me. I was the sort of girl of whom people said, 'She wouldn't say 'boo' to a goose!'

But there comes a time in most people's lives when the scales fall from their eyes, and they see themselves from the outside looking in.

I suddenly saw that if I didn't grab this opportunity, I could find myself stuck in this Marconi office until I retired, unless marriage and children intervened; and so far, the men I had been out with had been lame ducks!

As soon as I got to work that morning, I typed out my letter of application and CV and put them in the post. The reply came within days and I was called to an interview with the Crown Agents in London.

Going to London was a big adventure for me, and my Mum and Auntie Edna came with me, Auntie Edna travelling from Surrey, while Mum and I caught the train from Essex.

I had bought a short, curly wig especially for this interview. My long hair had a mind of its own, and couldn't be relied upon to behave itself, and I wanted to look the part – confident, self-assured, well-groomed!

Mum believed in allowing plenty of time for any important appointment, so we left very early; but halfway there, the train rattled to a halt, and over the tannoy came the announcement that there was a delay and they didn't know how long it would last!

Mum and I panicked and I could feel myself sweating with nerves. I had wanted to arrive in good time so that I'd have the chance to compose myself before being called in to the interview. I didn't want to have to dash in at the last minute, red-faced, out of breath and with dark patches of sweat under my armpits! But in fact, that is exactly what happened! I didn't have time to feel nervous. I just galloped in, all guns blazing.

Years later, Mum said that she always wondered if I would have changed my mind if we'd gotten there early and I'd had time to reconsider. We'll never know, but I think my mind was made up. I wanted to grab life with both hands!

I faced the panel of interviewers: four friendly-looking men sitting behind a desk. They asked all the usual questions and then asked if I had anything I wanted to ask them.

'Well,' I said, a little embarrassed. 'I'm afraid of insects, moths, and spiders. Will there be lots of those?' They smiled indulgently.

'You don't need to worry about insects. All the houses and offices have mesh at the windows to keep them out.'

Reassured, I said that I had no further questions; I just really wanted this job!

AFRICAN ADVENTURES – NON-SAFARI

But first of all, they said, I would have to sit a shorthand-typing test. Oh, dear, I dreaded tests of any kind. But I couldn't afford to fail. I'd set my heart on going to Zambia.

I had read somewhere that if you aren't the person you want to be, just act as if you are.

Summoning up every ounce of courage I possessed, I acted as if I had confidence by the bucket-load.

'Do I really need to take a test?' I asked. 'I'm a very good shorthand-typist!'

'We know you are, my dear; we've received your references!' they replied. They then went on to explain that there was a pay scale, and my position on it would depend upon the result of my shorthand-typing test.

I was sent to another room, where a man gave me ten minutes' dictation, and I was told to type it out as accurately as I could. As any typist of those days will know, different makes of typewriter differed in small ways, keys would be in different places, and it was easy to make mistakes when using an unfamiliar machine.

My heart leapt for joy when I saw the typewriter they wanted me to use was exactly the same as the one I had always used at Marconi – the familiar, pale green Imperial.

I rattled away, finishing in double-quick time. I had always been a fast typist.

The interviewers called me back in to their office. 'Well, Miss Norton, we are pleased to tell you that your test was 100% accurate, and this means that you will be on the top rate of pay - £1500 per annum.' (A fortune, and more than three times my Marconi pay)! This was 1968.

'The contract will be for three years, and you will receive a tax-free gratuity at the end of your contract of £750.'

Mum, Auntie Edna and I went for a celebratory lunch. I felt I was walking on cloud nine. Was I really going to darkest Africa? Little old, timid me? Yes, I was!

But one dark cloud appeared on the horizon, in the shape of Mum's next-door neighbour, 'Auntie' Margaret. We called all adult neighbours 'Auntie' or 'Uncle'.

AUTOBIOGRAPHY

Auntie Margaret was determined to put a dampener on my excitement.

'Aren't you being selfish, leaving your Mum and Dad to go halfway around the world, and you being an only child?' she accused. Her face was set in a disapproving frown.

I started having second thoughts. Perhaps she was right, and I was being selfish and thoughtless. Was I wrong to want an adventure while I was still young enough? I was twenty-four. Perhaps it would have to remain a dream. Maybe girls like me didn't have adventures.

I told Mum what Margaret had said.

'Don't you listen to her, my dear,' retorted Mum, anger rising in her voice.

She went on to say, 'I had always wanted to travel, but in my day it just wasn't possible for a young girl. You go, love, and have the time of your life. Pay no attention to her next door. I'll have words with her!' And she stomped round to give Margaret a piece of her mind.

Mum had been angry with Margaret ever since Margaret's son, David had wanted to emigrate with his wife and baby to Australia, but Margaret had said, 'What about us? How can you even think of leaving your poor old Mum and Dad alone?' And so David didn't go. My Mum never forgave Margaret for that. 'Selfish old woman!' she called her.

In due course I received a letter of confirmation, asking if I would be ready to fly out on the 24th December, 1968.

I knew that this would be my last Christmas with my parents for three long years, so I wrote back and said I didn't want to go on the 24th, and asked them to suggest a later date. Of course, they could have said, 'Absolutely not. Take it or leave it!' I hadn't thought of that.

'No problem,' they wrote back. 'Can you travel on the 1st January?' Being English, New Year didn't mean as much to me as Christmas, and I wrote back that I could.

They sent me a £50 voucher to buy household goods for the house I would be allocated when I arrived in Zambia, although at first I would stay in a hostel. With this money, I bought pots and pans, crockery, cutlery, sheets, towels, blankets – all the things I would need to set up home. Mum gave me my Granddad's old sea-going wooden trunk. He had been a deep-sea fisherman, sailing out from Lowestoft to catch herring. My trunk was sent on ahead to Lusaka, Zambia's capital city.

Using my Granny's old Singer sewing machine, I had made myself fifteen summer dresses, all from the same Simplicity pattern, but with different fabrics and necklines. Being slim, and with the mini being in fashion, I had needed only a yard and a quarter of material for each dress. And at about five shillings a yard, it was no great expense. But I would later regret that they were all made from synthetic fibres instead of cool cotton!

The first day of January arrived. It was 1969, a brand-new year, for a brand- new life. Mum and Dad, and my Surrey cousins with their children all came to Gatwick Airport to see me off on my evening flight. No one in our family had worked overseas before, so it was a big moment. I had a brief twinge of sadness that I was leaving Mum and Dad, but assured them that on my return, after three years, I would have enough money to send them on holiday to Australia, where Mum had always longed to go.

At this stage, I still couldn't really believe it was happening. I had well and truly tossed aside and buried the old Rosemary and had morphed into the devil-may-care, brave new Rosy (although Mum always called me Roe). I liked my new persona. I had climbed out of my cocoon, like a caterpillar turning into a butterfly. If I could do this, I could do anything!

I had a window seat in a row of three on the plane, and the two people on my right – a young South African woman and a young English man – spent the entire time flirting with each other, and were practically engaged by the time we arrived. Playing gooseberry is a bit of a bore!

When we reached Uganda, the stewardess said we would be getting off while the plane refuelled. We all reached for our coats from the overhead racks. After all, it was January; surely it would be chilly outside?

AUTOBIOGRAPHY

The stewardess laughed. 'You won't be needing those!' And as we climbed down the aircraft steps, we found out why. It was like walking into a Turkish bath or a sauna, as a blanket of hot, moist air enveloped us.

We trooped into the airport bar, where, suddenly thirsty, we gulped down glasses full of warm orange juice - their fridge had broken down. The barmen looked curiously at us pale-skinned passengers, while we looked just as curiously at them. I had never seen a black person before, except on television. I wondered how they tolerated this heat. We all felt like limp rags, and couldn't wait to get back on the plane, where there was air conditioning. It did cross my mind that I was about to spend three years living in the African heat. Would I be able to stand it?

At about 5.30 in the morning, the pilot announced that we were all to look to our left to watch the African sunrise. Oh, what a sight it was! Brilliant hues from purple to red to orange filled the sky. 'African sunrise!' I repeated to myself. It was really happening. I wasn't in a dream.

When I disembarked at Lusaka Airport, I discovered that I was not alone; there were four other girls from England, all coming to work as shorthand-typists in the Zambian Government. We marvelled at all the copper sculptures – Zambia is famous for its copper mines.

An Englishman, resplendent in a safari suit and floppy hat, came to meet us and escorted us to a minibus. As we drove along the airport road, we saw what appeared to be chicken huts on each side of the road. 'No, those aren't chicken huts,' said our escort. 'People live in them, whole families.' Our jaws dropped. How could the government allow this?

Driving along the main road into Lusaka, we passed many Zambian couples walking along the grass verge. I say walking, but actually the man would be on a bike, free as a bird, and his wife would be walking beside him with a mattress on her head, a baby on her back, and her hands occupied with some knitting or crochet, so as not to waste any part of her anatomy. Women's Lib was emerging in the UK, and I was shocked to see women being used as pack horses! Why didn't the men help carry the heavy goods? 'It's not their culture,' the escort explained.

We were taken to a hostel – I think it was called Highlands - on the outskirts of the city, and shown to our rooms – one for each of us. Mine was on the ground floor, with a thick hedge outside the window.

The only names I remember of the other girls are Sandy Moorhouse from Yorkshire and June Mulroy from Birmingham. Another girl was from Cheltenham, and had led a very sheltered life, with rather old parents. Let off the leash for the first time in her life, she went wild, and ended up having several abortions in a short space of time.

We spent our first weekend sunbathing for hours, not realising the power of the African sun, and some of the fair-skinned girls got sunburnt. After all, we had just come from an English winter. We smiled at the sheer novelty of sunbathing in January! It took us a while to grasp that, as this was Africa and not England, every day would be a hot and sunny day!

Sandy Moorhouse had brought her sewing machine with her, and in no time at all had run up some dresses for June Mulroy, who had a very big bust but a very narrow back, and found it difficult to buy dresses that would fit.

As I sat in my room, my clothes unpacked, I saw that the interview man had been telling the truth – the windows did indeed have insect mesh on them. Phew! Nothing to worry about there.

But during the night, almost from the moment I put the light out, what sounded like a huge swarm, nay, a whole herd of insects, started buzzing and whining, bouncing off the bedclothes and thudding against the walls and ceiling. They sounded like winged elephants! I was too scared to look.

I wanted to scream. My heart was pounding. I silently called for my Mum. I just couldn't bear it!

Back home, if even the tiniest moth flew into my bedroom, I would yell for Mum to come and remove it. Mum would fly up the stairs with her yellow duster, gently trap the offending moth, and put it out of the window. Oh, how I needed her now!

I spent my first night in Zambia quivering with fear, with the covers pulled up over my head, hardly able to breathe, and cursing that hedge. In my imagination, that was where all these enormous creatures lived, just waiting for darkness to fall, so that they could fly into the nearest bedroom and practise their swooping and diving and trampolining skills.

The next morning, my bedroom floor was thickly covered with the dead bodies of various flying insects.

At breakfast, we talked to a seasoned old hand, who had done many contracts in Zambia. He decided to warn us about the many dangers awaiting us in the tropics. First, there was a disease called Bilharzia, or Schistosomiasis, which you could get by swimming or paddling in rivers, where there might be a certain type of fresh water snail. Somehow, a parasite in these snails could enter your body and cause disease, even death. We finished our breakfast and left the table, not wanting to hear any more. We could tell that this old boy enjoyed frightening us out of our wits!

First insects, and now snails! This was all too much for me. I wasn't as brave as I'd thought I was!

But, having come all this way, I decided I had to give it a fortnight, and if by then I hadn't got used to the insects, I would go home, and face the shame of admitting I couldn't hack it. Auntie Margaret would gloat. 'Serves you right!' I could imagine her saying with a smirk.

Miraculously, long before the fortnight was up, I had grown used to the insects, the giant moths, the huge praying mantises, the big, brightly coloured spiders, even the mosquitoes and cockroaches! I'd come to accept that everything in Africa was larger than life.

And I learned not to sleep with the window open.

We were sent to work in different offices in Lusaka. On my first day, I had to take dictation from an African Government official, but I could scarcely understand a word he said, so I had to just scribble down what little I could grasp.

'Excuse, me Sir,' I said, 'but I noticed that you were dictating from your notes. Do you think I could borrow them, just in case there is an unusual word that I'm not familiar with?'

'Oh, of course!' he said, handing me the notes. Phew! That could have been awkward!

I simply typed his letter from his notes, expanding it a bit with my own shorthand notes, and he was none the wiser. But I soon got used to his accent and had no trouble understanding him again.

There were two white South African ladies in my office and two Zambian ladies. We all got on very well, and again I had to pinch myself. I would look out of the window at the Zambian streets, with a feeling of disbelief. It seemed like only yesterday I was sitting in my boring Marconi office, and yet here I was, working in Africa, and amazingly, on yet another familiar Imperial typewriter. The company must have sold their machines all over the world!

I wrote twice weekly to Mum and Dad, and once weekly to my Marconi colleagues, telling them of all the sights I had seen. One, which seemed outrageous to me at the time, and shocked the girls back home, was the common sight of African mothers breastfeeding their babies anywhere and everywhere.

If a baby cried when Mum was in a queue at the shops, or at a bus stop, out came a generously milk-swollen black breast and the baby would grab it with both hands and guzzle away contentedly. 'Plug in for happiness!' as my friend remarked. The mum wouldn't necessarily tuck it away afterwards, either. Why bother, when the baby might fancy another gulp later?

It could be a little disconcerting if you turned around in a shop queue, and found yourself nearly poked in the eye with a milk bar! Disconcerting to me, because I had never seen any other breasts than my own modest pair, and also because I was from buttoned-up Britain! Here, it was no big deal.

Babies were never left to cry. The breast was the answer to their every need. No one bothered about four-hourly feeds, or dummies – if the baby was hungry, it was fed, and that was that. And even if it wasn't hungry, the breast was still the answer. I had never seen such happy, peaceful babies!

There was no attempt at 'English-style' modesty, or discreetly popping the breast out from under a baggy top. Oh, no, they just whipped them out, full and magnificent – and why shouldn't they indeed! No one batted an eyelid, even when a mother walked along the street breastfeeding twins! No hands! She just used the sling method that I describe below.

But although their boobs were revealed for all to see, African women were modest in a different way from us. They wore long dresses that covered their legs, and probably considered us English girls, with our thigh-high mini dresses, to be the sluttiest of trollops!

Babies were carried on their mothers' backs in a sort of sling. I watched in amazement at how this was done.

The mother would pick her baby up by one arm, sling it round to the rear, where the baby would settle on its mother's flat back, with its legs wrapped around the mother's waist, and its arm, incredibly, still attached to its body; then the mother would expertly fling a length of blue cotton cloth around the baby and herself, and tie it in a knot at the front.

The baby, meanwhile, would bounce around as the mother walked, and, being in an upright position, was able to see all that was going on around it. So much more exciting than lying on its back in a pram! I think it is for this reason that African babies are much more advanced than western ones, and are able to hold their heads up from an early age.

When the mother needed to feed the baby, she would deftly swing the cotton sling to the front of her body, pop out the breast from the top of her dress, and let the baby get on with it.

Another sight that I wrote home about was African men walking along holding hands. I asked one of my Zambian colleagues if this meant they were gay, or just friendly? 'Oh,' she said. 'They're just friends. We don't have any gay people in Africa! It's only white people who do those disgusting things!' And for a long time, I believed her.

Just as we had got used to living in the hostel and working in the Lusaka office, June Mulroy and I were posted to a bush station called Mansa, formerly, in colonial days, called Fort Rosebery.

(Once Zambia had gained its independence, it set about changing colonial place names to African ones. Fort Jameson became Chipata; my favourite was Bancroft, which they renamed the tongue-twisting Chililabombwe)!

I was told I would be secretary to the Cabinet Minister for Luapula Province, and June, being younger, would work for his deputy, the Minister of State.

But I was perfectly happy where I was, and really didn't want to go. I disliked change, and feared the bush would be a little dull, and without modern facilities, and proper loo paper (would we have to squat in the bushes and use bug-covered leaves?); but June, ever the optimist, insisted we would love it.

My trunk was sent on ahead, and June and I boarded the Dakota plane which would take us to the back of beyond.

The airport at Mansa seemed to be in the middle of nowhere, just as I'd imagined it would be, in contrast to the bustling Cairo Road (not that it led to Cairo) in Lusaka, with its Bata shoe shops and Zambiri, a shop which sold everything Zambian.

As we walked down the steps of the plane, we saw a skinny man with ragged shorts standing by. He was heard to mutter, 'I think I'm going to marry that girl.'

We had been told that a government vehicle would come and collect us, and that a bungalow would be ready for us to move into; but no vehicle appeared, and I marched into the airport manager's office in a bit of a strop – remember, I was now confident and no longer shy - and demanded, with hands on hips: 'Where's our transport, then?'

'How should I know?' he replied, grumpily. 'I'm hungover and I'm off to the Copperbelt for a party at the nurses' hostel in an hour.'

Taking pity on us, he told us to go up to his house, which was about fifty yards away, and his houseboy would make us a cup of tea.

A few minutes later, the grumpy airport manager, who we had now discovered was a Scotsman called Charlie Baxter, joined us and said that he had investigated on our behalf, and confirmed that no transport was forthcoming, and that our promised house was not quite finished, having only recently been built.

But he had contacted some friends, Pat and Henry, an elderly

South African couple, and they would not only pick us up, but let us stay with them for a couple of weeks, or however long it took for our house to be ready.

He reminded us that we were not in the UK now, and things didn't always go according to plan in Africa. In other words, stop complaining!

On the Monday, we were shown to our spacious office and introduced to the two Zambian ladies who would show us the ropes – Maggie Bwalya and Edna Mubonda, wearing beautiful ankle-length dresses and elaborately coiled, matching headscarves.

Maggie explained that she and Edna were cousins. Maggie was unhappy because she had fallen in love with a man from another tribe, but her family had forced her to give him up and marry a man from her own tribe – the Bemba – 'and he drinks!' she said with disgust, almost spitting out the words.

My boss would be Fwanyanga Mulikita, and June's would be Mr Monga (not to be confused with Mongu, which is a place, they explained).

PART 2

We each had a large desk, and we could choose which one we wanted. One desk had a brand-new Adler typewriter on it, and the other had an older, pale green Imperial. As the most senior secretary, I was expected to choose the Adler, but I opted for the good old, familiar Imperial!

Our bosses had their own personal toilets near the offices, but everyone else was expected to use the general toilet in a separate block. June and I went to inspect this toilet. A sign had been stuck to the wall – *'Please Flash Your Big Lumps.'*

But there were, in fact, some big lumps lying un-flashed, and June said that no way was she going to use this toilet, even after she had pulled the chain and given it a good scrub with Vim, so we secretly used the Cabinet Minister's loo when he was away, and kept our legs crossed when he wasn't.

My boss, Mr Mulikita, was often away on cabinet business in

the capital, and so most of my dictation came from Mr Evans Willima, the Secretary of State for the province. I had got the hang of the Zambian accent by now, and there were no problems with the dictation.

Mr Willima was studying the Law of Torts in his spare time, and was a very learned, serious man. He used to give me reams of complicated dictation. I grew quite fond of him, and I like to think he was fond of me, too. When I resigned on marriage a few months later, he gave me the most glowing reference and I wish I still had it!

I never lost the feeling of unreality, as I compared my previous life, sitting in a Marconi office in England, with my life in Mansa, Zambia, working for a Secretary of State. Was I even the same person? It seemed that only a few weeks ago, I was the shy secretary who wouldn't say 'boo' to a goose, and was scared to leave the security of a company I had worked for since the age of 15; and now here I was in 'darkest Africa' brimming with confidence and feeling completely at home, as though I had lived in Africa all my life!

In the past, the British expatriates, having no television, had entertained themselves over a few dozen beers in the Mansa club house, but for some reason, this had been closed down. Some bright spark thought of a simple solution – each expat would take turns holding a party at their house every night.

June and I didn't drink, much to the consternation of the others. 'You don't drink? We'll give you a fortnight, and you'll be knocking it back the same as the rest of us!' they said.

'But why would we?' we asked, baffled.

'Well, let's face it, there's nothing else to do here, is there? That's why we get paralytic every night!'

June decided she might manage a couple of port-and-lemons, but I settled for a Coca-Cola, something I had never tasted before. Mum always gave me Tizer at home.

Because I had never had a Coke before, I didn't know what it was supposed to taste like, and so was completely unaware that the person manning the bar was adding a shot of brandy to my drink, for a lark. I did wonder why, after a few Cokes, I found it difficult to stay upright during the dancing, but thought nothing of it.

The oddest thing was seeing a room full of men all wearing shorts and showing their hairy legs.

Charlie told me that, in readiness for his job in Zambia, he had bought a couple of lightweight suits from Burton's the tailors, but his houseboy had washed them in the bath and hung them on the line, and they were ruined. But it didn't matter, because no one wore suits here, only shorts!

I had never been to a party before, apart from my own 21st birthday party at my home. I'd lived a very quiet life, being a bit of a bookworm, and usually only went to a party on New Year's Eve, mainly because it gave my friend and me the opportunity to be kissed and cuddled by several men!

Here in Mansa, I discovered that I loved parties and I loved dancing; and the more Coca-Cola I drank, the merrier and more uninhibited I became, flinging myself about with gay abandon to Stevie Wonder singing 'For once in my life.' It seemed an apt title. I briefly wondered what the girls in the Marconi typing pool would think if they could see me now!

One result of the nightly parties was that June and I seldom got home before 4 o'clock in the morning, and we struggled to get ourselves up in time to go to work. Our hours were 8.30am until 4.30pm, but we never arrived before 9, and usually knocked off at 4pm, to allow plenty of time to get ourselves ready for that night's party.

By 10 o'clock in the morning, having typed several letters, we couldn't keep our eyes open any longer, and would fall asleep with our heads on our desks.

We had the embarrassment of receiving a letter, addressed to us both, from one of the ministers, called Edward Lubinda.

In this letter (which I wish I still possessed) he said it had come to his notice that we always arrived late and left early, setting a bad example to his African staff.

He said that this was not a trivial matter, and if we carried on like this, our lack of self-discipline would affect other areas of our lives, to our detriment. He realised we were respectable girls, who had fallen into bad habits in an unfamiliar country, and he hoped that we would reflect on this and reform our behaviour.

What wonderful, wise words! I have never forgotten them, and ever since then I've had a reputation for reliability and conscientiousness, all thanks to him. Of course, Mum had brought me up to be reliable and conscientious, but Mr Lubinda was right to say that in a foreign country, we can find ourselves behaving in ways that we would not in our own country.

Thank goodness he had never seen us dancing! He might not have considered us quite so respectable then!

I always seemed to end up dancing with 'grumpy' Charlie Baxter, who, after a few beers, had a struggle to hold me up on the dance floor. Charlie only had one dance step, really.

They all called him 'snake-hips' because of his peculiar combination of the twist and a hip thrust. He had the skinniest knees I had ever seen – not that I had seen many men's knees (well, actually, none at all) – and he said that he had won last year's Knobbly Knees competition.

The breathalyzer had recently been introduced in England, but it had not arrived in Zambia, and especially not Mansa. The most frightening thing was seeing men (it was invariably men) staggering out of parties, barely able to put one foot in front of the other, climbing into their cars and driving off home.

One of them insisted the reason they always got home safely was because 'the cars go on autopilot.' And he must have been right, because we never heard of a crash, although sometimes a car would end up in a ditch, and the driver would just climb out and complete his journey on foot.

It used to baffle me that during these parties, the men kept saying, 'I'm just nipping out to check my tyres.' I thought that maybe the tyres in Mansa were of poor quality and likely to burst at any minute. I didn't realise that 'checking the tyres' was a euphemism for going for a wee in the bushes, which I only discovered when I went outside to see for myself these dodgy tyres which needed checking every few minutes.

By now, our bungalow was ready for June and me to move in to. It had two big bedrooms, a basic kitchen and a bathroom, plus a garden at the back with a clothes line. Prior to coming to Zambia, my Marconi boss, who had at one time worked in Kenya, told me that we would have to employ a houseboy.

But June and I didn't want a houseboy. How weird to have a strange, adult man roaming about the house, we thought. How hard could it be to do our own housework? Not that we knew! Both June and I had had similar mothers, who had never let us do any housework at all, so we were clueless.

It was the same with cooking. June was convinced that you needed to boil an egg for an hour if you wanted it hard-boiled. I'd never even boiled an egg, so I believed her.

Charlie often used to receive gifts of meat from pilots, grateful for his good service at the airport, and as he couldn't possibly eat it all himself, he would pass most of it on to us. There would be great packs of T-bone steaks and fillet steak, all in neat slices, wrapped in greaseproof paper. We didn't see the need to separate the slices, and just tossed the whole package into the freezer.

We only found out how daft this was when we decided to cook ourselves steak and chips for tea. We couldn't separate the frozen slices! We found the only way they could be broken up was to hurl the whole lump on to the floor from a great height several times, and by the third throw, the meat would fall apart into slices.

You would think that we would learn from this; but no, we made the same mistake every time! It's a miracle the vinyl flooring didn't crack, with the amount of frozen-solid meat that was flung onto it.

But our plan to manage without a servant proved to be impossible.

Every day, morning, noon and night, there would be a steady flow of 'boys' (men, really) begging us to employ them as houseboys.

'Oh, madam, madam, please give me job! Madam, at home I have wife and many, many children to feed, very, very hungry!' was the usual refrain, accompanied by much rubbing of the stomach.

How could we let a poor family starve?

Feeling guilty, and also because we had grown bored with washing and cleaning, we eventually gave in and hired one of them. He was called Sixpence.

Sixpence was a brilliant worker, and he loved cleaning. But with just two girls to work for, he didn't have enough chores to keep him occupied all day. His solution to this was to clean everything all over again. He would take all the clean bed linen from the airing cupboard and re-wash it and re-iron it, or he would keep re-polishing the floor.

He had a novel way of doing the floor. First, he would get down on his hands and knees and spread polish all over the vinyl tiles. Then, he would tie dusters to his feet and dance a fandango (well, more like the Twist) all over the floor until it shone like glass.

The trouble was, it was as slippery as glass, too. One day, June and I came home from work, stepped inside the house, and promptly fell on our backsides! We had to tell Sixpence not to polish the floor every day. He couldn't understand why, and seemed taken aback!

I've just written, 'We had to tell Sixpence,' but there was no 'we' about it! Sixpence would only take orders from June. Although she was younger than me by three years, she had a more forceful presence, and a loud, assertive Brummie voice, which carried an air of authority that my Essex voice just didn't.

Sixpence would simply ignore me when I asked him to do anything, such as make the tea. There is something uniquely humiliating about being 'dissed' by one's own houseboy! Obviously, my new-found confidence didn't cut any ice with him! Maybe he just felt he couldn't serve two masters (or mistresses).

June and I always washed our own knickers and bras. Somehow, we felt it was demeaning for a man to have to wash our undies. Knowing Sixpence, he probably felt offended, and we didn't know how to explain our reasons. He had limited English, and we knew nothing of his Bemba language. African languages are extremely complex and hard to learn, and most rural Africans know at least a little English.

According to some old hands, Swahili was the language to know. They said that if you could speak Swahili, you could converse with any African, regardless of their native language. If only we'd bothered to learn!

I had an episode when, briefly, my fear of spiders and flying creatures re-emerged. I'd had a bath, and was sitting in the living room wearing my fluffy dressing gown. I felt an itch on my back, and rubbed myself against the sofa, but it wouldn't go away. Eventually, I went in to the bedroom and took off my dressing gown and glanced in the mirror, expecting to see a pimple or insect bite on my back.

But it was a huge spider!

I had never moved so fast.

'June, June!' I yelled. 'Get this thing off me!' June saw the monster, dashed to the kitchen, grabbed a broom and swept the flipping thing off.

Feeling a bit mucky after that, I went to have another bath. I was lying there, luxuriating in the bath bubbles, and I glanced up at the ceiling. I noticed a big hole in the ceiling which I had never seen before, perhaps because normally I didn't look up in the bathroom.

As I stared at this hole, a giant bat, with a six-foot wing span (all right, a slight exaggeration) flew out of it and started to whizz around the room, swooping down at me. Thoughts of rabies flew into my mind. I mustn't let it bite me!

If I thought I'd moved fast with the spider, I positively shot from that bath like a bullet from a gun and skidded, with my wet feet, into the bedroom.

I screamed to June about this enormous bat, and she had the good sense to shut the bathroom door. She ran down to the houseboy's little hut at the bottom of the garden, and shouted at him to come to the house.

Shoving him into the bathroom, she said: 'Sixpence, I want you to get rid of this bat!'

He probably didn't understand a word, but she pointed to the wall, where the bat had come to rest.

'There it is! Do something!'

He just laughed at us silly white girls, and calmly picked up the bat and took it away with him. For all we knew, he would make a bat stew with it!

The big drawback of having a houseboy is that you have to make sure you are decently dressed whenever they are around. You can't just leap out of bed in your nightie and walk to the kitchen, where the houseboy is making the tea. Decorum is the name of the game!

We had some Danish neighbours in the house next door, and they (or at least the voluptuous, middle-aged wife, Inga) didn't seem bothered about decorum.

We popped round one Saturday morning to see if she could spare a jug of milk, and she opened the door wearing a completely transparent negligee and nothing else. Ordinarily, this wouldn't have mattered, except that as she bent down to scratch her legs, her houseboy was standing right behind her, his eyes out on stalks.

Inga's husband passed by at that moment, and I thought he would whisper to Inga to put some clothes on, but he didn't. Perhaps he thought that as their houseboy was a married man, it didn't matter.

Were June and I wrong to respect African customs? It was certainly the custom for African women to dress modestly, and it would be easy for us foreign girls to give the wrong impression, with our more revealing attire. Looking back, I cringe a bit, and feel that we should at least have draped a sarong over our mini dresses. 'When in Rome,' as they say!

Charlie, being keen on me, had bought me a second-hand Volkswagen Beetle in pale blue, which I promptly decorated with painted flowers. In England and the USA, it was all about Flower Power, so I felt that Mansa should have some of that.

Charlie's eyesight wasn't good enough for him to drive, and he had always relied on friends to pick him up from his airport house and take him to parties, so it seemed logical that he should buy a car of his own, and that I, being teetotal, should be the driver.

I'd had a couple of lessons in England, and I now practised my skills by driving up and down the airport runway. When I felt I had reached a decent level of competence, I applied for my driving test.

The examiner was a South African chap who knew Charlie well, and felt he owed him a few favours. He knew I was Charlie's girlfriend, and when I turned up at the test centre, he said, 'Well, Rosemary, I have seen you driving on the runway, and you seem competent enough to me,' and with that, he handed me my Zambian driving licence!

Zambian bush roads were just wide dirt tracks, and after a few hundred trucks and cars had driven on them, they tended to form 'corrugations' which resembled waves. It was extremely uncomfortable to drive on these corrugations, and they didn't do the cars much good, either.

One day, we were driving along in our little Beetle, with Charlie in the front and three passengers in the back, when all of a sudden I saw a wheel go rolling along in front of us, ending up in the ditch.

'Oh, look at that!' I said. 'I wonder where that came from?' I soon found out, because seconds later the car rumbled to a halt in the middle of the road with a thunk – the wheel was from our Beetle! The vibration caused by the corrugations must have made the wheel nuts fall off, followed by the wheel itself.

The men leapt out of the car, found the tyre and the wheel nuts and put everything back on.

As my only driving experience had been on the airport runway and the dirt roads of Mansa, I found it confusing when we drove to Lusaka and I was confronted with roundabouts and traffic lights.

Approaching a roundabout, I saw a sign saying, 'Keep right.' It probably meant 'Keep to the right-hand lane,' but I took it literally, and turned right to go round the roundabout instead of left, and couldn't understand why other cars were sounding their horns.

Further up the road, we sailed through a red light. I hadn't even noticed the traffic lights, let alone the colour.

A police car flagged me down. 'Excuse me, madam, do you realise you've just driven through a red light?' I panicked and didn't know what to say, but Charlie took over, explaining, 'I'm so sorry, sir; we've just driven down from Mansa – we don't have traffic lights there!'

'That's quite understandable, Bwana,' the policeman said with a smile. 'Carry on, but don't let your lady friend miss them next time!'

To cut a long story short, both June and I ended up getting engaged – June to Stuart Irvine, whose father owned the local petrol station, and I to Charlie Baxter, the grumpy one who ran the airport!

But before we could get married, June and I had to have an engagement ring. June's fiance drove us all to the Copperbelt to buy the rings, as there were no jewellers in Mansa.

As an aside, there weren't many shops of any description in Mansa, and those that did exist carried a very small range of goods, giving very little choice. This may sound like a disadvantage, but in fact it made shopping a stress-less experience! If you wanted washing powder, for instance, there would be only two brands to choose from.

A friend went for a short holiday in England, and found herself completely overwhelmed by the vast range of goods. She went into a little corner shop to ask for a packet of salt (of which there was only one brand in Mansa), and the shopkeeper said, 'What kind of salt? We have Maldon sea salt, Cornish salt, pink Himalayan salt, iodised salt...' She panicked. 'Salt! Just salt! That's all I want! Any old salt will do!'

To reach the Copperbelt, you had two choices – you could stay in Zambian territory and go the long way around, involving probably over a thousand miles, or you could take the short route of a couple of hundred miles, which involved crossing the Congo Pedicle. I cannot now remember whether we went to Ndola or Kitwe, but either way it involved crossing this dangerous road.

The Congo Pedicle is a little spit of land which intrudes into Zambia, cutting it in half at one point. I'm probably not explaining this very well, and I'm sure I could find a map, but I don't want to bore everyone!

People wanting to cross the pedicle had to bribe the Congolese border guards to let them through, in both directions. Apparently, they were unpaid, so they had to make their money somehow.

Arriving in the Copperbelt town, we found a jewellery shop.

June chose a big ruby and diamond ring, and I chose a sapphire. June liked bling (a word not invented then) but my ring was more modest – and we got it in the sale, with one third off!

June was a Catholic, and her fiance was not, so Stuart had to have instruction from the local priest before they were allowed to get married in the local Catholic church; but Charlie and I had a civil ceremony in the registry office, where the registrar gave us a carbon copy of our marriage certificate instead of the original by mistake.

I had to borrow a wedding ring from our female witness, and Charlie borrowed a blazer from her husband, which was a couple of sizes too big. I wore a navy-blue silk dress that I had made myself from a length of material bought from a Chinese exhibition in Lusaka.

Our wedding reception consisted of sandwiches and a trifle, which we really appreciated, because it wasn't easy for our friends to get hold of the ingredients.

I told Maggie Bwalya at the office that, like her, I had married a man from another tribe – the Scottish tribe! She found this hilarious.

My Mum and Dad detested the Scots, possibly because of our neighbours opposite us. They were a married couple, the wife being from Manchester and the husband from Glasgow. We knew that the husband beat his wife up when he'd had too much to drink, and my parents had tarred all Scotsmen with the same brush. They were all drunken wife-beaters in their minds!

I can only imagine their faces when I wrote to say I had married one of 'the enemy' – and the reason for the rush was that Charlie's contract was coming to an end, and if we hadn't married when we did, he would have been sent to another posting, and we might never have seen each other again. Well, that was his excuse anyway; I think he felt he'd been a bachelor long enough!

Regarding his remark, 'I'm going to marry that girl,' when June and I arrived in Mansa, he said that he just fell in love with me at first sight as I walked down the aircraft steps. I said I was surprised that he didn't choose June, she of the big bust. 'Ah,' he explained.

'But I'm a leg man, not a bosom man – and you've got smashing legs!'

PART 3

Looking back, it seems a flimsy excuse for marriage, but we were still together 45 years later, until his death in 2014, and when he was ill, we often reminisced about our mad courtship days in Mansa.

Prior to our weddings, June had somehow got hold of a booklet from the library on what to expect on our wedding night, and insisted on reading it out loud in the office. She mispronounced some words, and kept going on about the female organism. According to this book, it could be some weeks before a wife would 'learn to enjoy the experience.'

Well, they got that wrong!

I moved into Charlie's airport house. He carried me over the threshold with ease. He may have been skinny, but he was strong. I weighed eight stone and was five foot three, and Charlie probably weighed half a stone less and was five foot eight. In his youth, he had been the Cross Country Champion for Fife, and had muscles of steel.

In his garden, I remember seeing a huge praying mantis in a tree catching an equally huge butterfly, and munching it hungrily. I could hear every crunch! But of course, after my baptism of fire in the hostel, I was no longer freaked out by creepy-crawlies. Nature is red in tooth and claw, so they say, and never more so than in Africa, where nature is not just red, but super-sized as well!

Charlie owned a dog and a cat. I could never have married a man who didn't love animals. The dog (a bitch), Kiska, was accustomed to sleeping on Charlie's bed, and every time Charlie and I got into bed together, Kiska would growl and look daggers at me. She was in love with her master, and I had taken her place. Poor Kiska! She never did get used to sharing Charlie with me.

Because June and I were civil servants, the rules were that as females, we had to resign on marriage, which seemed terribly unfair, because this didn't apply to our husbands, who were also civil servants.

Shortly after our wedding, Charlie's contract came to an end, and the Zambian government paid for him to have six weeks' leave, on full pay, with all flights paid for. We could go wherever we wished.

We thought it best to go and see my family in Chelmsford, so they could meet my new husband. This tied in nicely with the fact that one of Charlie's ex-girlfriends, Irene, who hailed from Guernsey and had worked as a nurse in Mansa, was getting married to a South African chap in Guernsey, and they had invited us to their wedding.

We had a week or two with my Mum and Dad first, and Mum said, 'While you're here, why don't you have a wedding blessing in the local church?'

I wasn't particularly bothered, and not very keen, really, as I hated being the centre of attention or being stared at, and the idea of walking up the aisle petrified me; but to please my Mum, Charlie and I agreed to do it.

But first, I had to find a wedding dress. The vicar had been to see us, and he said that, as I was already officially married, it wouldn't be appropriate to wear a long white dress, but I could wear a short one.

Mum, knowing I had no sense of style, asked her neighbour, Daphne, to go with me to choose the dress. We found a white lacy mini-dress from the bridal shop. It had long sleeves and was very pretty. I hate tight clothing, so I picked a size 12, which was comfortably loose on my slim figure. In those days, a size 12 was for 36 inch hips (today a size 12 is for 40 inch hips)!

We went on the ferry and hovercraft to Guernsey and attended the wedding, which was in a Catholic church. Having no clue what the routine was, we just copied what other people did. There seemed to be an awful lot of jumping up and down – first we were kneeling, then standing, then sitting, then kneeling again. I thought to myself, if this is what church is like, I'm never going again!

The wedding couple had booked us into a hotel beforehand, so we didn't have to worry about finding somewhere to stay in this busy holiday season.

This hotel provided three square meals a day, with several courses at breakfast, a three-course lunch and three-course dinner. Charlie wasn't used to eating all this food, but his Scots blood came out, and he ate everything put in front of him, as he had paid for it! We spent three weeks in Guernsey, and regarded it as our official honeymoon.

On returning home, I found that Mum had organised everything for the wedding blessing. She didn't know the phone numbers of my friends, so, panicking that there would be no one to come to the wedding, she contacted all my old Marconi colleagues and invited them instead! I did contact my 'proper' friends, of course!

On the day, my relatives congregated in the front room while Mum served tea.

I had already been to the hairdresser, but to my dismay she hadn't managed to copy the picture I had shown her, and I felt I looked ridiculous, which wasn't a good start to the day!

The real disaster came, though, when I put on my wedding dress. Unbeknown to me, all the food at the hotel had made me pile on a stone in weight, and the dress was now uncomfortably tight. Still, it was too late to find another dress, so it would have to do.

As I walked up the aisle with Charlie on my arm (because, remember, we were already a couple), I heard a neighbour, Mrs Theobald, whisper to Mum, 'When is Rosemary's baby due?'

Mum said, 'What baby? Rosemary's not pregnant!' I could imagine Mrs Theobald, the village gossip, saying to herself, 'Pull the other one!'

And I wasn't pregnant, but all the extra weight had gone to my tummy, and in the too-tight dress, I did indeed look as if the 'baby' could arrive any minute! I should have picked a bigger bridal bouquet! Even my legs looked chubby in the photos. They had always been my best feature!

What with the bad hairdo and the tight dress, and Mrs Theobald's remark, my wedding day was far from the happiest day of my life. If you look at my wedding photos, there are only one or two of me smiling. Such a shame! But as Mum would say, 'There are worse troubles at sea.'

By then, Charlie had received a letter from the Zambian government, telling him where they would be sending him on his return. It was to be Lusaka, where I had originally worked.

I was heartbroken not to be returning to my beloved Mansa. I had grown so attached to our friends there, and the simple, rural life, and never dreamed we would be sent elsewhere.

We were given a government flat in a block with other expats, and we settled in. We didn't have parties every night any more (oh, how I missed those parties!) but Charlie did shift work at the airport, with four days on and three days off, and during those three days we entertained our new friends. Charlie had taught me how to cook, and my speciality was Steak Diane, which always went down well with guests.

I had found a job at Shell & BP as a shorthand-typist, working for a smashing Dutch manager called Mr Blok. He once had a meeting with a Mr Wood, and it amused me when he dictated a letter entitled Re: Meeting Wood-Blok!

We employed a houseboy called Solomon who, if not as wise as his Biblical name implied, was certainly crafty. We would arrive home from work to find Solomon waving a sponge cake aloft.

'Look what I've made for you, madam!' he'd proudly announce. We'd take a bite, only to find it so sickeningly sweet, we couldn't eat it. He had used about a pound of sugar to four ounces of flour!

'You have it, Solomon,' we'd say. 'Take it home for your wife. She'll love it.' Solomon would make an identical cake every week. Was he daft, or were we? Solomon's wife had probably doubled her weight by the time we left!

Solomon liked to make us pots of tea, in an unusual way – everything went in the pot at once: the tea, the milk, the sugar. We grew used to pouring our milked and sugared tea straight from the pot, and wondered why we'd never thought of it ourselves!

We brought my Mum and Dad out for a holiday, and they had the time of their lives. We had a Fiat 600D (our Volkswagen Beetle having been stolen not long after we moved to Lusaka), which resembled a little bus.

In this vehicle, which had comfortable bench seats, Dad and I took turns driving the 350 miles to Livingstone, to see the Victoria Falls. Mum and Dad were entranced. Never in a million years, she said, did she imagine she would be walking about in Africa, which was much the same as I had felt, and in fact still did!.

(Years after they had died, I found that Mum had kept the receipt for the hotel (although we had paid, of course), and even the receipt for her laundry, as a memento).

Mum had thoughtfully brought some Marks and Spencer shirts out with her, especially for Solomon, and he seemed very pleased with them, thanking her profusely. Mum was a very generous lady, and she liked to spoil people.

If only Solomon had been honest . . .

Some colleagues at Shell and BP were talking about a scam that some houseboys were involved in. Apparently, if they saw that 'madam' had a lot of clothes (perhaps too many, in their opinion), when they did the laundry, they would hold back a dress or two and hide it in their cleaning cupboard, where they knew madam would never look. If, after a fortnight, the missing dresses had not been remarked upon, the houseboy would take them home for his wife, or sell them.

Although Solomon had his funny little ways, I did not really believe that he would do such a thing, but then again, I did still have the fifteen dresses I had made in England, plus a few more besides that I had bought in Zambia, and maybe he thought I could spare a few.

Hardly daring to look, I opened the door of the cleaning cupboard when Solomon was out, and there, rolled up among the dusters, were two of my dresses.

Why did he do it? We paid him well, gave him good food, did not make him work hard and Mum had given him brand new shirts.

We had no choice but to ask him to leave.

After he had gone, we discovered that he had also stolen a beautiful cigarette lighter that Mum had given me. It left a nasty taste in the mouth; but after all, he was the only one who had ever abused our trust, so we refused to feel bitter.

But going back to the Fiat 600D car, I had a little problem with it.

I used to take my friend, Heather, to town with me when I went to work, as she worked as a nurse not far from my office.

As we drove along, a terrific hum started, a sort of buzzing sound, coming from the engine. It got louder and louder.

'Heather!' I yelled. 'We must have a swarm of bees in the engine! We'd better stop at the next garage and get them to do something! We'll be stung to death if they escape!'

Not that I was panicking. Oh, no, not me.

Heather shouted, 'Drive faster! Hurry up! They'll come in through a gap in the dash board!'

I pressed my foot hard to the accelerator pedal, but the faster I went, the louder the buzzing became.

I pulled in at the next service station, roaring in like a bat out of hell. We leapt from our seats and ran to find a mechanic.

'Quick, lift the bonnet and look in the engine!' I begged. 'I think we've got a swarm of bees or wasps in there!'

He calmly lifted the bonnet and scratched his chin. We stood well back, expecting this huge swarm of giant African bees to come swooping out, furious at being trapped in a hot engine and unable to escape, and looking for someone to sting.

The mechanic spoke. 'Madam, when did you last put water in the radiator?'

I looked at him in puzzlement. 'What do you mean, water? I've never put any water in it. I didn't know I was supposed to!'

I added, 'I never used to put water in my Volkswagen Beetle and that seemed OK!'

'Ah, madam,' he said with a patronising tone. 'That's because VW Beetles are air-cooled; but most cars, like this Fiat here, are water-cooled. Your engine has overheated and the water has boiled dry. That's what caused the buzzing sound. You were lucky it didn't explode or catch on fire!'

Well, as I am very fond of saying, you learn a new thing every day!

Another thing I learned the hard way was that money doesn't grow on trees, but my spending grew like a weed!

Charlie went to the bank to withdraw some money. We had separate bank accounts. The teller said, 'Mr Baxter, I'm afraid I cannot let you withdraw any money, because your wife is overdrawn on her account! You must put some of your money in her account.'

I had never had a cheque account before. In England, I was with the Trustee Savings Bank, and had a passbook, so I could always see at a glance how much money I had left.

In Lusaka, with all the shops, I was writing cheques left, right and centre! It didn't feel like money. Of course, as we entertained a lot, I was always buying fillet steak, and beer and wine for the guests, and I had lost track. Charlie had to sit me down and explain how to fill in the cheque stub, so I would know where the money had gone and how much I had left.

I still keep to this routine, and am always amazed at how many of my friends have no idea how much money they have. Budgeting and cooking are the two main things that Charlie taught me – probably my parents should have done, but they didn't!

One day, I was walking along the Cairo Road (which didn't lead to Cairo) in Lusaka, when who should I see coming in the opposite direction, but Jeremy Thorpe. At the time, I think, there was a big hoo-ha in England about him having arranged to have a boyfriend called Scott bumped off. He looked a very miserable man, and wore a hat, just as he always did in England.

But the most amazing coincidence occurred the next day. I was walking along the road to work when I couldn't believe my eyes – there, coming towards me, were two of the Marconi engineers I'd worked with a couple of years ago! There was Peter Chapman, and a little Turkish engineer whose name escapes me. They were as shocked to see me as I was to see them.

I asked them for the number of their hotel and said I would be in touch later. I told Charlie, and he wasted no time in ringing them up and arranging to take them out for the day. We packed a picnic and a rug, picked them up from their hotel in the Fiat, and took them to a grassy spot, where we chatted away as if we were still at Marconi.

Charlie was very sociable and easy to talk to, and he got on really well with them, as though he had known them all his life. I just could not believe this was happening; it seemed so surreal to be sitting in Africa with two men for whom I'd been typing letters not long before!

How could it possibly happen that in a country the size of Zambia, we would bump into each other? If I'd been a few minutes earlier or later, I would have missed them.

About this time, I started to feel a bit broody, but Charlie didn't seem to want children at the time, and so I put the idea at the back of my mind.

At the end of the Lusaka contract, we were posted to Mongu, the capital of the Western Province, formerly known as Barotseland in the colonial era.

There was just one road leading from Lusaka to Mongu, and this road was about 600 miles long. A friend of Charlie's drove our car there, loaded up with our worldly goods, and I went separately on the plane.

When we arrived at Mongu airport, we found that the outgoing people had left a pantry full of supplies – loo rolls, herbs, spices, flour and cooking pots, etc. We also took on their lovely dog – a female Rhodesian Ridgeback called Sandy.

Their houseboy asked if we would let him stay and work for us, and we agreed. I can't remember his name, but let's call him Tembo – a fairly common name in Zambia.

I immediately found a job as secretary to the manager of the local Standard Bank. I loved my work there, but there was one snag. I can't do arithmetic, but if one of the tellers was off sick, they always asked me to help out. Time and again, an African customer would complain that I had given him the wrong money, or had made a mistake in his bank book, and I would sheepishly correct it.

Sometimes, customers would bring in a heap of notes – the currency was 100 Ngwee to the Kwacha – and the notes would look as if they had been nibbled by rats; and indeed, this was often the case, as they had usually been buried under the bed in a mud hut.

The pronunciation of ngwee was a bit hit and miss. It was supposed to be pronounced 'enggway' with a hard 'g' (that's the nearest I can spell it!) but some newcomers thought it was pronounced nugee, or even en-gee-wee!

One of my jobs as secretary was to keep a record of postage stamp usage. I had a little locked box with stamps and some loose change in it. Once a month, I was supposed to count up the stamps and count the money – balance the books, in other words.

But I never managed to get it right, never having done this before. It was mostly guess-work! So when I ended up with less money in the box than I should have had, I simply made up the deficit with cash from my own purse.

It was Chris Coulson, the Accountant, who found me out, although I've no idea how he could possibly know.

He said, 'Rosemary, if it doesn't balance, just tell me; you're not meant to use your own money!' To this day, I don't get it. How did he know? Thank-goodness I wasn't in charge of millions!

Some of the customers had names that seemed odd to our ears – the oddest one being Fuxon Moyo. I wonder which swine with a warped sense of humour chose his Christian name?

It was the custom, apparently, for a houseboy or gardener, if his wife had just had a baby, to ask the white employer to choose a name for the new baby. There was a story, possibly apocryphal, of a houseboy whose surname was Banda. When he asked his employer to pick a name for his new baby, the employer allegedly said, 'Call him Elastic!'

One of my African colleagues at the bank was called Mercy Munyimba. Now, that was a nice name!

Tembo did all the cooking for us, and it was a treat to come home from work in the lunch hour to a hot meal, full of flavour. But sometimes it had rather an unusual taste.

When we sat down to a beef casserole, we detected a subtle hint of cloves; not unpleasant, but a bit odd.

The next day, it was a delicious chicken dish, tasting weirdly of cinnamon.

Tembo was familiar with all the spices and condiments in 'his' pantry, and he knew how to use them. When we moved in, naturally I had put all my herbs and spices next to the others on the same shelf.

I asked, tactfully, 'Tembo, do you know the difference between savoury spices and sweet ones?'

He looked at me blankly. 'Madam, I cannot read. When I cook, I put a little bit of everything in the meat!'

But he was a brilliant cook. I've never tasted meat so tender, or gravy so rich. And who cared if it tasted a bit like dessert?

The airport manager's house was a huge affair, and it had a wide room which stretched from one side of the house to the other. The previous occupant had turned this area into a bar, complete with fridge, and so we soon got back into the habit of partying every night! Guests would take turns to bring crates of Lion or Castle beer. Lion was said to be a bit too sweet, so Castle was the more popular drink. I never wanted to see a Coke again, so I stuck to water or tea!

We often had to entertain pilots, if they had a few hours to spare before take-off. We had one young pilot who was Australian. I asked him if he would like a beer or a cup of tea.

'Well,' he said, 'What I'd really like is a cup of jasmine tea, but of course that's the last thing you'd have in a place like this!'

You should have seen his face when I went to the pantry and showed him an unopened packet of jasmine tea! I had bought it at the Chinese exhibition in Lusaka, at the same time as I had bought the Chinese silk for my wedding dress!

One day, we went down to the Zambesi River and were privileged to see the amazing sight of the King of Barotseland, Lewanika II, in his royal barge, painted in black and white vertical stripes, floating up the river with his entourage. Thousands of people turned out to watch him, just as they do in England for our Queen. I have some photos somewhere. If I can't find them, I will download a photo from the Internet and put it on separately.

We had acquired an old beach buggy, and regularly drove to the 'beach' at Lake Makapaela. Initially, this was a lovely beach to stroll along, or to sit eating a picnic.

But one day, a farmer came walking along the beach, leading a herd of cattle, who all did what cattle naturally do, and once those steaming, stinking heaps appeared on the sand, so did the flies, by the million! The beach was never the same after that; it was fly heaven.

But still, we continued to go, hoping the flies would have moved on to other aromatic heaps on other beaches; but they never did.

We always took our good friend along with us - the Bank Accountant, Christopher Coulson, who had developed a huge crush on me. He used to go all dreamy-eyed every time he looked at me, apparently!

I must have been really thick, because I didn't notice this myself. It was Charlie who told me: 'Chris is in love with you!'

Christopher's desk was next door to the Bank Manager's office, just a few yards from my desk, and now that I knew about his crush, I couldn't help noticing that he did keep looking at me.

Christopher wore glasses, as did my Charlie, and a memory sprang into my mind of a remark one of the girls in the Marconi typing pool had made to me years before.

'Rosy,' she said one day, 'have you ever noticed that all your boyfriends wear glasses?' She might as well have asked if they carried a white stick! Cheeky monkey. And anyway, they didn't all wear glasses; there was one who didn't – just the one.

But a new employee was about to arrive, whose desk was between Christopher's and mine, to my relief. We had been told to expect a new Deputy Manager, a Zambian called Henry Mufalo.

We had imagined that his surname would rhyme with Buffalo, and so we were anticipating a swashbuckling character, in the mould of Errol Flynn.

He turned out to be about five feet tall, quietly-spoken, and far from swashbuckling! And his surname didn't rhyme with buffalo! He pronounced it Mu-FAH-lo.

One funny incident involving Henry has just come to mind. Henry was a stickler for tidiness, and he would regularly inspect everyone's desk and the drawers therein. He was shocked at the untidy state of them, full of sweet wrappers, old Fanta cans, cigarette stubs, etc.

He came to my desk, which was a model of tidiness. He opened the drawers and gasped.

'Come over here, everyone!' he ordered. 'Come and look at Mrs Baxter's drawers! This is how your drawers should look!' And all the African staff came over and looked approvingly at my drawers.

There was an Irish lady there, called Theresa Ring. Theresa, Christopher and I were helplessly chortling with laughter, and poor Henry was baffled. I had to explain that in England, the word 'drawers' is another word for knickers. He looked a bit embarrassed, but joined in with the laughter. He may have blushed – but who could tell?

Years later, we heard that Chris had caught Blackwater Fever (a dangerous form of malaria), and had died on the plane on the way back home to Cheltenham. The sad thing was that, once we were back in England, we sent Christmas cards to him for decades, not knowing why he never sent one back.

PART 4

The Manager of Standard Bank was an Englishman called Peter Witt, who had been seconded from the UK branch. His wife was called Rosemary Witt. The bank treated its managers very well, and in addition to their large house, they were given a swimming pool.

This was the kind of pool that is erected above ground, and it would need many hands to put it up. Peter asked if the expatriate men of the village would be willing to come and help. There would be free beer for the men, and Rosemary Witt would provide tea and cakes for the wives.

Putting up the pool and attaching the pump took several hours, and we ladies had an enjoyable time scoffing cakes and drinking tea while the men slaved away in the heat.

A group of us were chatting together, and several ladies mentioned that they thought Rosemary Witt was a bit eccentric.

'You can say that again!' I agreed. 'She even washes up her teapot!' (I had seen her do this in the kitchen).

There was a sudden silence, and the sound of brains clicking, trying to make sense of what I had just said. I might as well have written the word 'weird' on my forehead.

The other ladies looked at each other, then at me, and said, in a puzzled tone, 'But doesn't everyone wash up their teapot? What sort of dirty person wouldn't?'

But in my own home, Mum never, ever cleaned the teapot. Dad used to say that washing it up would make the tea taste funny, and so it was only ever rinsed under the hot tap, never washed. I didn't know anyone else who washed up their teapot, so obviously it was a normal custom in our neck of the woods.

Blush? I must have looked like a beetroot!

Charlie had joined the Round Table, a club for men who wanted to help the community. There was a hospital in the village, run by nuns. These nuns had asked if the Round Tablers would help to erect a covered walkway from the garden area to the hospital. They promised to provide beer, so there was no shortage of takers!

It was thirsty work, and a great deal of beer was consumed. Charlie remarked on how deliciously chilled the beer was, and asked one of the nuns how they managed to keep it so cold.

The German nun replied in her thick accent: 'Vell, you see, ve alvays keep ze beer in ze mortuary, mit ze dead bodies!'

All the men spluttered into their glasses.

By now we had been married for four years. It was at one of our many parties that an elderly gentleman asked if we'd thought about having children. I said that I had thought about it a few years ago, but Charlie didn't seem bothered, although he was now 36, and I was 28.

'Well, my dear,' he said, including Charlie in this. 'Have you ever thought that perhaps this party lifestyle won't last for ever, and that one day you will be old and wish you'd had a family while you were young?'

This made Charlie think hard, and he said, 'Let's do it!' So we did.

Charlie's contract came to an end, and this time we decided to go to Australia to meet his folks for the first time. They had all emigrated from Scotland to Australia in the days when you could go for £10. I was three months pregnant when we set out in November.

We travelled by train down to Durban in South Africa, passing through other African countries on the way (possibly Botswana and Malawi, but I can't quite remember – it was all a blur), and from there we went by ship to Adelaide.

We had a cabin with two single beds, mine on the starboard side and Charlie's on the port side. All night I had the weird feeling that I was about to tip out of my bed. Charlie insisted I was imagining it; but it happened night after night.

'Maybe it's something to do with being pregnant,' he suggested. I don't know why we didn't just swap beds, so he could experience it.

Two weeks later (of a three-week trip) the captain announced: 'Please accept our apologies. The ship has had a list to port for the past fortnight. We do hope this hasn't caused you any inconvenience. The problem has been fixed now. Thank you for your co-operation.'

I shot Charlie a filthy look. 'There you are! It wasn't all in my imagination, was it!'

After spending three weeks on the ship, we had a strange sensation when we walked on dry land in Adelaide - I think it's called 'sea legs.' We wobbled all over the place and couldn't walk properly for several hours!

Charlie's family – his Mum and Dad and three sisters – all welcomed me with open arms. They had all retained their broad Scottish accents, whereas Charlie, having joined the RAF as a boy entrant at the age of 16 and travelled the world, had lost most of his.

When I went out to go to the shops, his mum said, 'Ye'll be going to get your messages, then, hen?' I said, 'No, I'm just going shopping!' They mean the same thing, apparently.

When I returned home, laden with carrier bags, she would say, 'Ye've been spending your man's money again!' In vain did I insist that it was partly my money, as I had been working, too.

I loved my mother-in-law's accent. She called shoes 'shoon' and the floor 'flair' - it was an education for me!

She must have thought I was a lazy devil, though. I used to lie in bed until 11am and then make myself a big breakfast of bacon, eggs, beans, mushrooms and mushrooms. I suppose she made allowances because of my pregnancy, or the fact I was English!

Although Australia is a hot country, this time the heat exceeded all expectations. According to the television news, this was the hottest November in 75 years. Old people were dying like flies, they said.

We were staying with Charlie's parents, in their tiny flat, with no air conditioning. We would go and stand under a cool shower, and as soon as we had dried ourselves, we would be dripping in perspiration again. Even coming from Africa, we weren't used to this heat! The humidity level was sky-high.

When I did some washing in Charlie's mum's twin-tub, by the time I had hung out the last garment, the first one had dried!

But I didn't think the washing looked very clean. Charlie's mum had said to use a cap full of the liquid laundry detergent, and so I did. However, when I read the instructions for myself, it actually said to use a cup full!

But when it came to ironing Charlie's shirts, I hadn't a clue. Mum had never allowed me to go near an iron - 'You'll burn yourself, dear, using your left hand!' - and in Zambia we had a houseboy to do it. Mum-in-law had to show me how it was done, especially that tricky bit - the yoke at the back.

I would love to have known her thoughts - here I was, a grown woman of 28, unable to iron a shirt for her son, spending all 'his' money, and unable to drag my lazy carcass out of bed much before mid-day! We were surprised to find that Charlie's Mum only ever bought tinned fruit and vegetables. Her fridge was full of tinned peaches, tinned carrots, tinned peas, even tinned potatoes!

We had been unable to get fresh fruit in Mongu, and had been looking forward to eating lots of it in Australia. We asked why she used tinned fruit and veg, and she replied, 'Well, it's too much trouble to peel the fresh stuff!'

The heat was exhausting, and we found that the only way we could get cool was for me to go to the shopping mall, exotically called Tea Tree Plaza, while Charlie went with his Dad to the pub!

The pub was called The Highlander, and had a Scottish theme, with a tartan carpet on the floor and tartan wallpaper on the walls.

Both these establishments had wonderful air conditioning, so we had to go every day, for several hours. Oh, the bliss!

It was February when we returned to Zambia and I was by now six months pregnant. We discovered we had been posted to a beautiful, mountainous area called Chipata, capital of the Eastern Province. I felt very sad, because I was having to leave all my friends in Mongu, one of whom was also pregnant. Her name was Christine Pickering, but the Africans couldn't pronounce Pickering, and called her Mrs Pickling!

We landed in Lusaka, where we stayed with friends for a couple of days while we looked for a suitable car to take to Chipata. These friends had a beautiful white cat called Noddy, and they needed to find a new home for her, because they were returning home shortly. Noddy had been their little girl's cat. We both loved cats, so we didn't hesitate to take her. They gave us her cat basket to carry her in.

Just before we left for Chipata, I went to a shop in Lusaka to buy some nappies. I had read a book on babycare which insisted I would need three dozen terry towelling nappies and some muslin squares. I plonked the packets down on the counter.

The look on the shop assistant's face was a picture!

'Thirty-six nappies?' She looked at my modest bump. 'Exactly how many babies are you expecting, madam?'

But the childcare book was written for the English market, where, because of the weather, it might take many days to dry the nappies, so you would need plenty of them, whereas in the tropics, they would dry in an hour or so! But I decided to get three dozen anyway.

We bought a second-hand pale-blue Datsun 1600 and I drove the car (and Noddy) the 350 miles to Chipata.

When you have been driving at 80 or 90 miles an hour for several hours without stopping, on a completely straight road, it is extremely hard to suddenly start driving slowly.

As we approached a bridge, we saw a sign saying, 'Keep to ten miles an hour when crossing this bridge.'

Well, I tried my hardest to reduce the speed to 10 mph, but as I crossed the bridge, the lowest I could manage was 20 mph. When I reached the other end of this long bridge, one of the guards approached me, rifle in hand, and said, 'Madam, you were doing more than ten miles an hour.'

In vain I explained that I was pregnant, I had been driving for several hours at high speed, and 10 miles an hour was just too difficult; but he was adamant.

'Madam, you must reverse to the other end of the bridge and do it again. You must keep to 10 miles per hour.'

Now, everyone knows that women always find reversing manoeuvres very difficult, and with my six-month bump in front of me, almost touching the steering wheel, limiting my mobility, it was very, very difficult indeed. Not only that, but I have always hated doing any kind of manoeuvre when people are watching, especially men.

The bridge must have been at least a hundred yards long, and as I wove my way back along it, I veered first to the left and then to the right.

At last I reached the end without bumping into one of the guards lined up along it, and with my eye firmly fixed on the speedometer, I crawled along the bridge once again, keeping to this daft 10 mph speed limit.

The guard didn't even have the decency to say, 'Well done!'

There is an insect in Africa called the Putzi Fly. We hadn't encountered it before, because we had always made sure our clothes were ironed, and this killed off the eggs the fly had laid in the wet washing hanging outside.

Our houseboy in Chipata was called Samson. He had removed the loose covers from the Parker-Knoll armchairs and washed them, but he hadn't ironed them, presumably thinking that as we weren't going to wear them, it didn't matter.

However, Charlie had the habit of coming home in the lunch hour, throwing off his work shirt, and reclining in his favourite armchair. A few days later, his whole back was covered in itchy lumps.

The next day, a friend, Pete Sanchez, an ex-mercenary, arrived to stay for a few days. He took one look at Charlie's back and said, 'That's the bloody Putzi Fly!'

And he borrowed one of my sewing needles, held it in the flame of a match, and proceeded to pick out the hundreds of Putzi Fly maggots one by one. Was this painful? I reckon so! Charlie seemed to need a lot of beer to numb the pain, anyway.

Not long after that, I was sitting in the bath, and I felt a soft swelling on my right buttock. Thinking it was a boil of some sort, I gave it a gentle squeeze, and out popped an enormous, wriggling maggot!

'Charlie, help! I've found a ruddy maggot in my bottom!' I yelled.

Charlie inspected it and said, matter-of-factly, 'It's only the Putzi fly maggot, you daft thing. You're just lucky Pete Sanchez didn't have to dig it out with a needle!'

Samson obviously hadn't ironed my knickers properly. I still have the scar to this day, and often can't resist picking at it in the bath. I half expect another maggot to emerge, perhaps one that's been hibernating all these years.

Whenever I watch a bush tucker trial in 'I'm a Celebrity, Get Me out of Here!' on the TV, and someone has to eat those Witchetty Grubs, I always think of the Putzi fly maggot!

And talking of food, a friend of Charlie's used to bring us a leg of venison now and again. I did know, of course, what venison was, but I never gave it too much thought, and we always roasted it and enjoyed eating it.

However, one day this chap turned up with a small enamel bowl, covered with a cloth, and said, 'Sorry, Charlie, I didn't have time to prepare it this time.'

I took the bowl into the house, removed the cover - and there, in the bowl, was this tiny little Bambi lookalike, all curled up as though sleeping. I cried my eyes out! No way could I bring myself to eat this beautiful little creature, so I gave it to the houseboy for his family. He probably thought I was mad, giving away food! I think Charlie might have eaten it, but I just could not.

Up until this time, we had always taken anti-malarial tablets, but we were told that Chipata was a malaria-free zone, and, being pregnant, I didn't want to take them anyway, so I stopped.

When I was in my eighth month of pregnancy, I started to feel really ill, boiling hot one minute and freezing cold the next. I felt worse as the day wore on, and I waited for Charlie to come home in the lunch hour, as he usually did.

But on this day, he didn't, and by then I felt too weak to phone his office in the control tower, so I fell into bed and hoped the fever would pass. I became aware that I was bleeding heavily. At about five o'clock, Charlie came home and found me curled up in bed.

'Charlie, I'm very sick, and I'm bleeding,' I said. 'Where are you bleeding from?' he asked.

'Where do you think?' I replied. 'I'm worried I'm losing the baby.'

Charlie dashed to the phone and called the only person he could think of – Madge Law, an elderly, retired South African midwife. She drove over straightaway and took a blood sample, but she said she was sure I had malaria. It gives off a certain odour, apparently. She drove to the hospital to get the Chloroquine and gave me strict instructions not to move a muscle for a fortnight. During this time, she came daily to check on me.

Apparently, malaria can cause the womb to contract, and I could have lost the baby; but I didn't, and eventually I recovered. I wouldn't wish malaria on my worst enemy! Within a couple of weeks, I had lost a stone in weight. Even when I was well, all I could manage to eat was tinned fruit (there was no fresh fruit available) for a while.

Madge was worried that I might have a condition called placenta praevia, and recommended I go to Lusaka for the birth, rather than the basic Chipata hospital, but we just couldn't afford it, and with the optimism of (relative) youth, we decided to take our chances. And quite honestly, I couldn't face that 350-mile journey back to Lusaka (including that 10mph bridge!), and I would have been on my own, as Charlie couldn't have left the airport unmanned.

AUTOBIOGRAPHY

Our Sally was born, fit and healthy, and two weeks overdue, in May 1973 in the local African hospital.

Outside the hospital were little groups of wives and mothers, cooking their local food, mealie meal, made of maize meal, on cooking pots over a 'camp fire' ready to take to their relatives, as the hospital didn't provide food.

When I walked in, with the contractions a few minutes apart, the midwife cheerfully said, 'I hope there are no complications, my dear, because we don't have any equipment here.'

Fortunately, we didn't need any equipment. And as I was the only white woman in the hospital, there would be no chance of a mix-up with the babies!

It was not a happy experience. I was left alone all the time, in pain and wondering how much worse it was going to get. Charlie and I were supposed to be at a party that night, and Charlie did offer to stay with me, but I told him to go and enjoy the party. I was like an animal in pain, and just wanted to curl up and die on my own! Our beautiful daughter, was born at twenty to eight in the evening. I had been in labour since about half past three in the morning.

Later the following day, Charlie and his friend Duncan turned up in Duncan's car to collect me. No one offered to carry the new baby, and on the way out, walking over the rough, stony ground, I nearly tripped over and dropped her! I put her in the second-hand carrycot in the back of the car, and wondered how on earth I was going to cope!

I had already struggled to dress her in the hospital. Mum had sent me a tiny nightie, probably the sort of thing she had dressed me in; but it was long and tied in a bow at the back and went on over the head, and Sally screamed her head off. If only Mum had sent me a Babygro!

This was the first baby I had ever held in my life, and I didn't even know how to put a nappy on. The nurses did it in the hospital. For about three months, it kept falling off, or the contents would fall out! Luckily, a friend who had children of her own came to stay, and she showed me how it should be done. I think the nurses in the hospital must have assumed that white women know it all, and didn't bother to teach me, and I didn't think to ask!

Oh, how I wished I had my Mum to help! There were no health visitors to come and see how I was getting on, and at the time I knew hardly anyone in the village, which was eight miles away. I was unable to drive for some time, because I couldn't sit down on a low seat, on account of the tightness of the stitches. (Sorry, any men who are reading this – too much information)!

It was a miserable time, one way or another, and looking back, I can see that I was suffering from post-natal depression. I just couldn't find my usual happy self. However, I don't want to end this chapter on a sad note - after all, I had my beautiful, healthy, bouncing baby!

By this time, Noddy the cat had produced two litters of kittens. She was a wonderful mother, but a bit of a trollop; within weeks of giving birth, she would be out in the front garden, rolling on the ground waving her legs in the air! There was no vet available, so we couldn't have her spayed.

One day, a stray cat appeared on the doorstep, howling with hunger. I gave her some meat, and she ate it and disappeared.

A few hours later, she appeared at the door again – this time with four kittens! We couldn't turn them away. In due course, Noddy's kittens and the stray cat's kittens matured, and mated with each other. Within a very short space of time, we had sixteen cats and kittens, all needing food and shelter.

Our Sally probably thought these cats were her siblings, and once she was toddling about, she seldom walked anywhere without a cat or kitten in her arms. We bought her a second-hand doll's pram, and she started piling the cats in the pram and pushing them around the garden!

Two years later, in 1975, Charlie's contract came to an end, and we flew to England while we decided what to do next. Mum and Dad were thrilled to spend time with their only granddaughter, of course. We stayed with them for about six weeks, and I had hoped we could emigrate to Australia, and perhaps bring Mum and Dad out to join us; but it was not to be. Charlie was offered a job at the airport in what was then Salisbury, Rhodesia, and so that was where we had to go.

I was never very happy in Rhodesia (later to be called Zimbabwe) although I had some lovely friends, one of them originally from Nottingham. I missed Zambia and the simple village life. I think I was still suffering from depression, and to make things worse, I inexplicably gained about three stones!

When Sally was three, we had another lovely daughter, Fiona, and four-and-a-half years later, a gorgeous son, John. He came as a bit of a surprise. Charlie had a prostate problem, which required an operation, and had been told he wouldn't be able to father any more children. We weren't bothered - we were happy with our two little girls - and so it was quite a surprise to find the doctor had been mistaken!

The girls had been born in the African winter, but John came along in the steaming hot summer, in November. One day, when he was about three months old, I decided it was too hot for him to be wearing clothes, so I just put him in a nappy and a muslin cloth to shield his body from the sun. As I walked along the street pushing John in a pram, I got a lot of funny looks from African mothers.

African babies always seemed to be dressed for an English winter, no matter how hot it was; they would be wearing a woolly hat, cardigan or jumper and bootees, while strapped to their mother's back and covered in a cloth or thick towel, so it must have been a shock to see this white baby dressed so minimally! Thankfully, he survived.

I never managed to lose those three stones, which had mainly gone on my stomach, and I got quite used to people asking me when the baby was due!

THE MAGIC RAFT SERIES:
1 The Case of the Manic Monkey
Julie Hatton

One morning, the sun was shining brightly in the sky, yet four children were very bored.

'What can we do now?' asked Sam, of his brothers and sister. 'We've done all our chores. There's nothing to else to do.'

'How about we make a raft to sail on the sea?' asked Tom, excited.

'Great!' cried all the children, delighted with this novel idea.

'What shall we make our raft with?' asked Sam, looking around eagerly.

'I thought we could use that old table that's in the shed,' suggested Tom. 'Upside down it should make a good raft.'

'I'll see if I can find a tablecloth for a sail,' shouted Adele, as she left the room for the airing cupboard.

'I'll pack some food to eat,' said Toby, who was always hungry.

Tom and Sam left for the garden shed. They pulled open the door and dragged the old table onto the green grass. The boys turned the table upside down. 'What a great raft,' said Sam, pleased.

Adele ran forward with a very large white cloth billowing in the wind. Toby approached carrying a large basket. 'I have lots in here to eat and drink,' smiled Toby, delightedly.

The children were very lucky. The sea was not far from the back gate. They pulled and pulled the raft out of the garden, over the stones and onto the sandy beach. The basket was placed in the raft.

The white cloth was tied on for a sail. They were ready for an exciting adventure.

The intrepid four clambered in and pushed the raft out onto the sea. The raft was a little unsteady when they were standing up, but once they sat down, the raft was quite safe. The children knew the raft could easily sink beneath the waves and, when it didn't, they all sighed with relief. 'Our raft is magic! cried Adele, in delight. We actually have a magic raft!' The other children smiled and cheered. Toby was so pleased he jumped up excitedly, but he was quickly pulled down again by Tom who feared the raft, magic or not, might tip over.

The little raft with its children bobbed up and down happily on the blue ocean. The white sail caught the wind and pulled them along very quickly. Seagulls called loudly overhead. Toby gave everyone a bag of crisps. They eagerly opened them up and crunched on the salty snacks in the warm sunshine. Sam gave everyone a small bottle of orange to wash the crisps down. The children sat back happily together as the little raft bobbed along on the top of the white waves.

'Ship ahoy!' cried Tom, as he saw a ship far, far away. 'Hey! Ship ahoy!' he called, but his voice was lost in the wind.

'Look over there,' cried Adele, standing up and nearly upsetting the magic raft. 'An island!'

'Watch out!' cried Tom, grabbing her arm. 'You'll have us all in the water!'

'Sorry!' said Adele, sitting down carefully. 'Shall we sail over there?'

'I don't see why not,' said Tom. 'Does everyone want to go?'

'Yes!' they all shouted. 'Yes, yes, yes!!!'

Slowly, Tom steered the little raft with his oar, a light plank of wood he'd unearthed in the shed. The island was quite large. 'I haven't seen this before,' said Tom. 'I wonder how I could have missed it!'

'Perhaps the island is magic, too,' suggested Adele, hoping like mad it was.

The little raft drifted onto the warm, sandy beach. There were many palm trees on the shore and the children could plainly see brown, hairy coconuts high up in the branches.

'Are those bananas over there?' asked Toby, still feeling hungry.

'Well, they are yellow and look the right shape, so I suppose they are,' laughed Tom.

The children pulled the little raft high up the beach beyond reach of the sea.

'Let's explore,' said Sam. 'I wonder if anything lives here apart from the many seagulls?'

'Follow me,' called Tom, as he walked up the beach to a little wood. The others ran behind to catch up. 'Hey! What on earth is that over there?' asked Tom.

The children's eyes followed his pointed finger. 'I say,' said Adele. 'It looks like a monkey.'

'Yes, a monkey eating lots of bananas,' laughed Sam. 'He must be very hungry.'

'Shhhhhhhh!' warned Tom. 'We don't want to frighten him away!' but it was too late. The monkey had seen the children, but he didn't move away. He didn't seem to be afraid of them at all. Tom crept closer. The monkey offered Tom one of his bananas, but as soon as Tom held out his hand, the monkey naughtily snatched it back, chattering loudly.

Tom sat on a large rock and watched the monkey munching on his bananas. Tom picked a banana from the floor and began to peel it. Once he'd done so, the sneaky monkey jumped towards him and pinched it right out of his hand.

Tom threw up his head and laughed loudly. 'You're a very sneaky chappie, aren't you?' he said, smiling in amazement.

The other children were walking around nearby. Toby found a coconut on the floor and was banging it on a stone to try and break it. He didn't have much luck. He soon learned just how hard it is to crack a coconut. Sam was climbing trees and swinging from the branches like a monkey.

Adele discovered a swing hanging from a large tree branch. She took a small book from her pocket and began to read aloud.

AUTOBIOGRAPHY

Suddenly, a little rabbit hopped up to listen, followed by a brown, prickly hedgehog. Something suddenly jumped out of the grass. It was a large yellow toad. He wanted to listen, too. A squeak from high in the tree came from a squirrel peeping out of her hole to listen. A line of starlings flew from the sky and perched on a low tree-branch and cocked their heads from side to side as they listened to the story. Adele was delighted. The creatures were so close and seemed so interested in her favourite book! Tom and the monkey also listened to Adele's story. It finished with a little song, so Tom danced a jig. The monkey tried to copy him, but kept falling over, much to the children's amusement.

Tom began to pick up a few fallen bananas, but had to fight hard to ward off the manic monkey who wanted them all for himself. 'Get away, you greedy thing,' said Tom, laughing. 'We want some, too!' Annoyed, the manic monkey jumped on Tom's bent back and began slapping him hard over and over again. The boy laughed and stood up. The monkey hung on for a while, then leapt off. It was so cross, it turned his back on the children and began to sulk.

To be continued . . .

Please visit our website at www.bugs2writes.co.uk where you can find information about us, our charity, other books in our collection and short extracts from the stories.